The Identification of
English Pressed Glass
1842-1908

Jenny Thompson

Published by:
Mrs. Jenny Thompson

Printed by:
Dixon Printing Co. Ltd., Kendal, Cumbria.
Reprinted 1993, 1996 and 2000 (including Supplement)

ISBN 0 9515491 2 X

Front Cover Pictures:
Taken from the "*Encyclopaedia of Practical Cookery*" published in the reign of Queen Victoria.

Back Cover Picture:
Sowerby & Co. Pattern Book c 1879 gold colour.

Foreword

Unlike most other items of Victorian glass, pressed glass can nearly always be precisely identified either by Patent Office Design Registry marks, or by the maker's trademarks, which could easily be incorporated into the iron moulds. It is this aspect of pressed glass that makes it a fascinating subject for a collector, and although some of the rarer objects, such as the Derbyshire 'Winged Sphinx' paperweight, fetch high prices, the majority of pieces are within the price range of collectors of modest means.

Jenny Thompson's book is to be welcomed as providing a concise, clear and comprehensive guide to the identification of pressed glass objects, with an analysis of the characteristic designs of the individual firms as well as details of the actual registrations. The publication of some of the original drawings from the Patent Office Design Registers is a new feature, not included in previous volumes on the subject. These drawings are especially fascinating as they show exactly what was registered, sometimes merely the shape, sometimes just a pattern which was then applied to a number of different articles. This book will undoubtedly be an invaluable tool for the keen collector of pressed glass.

Mrs. Barbara Morris
March 1989

Acknowledgements

I owe many thanks to the Ceramics department of the Victoria and Albert Museum when Mr. John Mallet was Keeper, and especially to Ann Eatwell, for all the help given to me over the many years that I was studying the registrations. I thank the Trustees of the Victoria and Albert Museum for their photographs of pressed glass in the Museum.

I am very grateful to Mrs. Barbara Morris for her encouragement and help in many ways and always for her sound advice; to Nicolas Powell for his photographs, and to all those who valiantly coped with my handwriting and typed sheets of numbers.

I must acknowledge the custody of the Design Registers and the Representations by the Public Record Office and thank them gratefully for permission to publish these lists and for their cooperation.

The cover to this book is from the Victorian "*Encyclopaedia of Practical Cookery*". In lieu of an author my reference goes to Messrs. Ring and Brymer, Caterers then and today, who assisted in the original volume.

Finally this book is for Martin with my very best love and thanks, for all his splendid help, and for our family.

I hope all lovers of pressed glass will find it useful.

Jenny Thompson.
July 1989

References

1) The Design Registrations and Representations.

2) *English Pressed Glass.* Raymond Slack

3) *Glass Circle Paper No. 4*, March 1980. Roger Dodsworth.

4) *History of the Homeland.* Henry Hamilton.

5) *Sowerby Gateshead Glass.* Simon Cottle.

6) *Victorian Table Glass & Ornaments.* Barbara Morris

The Identification of Victorian and Edwardian Pressed Glass up to 1908

Pressed glass belongs to that golden age of Victorian industrial and commercial expansion which came in with the aftermath of the Industrial Revolution.

One of the main characteristics of that time was the greatly increased use of power driven machinery and therefore, the expansion of the factory system as opposed to the workshop, in which previously it was usual for the worker to own his own tools and work was on a much smaller scale. With costly machinery this was no longer possible so the industrialist owned the machinery and directed his workforce. This led to a further feature of the period, that of industrial concentration and considerable urbanization.

The population of Birmingham was 144,000 in 1831 and 233,000 in 1851 and that of Manchester and Salford for the same years was 238,000 and 401,000. People poured into the towns from the countryside as streets of Victorian houses bear witness.

At that time Britain stood unique in the world, confident of supplying any goods required and sure that she would be able to meet any foreign competition. There was great industrial and commercial prosperity and with it a new and ever increasing middle class. Indeed, there were several divisions within that class and because the Victorians crammed their houses with objects and decoration, these people desired for themselves what had been the prerogative in the 18th century of the gentry, merchant, clerical, banking and legal professions.

In the bigger houses it was necessary to have two or three large dinner services, three dessert services and dozens of glasses to cope with ale, water, sherry, wine, port and brandy apart from those for custard and syllabubs. Then there were the decanters, carafes, finger bowls, ice plates, chutney, marmalade and jam jars, comports, sweetmeat dishes and so on. Some of these items were made in silver and porcelain, but those in glass were usually cut or engraved and came from Ireland, where there was no glass tax, and the first class glass houses of Stourbridge, Birmingham and London, with names such as Richardson's, Thomas Webb, Bacchus, James Powell and Apsley Pellatt.

With the upsurge in the profits of steel, coal, railways, cotton, wool and commerce this new flourishing middle class market with its varied echelons wanted similar pieces but at a lower cost.

Pressed glass provided an answer; the tax on glass was repealed by 1845 which lessened the price and it could be made in vast quantities in moulds. Just before 1845, the excise duty on glass yielded some £600,000 but the remission of the duty meant an increase in production of glass for both home use and export.

The earliest British pressed glass was probably made about 1836 in the Birmingham area, although as early as 1831, mindful of American competition, Apsley Pellatt took out a patent for a new way of assembling moulds.

The Pottery Gazette of February 1st 1886 describes the making of pressed glass as follows:

"THE POTTERY GAZETTE" — February 1st 1886

"In glass making as in other industries many ingenious tools, etc. have at different times been invented with a view to replace hand labour. To obviate hand-blowing, for instance, a process of shaping with press and iron moulds was substituted. The beneficial results of this invention are incalculable. It placed manufacturers in a position to make regular and cheap wares while skilled labour became no longer necessary. The simplicity of the operation of pressing glass was such that in a short time men could be trained to perform the work. It does not require much knowledge to train men to gather glass, drop it into a mould and cut off sufficient quantity. The glass now being in the iron mould, a plunger is made to press the plastic mass, and in solidifying, by cooling, the objects retain the form of the mould and the plunger. Next came improvements in combining the different pieces of moulds, improvements in presses and in tools for holding the pieces while being fine-polished."

The process was not without hazards as an observer called George Dodd, writing in the 1840's put it: "If the quantity of glass be too large, the over plus gives considerable trouble, if too little the article is spoiled. If the die and plunger be too hot the glass will adhere to them, if too cold the surface of the glass becomes cloudy and imperfect" — As a method even the pressing of glass had to be controlled properly.

Not only was the glass needed for the home market, but most of the big firms had offices in Europe, in fact, pressed glass was destined for all over the world. In 1888, Sowerby's stated in the Pottery Gazette that their pressed and cut glass was suitable to be sent to the Colonies and India — in the days of a vast Empire there was no limit to what could be achieved. Indeed, an early report of about 1830 to the Commissioners of Excise stated that "our correspondent in New York advised us that the market for flint glass in that city is destroyed by importations from Newcastle and almost entirely from the Gateshead works. The exports of flint glass from the Tyne are immense". Later on this became a two-way business with the Pottery Gazette sagely commenting in April 1878 "Some months ago, we drew attention to the quantity of American pressed glass now in England and pointed out the necessity of our manufacturers giving the matter their attention. The warning we are happy to state will have a good effect not only in the present but on the future trade of England." Likewise, at the International Health Exhibition of 1884, the Pottery Gazette reviewing Sowerby's wares said "their fancy glass should have been in the art gallery but being of such a cheap and popular character we suppose they were inadmissable." Much of the glass was of very high quality, when made by the best firms, with an astonishing variety of colour, pattern and decoration.

The amazing variety of pressed glass in every way, from colour, shape, utilitarian and decorative items, ranging from poor quality to the superb, makes the collecting of the glass especially fascinating. The Sowerby Pattern book of 1882 advertises these colours: "opal, turquoise, gold, jet, venetian in several colours, giallo, blanc de lait, malachite and patent ivory Queen's ware." The Sowerby colours deserve explanation as for their vitro-porcelain wares they used gem terminology "opal, turquoise, gold, jet" all jewels in their own right. The opal in this context was white while the jet was black, but the confusion arises with their "blanc de lait" which because of the true definition of the opaque vitro-porcelain wares was meant to be opalescent like watery bluish milk. Yet in the Pattern book of 1882, "blanc de lait" is advertised as "decorated, opaque, stained, blanc de lait" — so it may be that "blanc de lait" could be opalescent but when decorated and opaque then literally it became 'milk white' glass. The malachite in blue and green looked like marble as did the purple, streaked glass and some of the ivory Queen's ware resembled carved ivory with raised decoration. Each firm had its own specialities, such as Sowerby's ivory Queen's ware and Davidson's blue and primrose pearline though certain colours, like opalescent, amber, clear blue, clear green, opaque white, opaque turquoise and marble wares were made by many of the firms, but the marbled glass items came mainly from the North Eastern glass houses.

Collections can be made in so many permutations that it is hard to suggest any one way. Anyone interested in social history can form a series of domestic items like the enormous sugar bowls, or tiny cream jugs, custard cups and many different salts, both flint and coloured. The colours of pressed glass are so varied a whole collection could be formed from the malachite and marbled pieces, Sowerby's

Pattern

OF

FANCY GOODS

Manufactured in Glass by

Sowerbys Ellison Glass Works,

Limited,

Gateshead on Tyne,

England.

Opal, Turquoise, Gold, Jet, Venetian in several colours,
Giallo, Blanc-de-lait, Malachite.

Patent Ivory Queens Ware,

DECORATED·OPAQUE·STAINED·BLANC·DE·LAIT,

and new

TORTOISE·SHELL·WARE.

OFFICES AND SHOWROOMS	
LONDON;	6, Coleman Street, City, E.C.
GATESHEAD ON TYNE.	
BIRMINGHAM;	10, Broad Street.
PARIS;	52, Rue d'Hauteville.
HAMBURG;	49, Gr. Reichen Strasse.

JUNE. 1882, BOOK IX.

Patent Queen's Ivory ware, or Davidson's Pearline. Some of these pieces are so elegant and attractive, along with the Sowerby nursery character ones that they are far removed from the popular concept of cheap moulded glass, the attention to detail being superb.

The most collectable pieces are probably the John Derbyshire famous paper weights "Lion after Landseer", Greyhound, Britannia, Punch and Judy (no design registration) and Winged Sphinx. The latter is, so far, the most valuable and sought after of the group, and one of the rarest pieces of pressed glass. Then there are all the pre-1884 pieces of glass with their distinctive Victorian diamond registration marks and the post-January 1884 ones with their numbers on the side or base. Some people just collect trade marked items; with the peacock's head of Sowerby, the lion rising from a mural crown of Davidson and the two lion crests of Greener. Equally, the commemorative and Royal occasion pieces form a pattern of historical events. One of the best and rarest pieces is the Greener "Marquis of Lorne" item, especially in marbled glass, like malachite and the "Gladstone for the Million" plates are still seen often enough to stir the imagination, along with John Bright "Peace and Plenty".

In fact so much pressed glass was made that it should be easy to decide and form a collection as rare, or simple, plain or colourful, as the individual wants. Naturally being originally made for a mass market, a considerable quantity of the glass found today bears the scars of use, and misuse, and therefore is chipped. The only maxim is to buy the best that is available and affordable. Prices are going up all the time as the glass gets rarer.

Identification is all important. From the registration marks and the pattern books of the glass houses and also just by looking, an amazing amount of visual information can be absorbed and stored up. There is satisfaction in knowing what individual pieces are and indeed recognition is paramount in the valuation of any piece.

For the purposes of discussing the design registrations, as the registrations are essential for identification, it is best to divide the principal factories making pressed glass into groups, those from the North East and those from Manchester. There are, of course, a number of lesser known factories.

The most notable firms in the 1880's were from the North East. They are Greener, Davidson, Sowerby, Edward Moore and also W.H. Heppell which name has to be included because of the firm's connection with George Davidson, but the first three names are the most important ones.

The Sowerby name is probably the best known of the North Eastern firms. The family had been engaged in the glass industry long before the invention of the machinery needed for pressed glass. George Sowerby owned a glass works in Pipewellgate, Gateshead in the early 1800's and was followed by his son John as owner in 1844, — it was during John Sowerby's lifetime that the famous Ellison Glass Works became the focus of the pressed glass industry, for certainly Sowerby's was the most prolific, imaginative and artistic of the firms. In 1850 Sowerby took on Samuel Neville, his former manager of the old Gateshead Stamped Glass Works and together they leased land from Cuthbert Ellison for the purpose of building a new glass house. This was in East Street, Gateshead and the new factory was known as "Sowerby & Neville" in the early 1850s. By the mid 1860s they had purchased the land outright and were set to become the largest manufacturers of pressed flint glass in the country.

In 1871 Neville left the company to start up on his own and Sowerby's reverted to being a family concern as Sowerby & Co. John Sowerby's son, John George Sowerby, managed the Works from the early 1870s on, and inherited the firm on his father's death in 1879.

In 1882, the firm became 'Sowerby's Ellison Glass Works Ltd.', the title by which it is best known today and by then the firm was the largest pressed glass manufacturer in the world.

Sowerby
1876-c1930

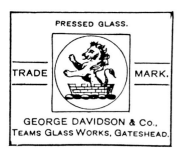

George Davidson
1880-c1890

Henry Greener
1st Trade Mark
1875-c1885

Greener & Co.
2nd Trade Mark
c1885-1900

George Davidson of the Teams Glass Works was the second best known of the firms from the North East. The firm was founded in 1867, also in Gateshead, and quickly became renowned for the manufacture of pressed glass. Apart from the already present demand, this was due to the energy and creativity of George Davidson, the founder of the Works. Starting with only a small workforce he succeeded in building an expanding major glass house over the following two decades. George Davidson died on February 22nd, 1891 aged 68, the day after his horse fell while he was driving home from Newcastle. It was a sad loss for the firm, though his son, Thomas was equally capable and succeeded him.

Despite the devastating fire of January 1881, which would have crippled lesser firms, new buildings commenced and production was able to forge ahead by the end of the year.

In December 1889 the firm's best known line in glass, the blue and primrose pearline was patented by Thomas Davidson, George's son. However, accounts of this new, special glass were reported in the Pottery Gazette as early as March 1889 so it was suitably advertised prior to the patent.

"Messrs. George Davidson & Co. have just secured provisional protection for a new fancy glass to which they have given the name of 'Pearline'. The base is in a rich blue and the edge is of a paler colour, to which the name of Pearline is most appropriate".

Essentially, George Davidson & Co. was a family firm at the top, and also succeeding generations of employees worked at the factory well into the twentieth century. At British Trade Fairs in the 1930's, the wares of both Sowerby and Davidson were admired and bought by Queen Mary and other Royal visitors.

The third firm of Angus & Greener of the Wear Flint Glass Works, Sunderland made some of the earliest registrations for pressed glass in the North East. Little is known about John Angus, but Henry Greener who was born in 1820 at Deptford came from a glass making family. He was apprenticed at the age of twelve to John Price, glass manufacturers at Pipewellgate. He became the firm's traveller and in his twenties he was employed in similar circumstances by Sowerby's the top Tyneside glass house.

In 1858 he returned to Sunderland and entered into partnership with James Angus as owners of the Wear Flint Glass Works. In 1869, following the death of John Angus, the firm traded as Henry Greener from mid 1869-84, then Greener & Co., from 1885 on, proprietors of the Wear Flint Glass Works, Sunderland.

All three of these firms had their own distinctive trade marks: in 1876 Henry Greener registered his first trade mark — a demi-rampant lion, balancing a star on one paw. After 1886, the lion is similar, but is holding an axe between his paws. George Davidson also used a lion crest, the torso rising from a mural crown. This mark was used for about ten years between 1880 and 1890. Sowerby & Co. had a crest trade mark of a peacock's head and that was registered in 1876. They were registering a large number of designs from the 1870's on, and even small pieces might have both the crest and registration date mark.

It is interesting to see in the Trade Marks advertisement of 1886 that Sowerby Ltd., and George Davidson & Co. are ranked with such pottery and porcelain marks as Crown Derby, George Jones, Minton, Worcester and also with Baccarat glass.

The Fourth firm Edward Moore & Co., of South Shields, was a medium sized glass works producing both pressed and blown glassware. The firm was established by 1860 and had three furnaces in working order by 1865. Edward Moore's business did well and in 1869 he exhibited at the Netherlands International Exhibition of Domestic Economy (held in Amsterdam) and won a silver medal.

EXTRACTS FROM REPORTS

BY

HER MAJESTY'S SECRETARIES OF EMBASSY & LEGATION

ON THE

Manufactures, Commerce, &c.,

OF THE COUNTRIES IN WHICH THEY RESIDE.

PRESENTED TO BOTH HOUSES OF PARLIAMENT BY COMMAND OF HER MAJESTY,
MAY, 1870.

NETHERLANDS.—Report by the Hon. T. J. Hovell Thurlow *on the International Exhibition of Domestic Economy, held at Amsterdam, in 1869.—(Page 306.)*

January 7th, 1870.

MESSRS. E. MOORE & CO., of the Tyne Flint Glass Works, South Shields, for Cheap Glass. This firm was established in 1860; has a very large home demand for its manufactures, which are distinguished for cheapness, durability, and beauty of design, and exports very largely to every part of the world. Its collection of Glass at Amsterdam was much admired by the Dutch, and it is to be hoped that the firm will reap, in a practical shape, advantage from their appreciation.

Despite a catastrophe in the late summer of 1881, when the largest cone at the Works fell with a resounding crash, Edward Moore was back in business by 1882 with many orders and able to provide competition for the Tyneside firms nearby. In 1888 Moore bought the moulds of Joseph Webb of Coalbourne Hill Glassworks at Stourbridge. The executors trading as "Jane Webb, Joseph Hammond & Henry Fitzroy Webb" continued to trade to 1888, and as would be expected from a Stourbridge firm, produced excellent quality pressed glass, so it was felt that the Moore acquisition of these moulds could only be advantageous.

Chiefly Edward Moore is best known for the registrations of 1887 and 1888. These are of importance for their classical design, reminiscent of eighteenth century silver, but produced at a time when other firms were experimenting with new shapes and colours.

On 14th February 1884, John Walsh Walsh of the Soho Vesta Glass Works, Birmingham, registered the 'arch topped, rolled over pillar, known as the "Queen Anne" and applied to glass'. Many of the Edward Moore registrations for 1887 and 1888 elaborated on this theme and the firm produced a series of sets of glass with pillars, curving gadroons and twists to the handles. These pieces look very handsome though they appear somewhat heavy for today's taste.

The fifth firm of W.H. Heppell, Newcastle Flint Glass Works, Newcastle is included because of the firm's unusual designs registered over ten years only, and because of the affiliation with George Davidson & Co., who in the mid 1880's bought the Heppell moulds and patterns after the firm foreclosed.

Before that in 1874, W.H. Heppell took over an existing glass works in Forth Street, Newcastle, which had been one of the most flourishing with five furnaces working in its heyday.

The Heppell family were reasonably well known in Gateshead where they had an iron foundry and it seems reasonable to suppose that moulds for the making of pressed glass were supplied from there to the new factory. In 1880, the firm was advertising in the Pottery Gazette their "blown, pressed flint, opal and marble, glass".

The registered designs were novel enough for George Davidson to want to buy up the Heppell moulds when the firm closed its doors in 1884, and certainly Heppell pieces should be in any collection for their originality.

The second group of glass houses consist of firms which were Manchester based. With good communications and access to the port of Liverpool, this group was just as important as those firms of the North East though less is known about the start of the firms and their owners.

The firms in this group are Molineux & Co., who first registered in 1846 and then became Molineaux, Webb & Co., Kirby Street, Manchester from 1864 and finally Molineaux, Webb & Co. Ltd. from 1890.

Their main rivals in Manchester were Percival & Yates who registered their first item in 1847, then as Percival, Yates & Vickers, and finally, Percival, Vickers & Co. Ltd., in 1867. Both firms produced excellent domestic wares as did James Derbyshire & Brother of Hulme, Manchester. In 1870 the firm became J. J. & T. Derbyshire and James Derbyshire & Sons in 1876. This firm produced some of the best quality services made in pressed glass.

John Derbyshire broke away from his brother and set up his own glasshouse in 1873 from Regent Road Flint Glass Works. He registered his first item in that year. By 1877, the works were known as the Regent Flint Glass Co. Apart from the very fine domestic pieces in 1873, John Derbyshire is known chiefly for his handsome paperweights of 1874 which, though they were registered as paperweights, were probably meant to be used as chimney piece ornaments. He too had a trade mark consisting of the letters JD and an anchor. His registered paperweights are probably the best known pieces of pressed glass, and his work is really in a superior class of its own.

Burtles, Tate & Co., Poland Street Glass Works, Manchester started in the 1850s but did not register a design until 1870. In the early 1880s the firm had a second glass house in Bolton known as the Victoria Glass Works. This was closed when they opened another works near the original one in Poland Street.

The firm is known for its flower holders both in blown and pressed glass. Several of their pressed glass items equal both Sowerby and Davidson in design and colour and they also manufactured good domestic items as the Pottery Gazette advertisements show.

In 1891 the firm's new "Topas opalescent" ware was described as a 'striking imitation of the old Venetian Topas'. In reality, it was similar to the Davidson Pearline of 1889, although the Burtles, Tate & Co. pieces are considerably harder to find today.

These firms form a tapestry of design, form, colour and pattern for Queen Victoria's reign and into the Edwardian era. Like a good weave, the colours and patterns intermingle and are dependant on each other. Each firm complements the other and it is necessary to take each firm separately to see how the registrations compare, and what the differences are.

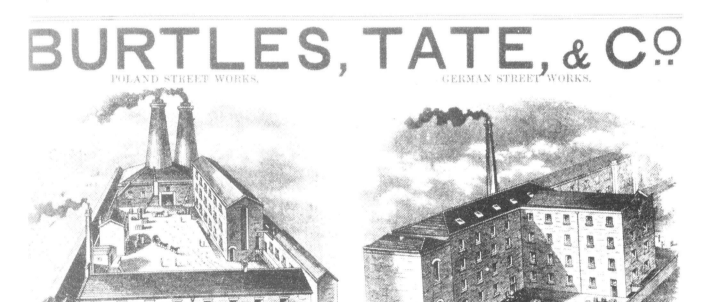

BURTLES, TATE, & Cº

POLAND STREET WORKS.   GERMAN STREET WORKS.

Manufacturers of

FLINT AND COLOURED GLASS, ALSO ORNAMENTAL FANCY GLASS.

GLASS NOVELTIES OF ALL DESCRIPTIONS FOR HOME AND EXPORT TRADE,

POLAND STREET, OLDHAM ROAD, MANCHESTER.

LONDON SHOW ROOMS, 17, ELY PLACE, HOLBORN, E.C.   TELEGRAPHIC ADDRESS: "BURTLES, MANCHESTER."

Greener

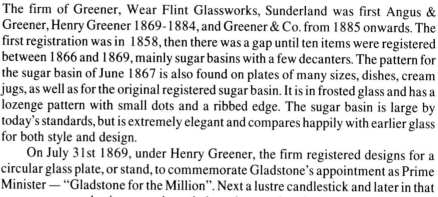

231430

31 July 1869

Design for "Gladstone" Plate showing detail even to raised dots.

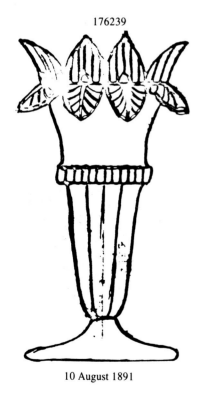

176239

10 August 1891

The firm of Greener, Wear Flint Glassworks, Sunderland was first Angus & Greener, Henry Greener 1869-1884, and Greener & Co. from 1885 onwards. The first registration was in 1858, then there was a gap until ten items were registered between 1866 and 1869, mainly sugar basins with a few decanters. The pattern for the sugar basin of June 1867 is also found on plates of many sizes, dishes, cream jugs, as well as for the original registered sugar basin. It is in frosted glass and has a lozenge pattern with small dots and a ribbed edge. The sugar basin is large by today's standards, but is extremely elegant and compares happily with earlier glass for both style and design.

On July 31st 1869, under Henry Greener, the firm registered designs for a circular glass plate, or stand, to commemorate Gladstone's appointment as Prime Minister — "Gladstone for the Million". Next a lustre candlestick and later in that year, a sugar basin to acknowledge the work of the Anglo-American Philanthropist, George Peabody. In 1876 they produced the vine and grapes decoration for a pierced dessert service, mainly to be found in opaque turquoise blue, milk-white and also in jet black. The registration is for the rim alone, as the diamond registration mark is found on other pieces with a different pattern. It is worth comparing them with the similar coloured plates of Sowerby. In June 1878, Greener registered a design for plates, butter dishes, spoon holders, sugar basins and cream jugs, and those which are commemorative, have medallion portraits of H.R.H. Princess Louise and her husband, the Marquis of Lorne to celebrate their visit to Halifax, Nova Scotia in November of 1878. The butter dish has portraits of the couple and a cartouche with the words "Marquis and Marchioness of Lorne landed Halifax N.S., 25th November 1878". In between the medallions are raised national floral emblems. The knob to the butter cover is a replica of the coronet of a Marquis and on the inside of the butter dish cover is Greener's first trade mark. It is one of the most striking pieces of pressed glass, especially in pale green marble, which is the colour best known for this particular piece, although it was made both in clear and coloured glass. As well that year the firm registered a glass plate and sugar basin with a portrait head of Benjamin Disraeli, Lord Beaconsfield, on it to commemorate the Congress of Berlin.

From then on to 1884, there is a remarkable change in policy as most of the entries (apart from 1881 when there was a design for ornamenting table glass) are for pavement lights and slabs of glass, probably necessary, but very dull. In fact, there is hardly anything of note in the design registrations until the pattern of the Silver Wedding plate for the Prince and Princess of Wales in 1888. In 1888 also, two patterns were registered with an aesthetic Japanese influence. It was at that time that the design for a rustic handle was registered; hence, baskets can be found in several colours, amongst them, a clear blue, amber and a smokey palest amethyst. Most of them have three registrations on them, not two, one for the handle, and two for the patterns of March and April 1888. The design for the patterns are very alike and motifs from one are incorporated in the other. It is as if two designs were needed to make up one elaborate pattern and as the patterns are typically aesthetic, it is an important piece. That same year, there is a bowl with shell shapes and chain decoration and a plate with cornucopia, flowers and fruit. The design of 10th August 1891 continues the naturalistic trend and is for a vase with a top formed by a double row of stylised leaves with the top row upright and the bottom row curving downwards. The registration is for the top alone as this piece may be found as a night-light holder in plain and coloured glass, but still with the same leaf rim. The leaf shape reappears in the same form in the pattern of 6th September 1893. However, in 1890 there is a chariot with gadroons and in 1893 a wheelbarrow with gadroons. It is interesting to compare them with the simple wagon and cradle shapes of W.H. Heppell ten years earlier. Both those of

Heppell & Greener are found in large and small sizes and certainly the smaller ones must have made delightful salt cellars.

Throughout the 1890s and into the 1900s Greener & Co. produced many designs imitating the contemporary, brilliant cut glass. Some are very elaborate and there is one swirly Art Nouveau pattern in September 1898. Few other firms attempted to produce these complex designs in the registrations apart from George Davidson & Co. It is impossible not to think of Greener and Davidson together, as their work was complementary, especially earlier on.

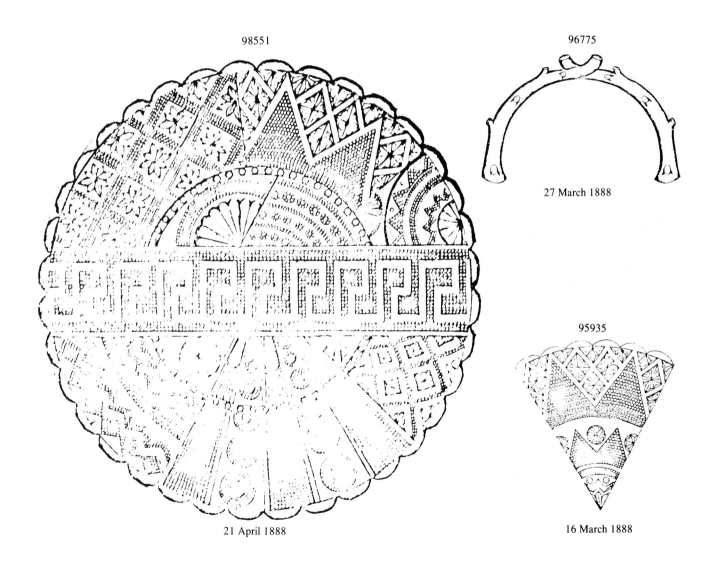

98551

21 April 1888

96775

27 March 1888

95935

16 March 1888

These three Registered Numbers may appear on those baskets which have this design.

197704

Shows early imitation cut glass.

Angus & Greener, Sunderland. Registrations

Registration No.	Date	Year	Parcel No.	Design
117501	21 December	1858	6	Dish
197703	24 May	1866	1	Bottom of decanter
197704	24 May		1	Decanter
200233	25 August		6	Dish or butter float
205812	26 January	1867	4	Decanter and stopper
209161	26 June		8	Sugar basin (lozenge pattern)
214357/8	26 November		9	Sugar basin foot & sugar basin
217728	1 April	1868	7	Salt cellar
218561	4 May		6	Sugar basin
221689	17 September		5	Sugar basin
228782	20 April	1869	9	Sugar basin

Henry Greener, The Wear Flint Glass Works, Sunderland.

231430	31 July	1869	8	Design for a circular glass plate or stand (Gladstone)
231927	12 August		8	Lustre candlestick
236921	7 December		7	Sugar basin (Peabody)
238105	14 January	1870	11	Glass basket
247081	10 November		11	Sugar basin (Friedrich)
250723	2 March	1871	8	Glass plate
268734	10 December	1872	7	Dessert dish
284695	27 August	1874	9	Plate
302199	29 July	1876	6	A dessert service (vine and grapes)
322393	8 June	1878	11	(Glass plate)
325547	31 August		8	A sugar basin showing both sides (Lord Beaconsfield)
330470	18 December		10	A slab of glass for reflecting daylight
337416	22 July	1879	7	A slab of glass
338015	8 August		12	A pavement light
340104	19 September		19	A tile made from a mixture of glasses
359361	8 December	1880	14	Drinking cup (tankard shape E. Hanlan, the oarsman)
362328	1 March	1881	12	For a "circular glass light"
364187	21 April		13	
366032	14 June		9	Design for ornamenting basins, cream jugs, butter dishes and covers, plates and all other descriptions of table glass
366408	24 June		10	Pressed glass light
374475	7 December		17	
378022/3	4 March	1882	10	A base or pavement light
381481	25 May		12	
383640	19 July		6	
394098	12 February	1883	9	
396305	31 March		9	(Slab of glass)
397604	1 May		16	(Slab of glass)
406944	14 November		12	(Slab of glass)

81160

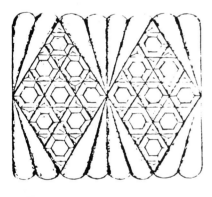

Shows gadroons similar to those of Edward Moore.

15 September 1887

Henry Greener, The Wear Flint Glass Works, Sunderland and 5 Farringdon Road, London.

Registration No.	Date	Year	Design
14390	3 October	1884	Ornamental design for glasses for pavement lights, floor lights, etc.

150277

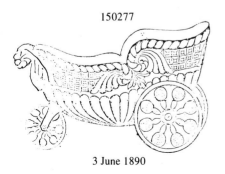

3 June 1890

Greener & Co., Sunderland

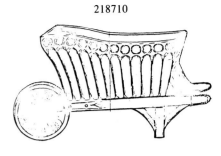

218710

38582	23 November	1885	Shape for a glass mould
48352	5 May	1886	Shape of glass dish
71736	9 April	1887	Design for the ornamentation of glass
81160	15 September		Pattern of table glass
88120	26 November		Pattern and shape of a dish (centenary)
91449	11 January	1888	Pattern of a plate (Silver Wedding)
94543	25 February		
95935	16 March		(Partly imit. cut. Part of pattern included in 98551)
96775/6	27 March		(Rustic handle)
98551	21 April		(Japanese influence)
103434	11 July		(Dish)
103975	17 July		
108018/9	14 September		
109461/2	29 September		(Decoration candle holder, 62 imit. cut)
113896	15 November		(Shell and chain effect)
115743	14 December		(Fruit and flowers with "peace and plenty" in words)
121985	23 March	1889	
128882 to 84	17 July		(Patterns)
138051	14 November		(Patterns)
145580	11 March	1890	(Rope handle)
150277	3 June		(Chariot with gadroons)
150401	5 June		(Pattern imit. cut mostly)
160244	3 November		(Patterns)
163075	16 December		(Mostly imit. cut)
176239	10 August	1891	(Vase, naturalistic top)
182002	30 October		(Pattern, mostly imit. cut)
196641	10 August	1892	(Pattern, mostly imit. cut)
210371	10 April	1893	(Fancy, rustic)
215154	18 July		
217749	6 September		(Free design, acanthus etc.)
218710	20 September		(Wheelbarrow with gadroons)
223742	11 December		(Pattern)
234231	14 June	1894	(Imit. cut)
241930	10 October		(Imit. cut)
258156	15 July	1895	(Imit. cut with star pattern and lines forming diamonds)
262018	16 September		(Imit. difficult cut)
276977	1 June	1896	(Imit. cut. Base diamonds and squares - sides shell or fans pattern)
284639	23 September		(Elab. imit. cut)
304505	3 September	1897	(Elab. imit. cut)
325194	9 September	1898	(Interesting free design Art Nouveau)
325539	15 September		(Very elab. imit. cut)
343063	11 August	1899	(Very elab. imit. cut)
360332	14 July	1900	(Fan shaped edge with gadroons. Imit. cut)
378765	27 August	1901	(Elab. imit. cut similar to 343063)
388197	6 March	1902	(Tumbler shape)
465892	26 September	1905	(Elab. imit. cut)
514796	31 October	1907	(Bowl, imit. cut)

325194

343063

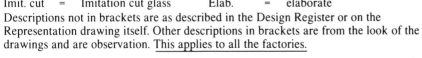

Imit. cut = Imitation cut glass   Elab.   = elaborate
Descriptions not in brackets are as described in the Design Register or on the
Representation drawing itself. Other descriptions in brackets are from the look of the
drawings and are observation. This applies to all the factories.

George Davidson & Co.

153858

2 August 1890

Between 1877 and 1878 this firm registered only four items, tumblers being the most interesting in 1878. For ten subsequent years there were no registrations for shape or design, but in 1888 appeared the very good Thomas Davidson pattern of 31st March and then in 1890 they registered the well known hobnail pattern, imitating cut glass. In 1891, there was an elaborate pattern of flower shapes formed by triangles which is not very different from the one of Sowerby of 1889 and in 1893 the flower trough with stylised shells round it. It is a pretty pattern and is often seen in pearline, both blue and primrose. From the 1st August 1894 until February 1908 there were fifteen registrations of patterns, mostly imitating cut glass and they are really very good. The articles, bowls, dishes, jugs and so on are sometimes very like the real thing with diamond and hobnail effects. They turn up in clear glass, coloured glass and in pearline. Pearline as the name implies, has a rim of opalescent glass, the glass itself being in pale blue and primrose yellow, which were the two registered colours, and less often, palest grey, like a moon beam. The primrose yellow must not be confused with vaseline glass which is a completely different type of glass. Though the firm did not register as much as Sowerby they were very prolific in the late 19th and early 20th centuries; earlier, between 1880-1890 they used their trade mark of a lion rising from a mural crown and many pieces have just this. Despite the bad fire in the factory in 1881 the use of the trade mark may be the reason for the lack of registrations in the 1880s, but the need for a luxurious looking glass, albeit pressed, in the late 1890s and 1900s more than made up for lack of registrations in the 1880s and the patterns for imitation cut glass were certainly rich looking, though the glass itself does not have the same feel of quality as the earlier pieces.

Advertised in the Pottery Gazette several years prior to registration.

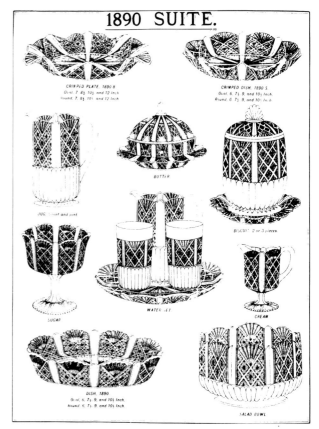

**George Davidson & Co., Teams Glass Works, Gateshead-on-Tyne.
Registrations.**

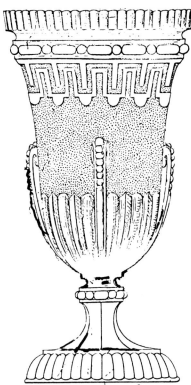

Registration No.	Date	Year	Parcel No.	Design
306884	16 January	1877	8	Vase
308104	28 February		15	Vase
326775/6	23 September	1878	6	Glass Tumblers
96945	31 March	1888		Thomas Davidson (imit. cut)
123198	10 April	1889		
126694	5 June			(Swirling leaf pattern)
130641 to 43	13 August			41 (Jelly mould shape)
153858	2 August	1890		(Pattern similar to hobnail imit. cut)
176566	15 August	1891		(Elaborate pattern imit. cut of flower shapes, formed by triangles)
193365	1 June	1892		(Pattern imit. cut)
207909	20 February	1893		(House shape)
212684	25 May			(Basket shape. Pattern of stylised shells)
217752	6 September			(Imit. cut)
224171	19 December			(Pattern of dots within a form similar to Greek key pattern)
237038	1 August	1894		(Some imit. cut, overlapping circular pattern)
254027	1 May	1895		(Imit. cut)
285342	2 October	1896		(Imit. cut, star centre)
303519	18 August	1897		(Imit. cut)
320124	10 June	1898		(Imit. cut in sections)
340825	5 July	1899		(Relatively simple imit. cut, linear radiating pattern)
360167	13 July	1900		(Imit. cut radiating pattern from centre)
413701	14 July	1903		(Imit. cut with pattern of eight petal shapes)
436804	12 July	1904		
444604	5 November			(Elab. imit. cut star centre)
464621	11 September	1905		(Elab. imit. cut diamond and ribbing pattern)
486298	1 September	1906		(Imit. cut)
512560	25 September	1907		
514848	1 November			(Imit. cut, daisy flower pattern on base area)
520674	25 February	1908		(Elab. imit. cut. Clear separation of motifs)

176566

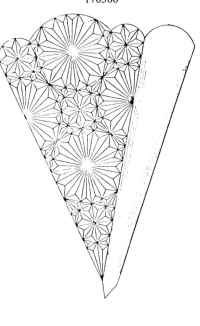

207909

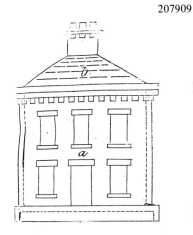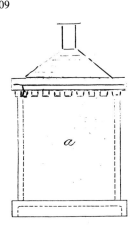

284672

SIDE VIEW

W.H. Heppell, Newcastle Flint Glass Works, Forth Street, Newcastle-upon-Tyne

This firm registered some fifteen items between 1874 and 1882. In February 1880, there is the coal scuttle shape and in the June of that year, the coal truck wagon shape as used in the collieries. They are in many sizes, the biggest probably being meant for sugar and the smallest as a salt cellar. There is a barrow shape and in 1881 a cradle one. These items are novelties. The 1882 Dolphin series, however, is heavy and not very attractive, but it did reflect the then current popularity of dolphins as a decorative motif. After the firm gave up in the mid-1880s George Davidson's firm acquired the Heppell moulds and patterns and some of these were later produced by Davidson's.

William Henry Heppell & Co., Newcastle Flint Glass Works, Forth Street, Newcastle-upon-Tyne. Registrations.

Registration No.	Date	Year	Parcel No.	Design
284672	26 August	1874	5	Dish (inverted thumb nail pattern round sides)
295362	23 October	1875	3	Butter dish and flower stand combined
295919	13 November		4	Plate or bowl
338286	14 August	1879	13	Tile
338287	14 August		13	Slide or top light
346543	17 February	1880	9	(Coal scuttle shape)
351191	19 June		16	(Wagon shape)
354935	7 September		1	
359806	18 December		15	(Wagon shape?)
370524	26 September	1881	1	(Indistinct cradle shape?)
372860	7 November		3	(Plate)
374437	6 December		13	
390584 to 86	24 November	1882	17	(Dolphin series)

Advertisement in Pottery Gazette, December 1880.

EDWARD MOORE & COMP?

TYNE FLINT GLASS WORKS

SOUTH SHIELDS,

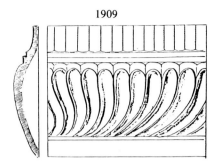

1909

Pattern of John Walsh Walsh of 14 February 1884 which influenced firms such as Edward Moore.

Edward Moore & Co., Tyne Flint Glass Works, South Shields

The earliest registrations are in June 1861 and are for patterns. One is an oval thumb nail pattern and the other a more complicated one of petal and crescent shapes. This pattern has been used on a decanter and it is a handsome looking piece, imitating cut glass. Apart from 1868, when there is a registration for a glass gas globe, there are no more registrations until October 1886. The pattern of the October piece is the first of the gadroon ones and was probably done for a gas globe initially. There were many of these registrations in 1887 for glass shades in bowl shapes with various patterns, such as the hobnail one of April 13th, and at that time there were several patterns registered for tumblers.

As mentioned earlier, the principal registrations are for September 1887 and for March 1888 when the firm registered classical designs with gadroons and pillars for bowls, covered bowls and jugs. Most of these bowls are in plain glass, but they were made also in an opaque caramel colour. This shade, however, is extremely rare and is not often seen. Edward Moore produced marbled glass like that of the Sowerby malachite items and also a clear emerald green. It is interesting to note as well that in the November of 1887, Sowerby's registered a sugar basin with small pillars and gadroons to the base, whilst in September 1887 Henry Greener registered a pretty pattern for table glass incorporating fan shaped gadroons. George Davidson & Co. made a fine sugar and cream set with pillars in August 1889. They come in clear glass but are often seen in pearline as well. It seems that the first registration of a new style or type of decoration was always followed swiftly by a similar one, from one or other of the glass firms, but the name Edward Moore is closely associated with the word 'gadroons'.

The last registrations are in 1889 and the most interesting one is that of September 18th, which is for a bowl imitating basket work and is reminiscent of Sowerby's many baskets. Sadly, there are no further registrations after the disastrous fire of 1891, although the firm continued to operate until the 20th century.

TERMS, &c.

Payment received in Cash only; less five per cent. discount, at one month from date of Invoice.

The Goods are delivered to the Carriers in South Shields; the Carriage from thence is payable by the Purchaser.

No allowance is made for Breakage.

Packages are charged :—Hogsheads, 6/- each ; Large and middle size Tierces, 5/- each ; Smaller Tierces, 3/6 each ; Casks, 2/6 each.

Empty Packages, can only be allowed for, if returned *in good condition* Carriage Paid, within one month from date of Invoice, addressed in full, EDWARD MOORE AND CO., TYNE FLINT GLASS WORKS, SOUTH SHIELDS ; with the name of the *Sender* added. They must also be advised to us by post.

BISCUIT BOXES, ICE PAILS & VASES
C 1870

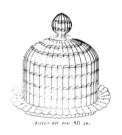

From Edward Moore's Pattern Book.

Edward Moore & Co., Tyne Flint Glass Works, South Shields.
Registrations.

217207

Registration No.	Date	Year	Parcel No.	Design
141573	27 June	1861	1	(Pattern)
141642	29 June		4	(Pattern)
217207	5 March	1868	11	Pressed glass gas globe

58275	7 October	1886		Pattern (all over gadroon pattern)
63543	15 December			Shape and pattern of gas moon or shade (similar to above)
65339	14 January	1887		Shape and pattern of pressed glass gas shade (bowl shape with horizontal ridging)
67425	7 February			Shape and pattern of pressed glass gas shade (similar to above)
68249	18 February			Shape and pattern of pressed glass lamp shade (similar to above)
71753	12 April			Shape and pattern of an oval covered dish (with gadroons)
71816	13 April			Shape and pattern of a gas shade (bowl shape with hobnail pattern)
72815	28 April			Pattern for a pressed glass shade (bowl shape)
72884	29 April			Pattern for a pressed glass shade (bowl shape with serrated rim and pattern of circles)
75015/6	8 June			Pattern (tumblers)
75091/2	9 June			Pattern (tumblers)
76878 to 80	13 July			Shape (oval, lobed)
76935	14 July			Pattern (gadroon base to tumbler shape)
77341	25 July			Pattern (tumbler shape with facets)
80012	1 September			Shape and pattern (swirling gadroons on bowl shape)
80013	1 September			Shape and pattern (jug and covered bowls with pillars and gadroons. Twisted handles)
81959	24 September			Shape and pattern (similar to 71816)
82606	30 September			Shape and pattern (similar to 80013 but more elaborate)
83773	12 October			Shape (jug and covered bowls in oval and lobed shape. Twisted handles)
88124	29 November			Shape (similar to above)
88125	29 November			Pattern (tumbler)
88730	5 December			Shape (similar to 88124)
92045	23 January	1888		Shape (imit. cut quatre foil shape. Twisted handles)
94820	1 March			(Set of covered bowls and jug with gadroons on bowls and covers. Twisted handle to jug)
95625	12 March			(Tazza shape)
95775	14 March			(Swirling gadroons. Twisted handle)
107316	5 September			(Double shell light)
109612	2 October			(Imit. cut dish with clear lobes)
120437	26 February	1889		(Comport shape. Elaborate imit. cut with plain swags)
129933	31 July			(Fluted hat)
132189	31 August			(Bowl imit. basket work with twisted handles)
133560	18 September			(Bowl imit. basket work with twisted handles)
139589	4 December			(Bowl shape - circular raised pattern)
141068	24 December			(Bowl shape with ivy or vine leaf and tendrils)

80012
Side View:

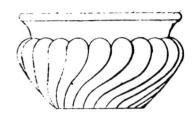

Underside View:

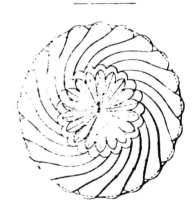

133560
Elevation.

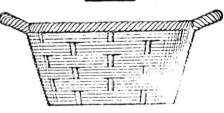

Plan.

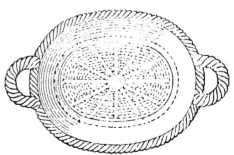

21

Edward Moore & Co.

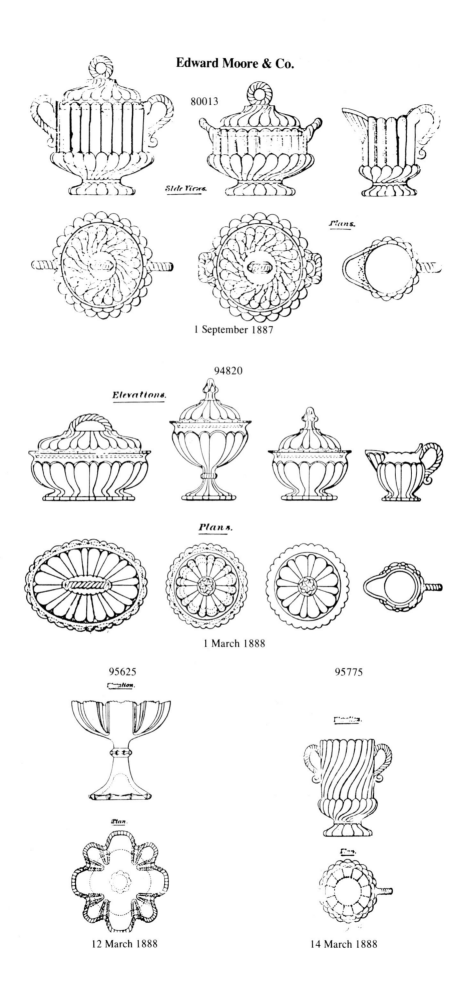

80013

Side Views.

Plans.

1 September 1887

94820

Elevations.

Plans.

1 March 1888

95625

Elevation.

Plan.

12 March 1888

95775

14 March 1888

Sowerby & Co., Ellison Glass Works, Gateshead-on-Tyne.

In 1882 Sowerby's Ellison Glass Works Limited

Sowerby & Co first registered a design in 1872, there were to be nine that year, 1873 had two, 1874 six, but by 1877 over sixty registrations. The pieces registered were various, ranging from a covered dish, decanters and bowl (these were the first items in 1872) through the gamut of sugars, butters, ice pails, sweetmeats, baskets, vases, celery vases, flower troughs, spill vases and so on to cater for the Victorian taste. The imagination was as prolific as the output and there are some delightful articles considering these were meant to be the day to day pieces of the ordinary home. For instance, some of the celery vases were made so that they could be upturned and a dish balanced on top to form a comport.

Sowerby's pattern books show in detail the decoration of the majority of their special pieces and also which of the items were registered. It is possible that they started to register more and more designs when they realized the success of the vitro-porcelain ware, which being opaque, gave the glass a substance similar to porcelain. It was pretty and delicate but did not look fragile.

The 1870s and 1880s were the important years. In 1877, and 1878, the most prolific years, there is a spill vase with basket work effect, a flower pot with figures and fan decoration, another vase with bullrush motif, items with angular bar shaped handles, many candlesticks and the inevitable butters and large sugars shaped like comports. It is not until later that the design of the sugars alters and they become stemless. 1879 was another important year with the plate with the design of geese and a scalloped edge, another with peacock feathers as well as different round and square vases. The 'new bowl' was in that year which is probably the best known of the Sowerby wares. It has upright ends shaped like hair combs and though the registration was just for the shape of the bowl, it is found in Queen's Ivory ware with a decoration of raised blossoms to simulate carved ivory. These pieces are typically 'aesthetic' with many of the motifs inspired by the art of Japan. In 1883 they patented the most unusual pyramid shaped glass cheese stand, in 1884 a glass post pillar money box and in 1886 a fan picture frame and the pattern and shape of a boat stand. The latter can be compared to other firm's flower trough boats of a few years earlier and that of 1888, albeit gondola shape, to John Walsh Walsh's registration in January 1887 of a boat with a space for a lamp in the centre.

Sowerby's is not as well known for their commemorative wares as Henry Greener and Greener & Co. but they produced a striking Golden Jubilee plate in 1887 with a portrait of the Queen in the centre and a rim of national emblems. There was a similar plate for the Diamond Jubilee, and also a plate and bowl commemorating the Scottish poet, Robert Burns.

The unusual items are interesting because they are rare but the charm of Sowerby glass lies in the enormous range of decoration and colour. There are the frosted angular sugars and cream jugs, with the clear glass ribbed ones, the frosted ice pails, the basket weave spill vases and hanging vases, and the flower troughs some with Nursery Rhyme and Kate Greenaway type figures. Many of the Nursery Rhyme pieces were taken from designs in the children's books by Walter Crane. These include Little Bo-peep, Jack Horner and Oranges and Lemons. Then there were country scene figures like the apple pickers or pieces with peacock, parrot, swan or bee patterns. The list is long and the pieces with patent office design registry marks often have the peacock's head trademark as well. Apart from clear glass there are many colours, some of which have been mentioned, as well there was an amber and a ruby with a hint of orange in the depths. Later on, in the mid 1920s they did iridescent orange items ('carnival glass') using the earlier moulds so that the glass continues the Victorian shape.

One of the first Sowerby items to be registered in February 1872.

393638

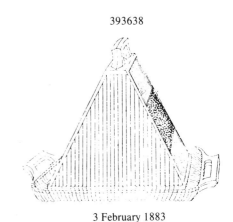

3 February 1883

Taken from drawings by Walter Crane.
See black and white photograph number 31 for Lavender's Blue.

These colours are all very distinctive and in addition there are some rare aesthetic colours which are not often found. Sowerby glass is the collectors' joy for the quality of decoration and for the range of shape and colour.

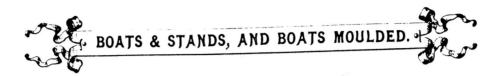

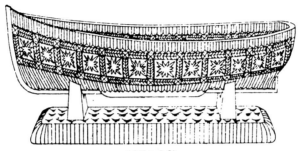

1874 *3 Sizes*
10, 12, 15 Inches and Stands.

One Stand fits all Boats.

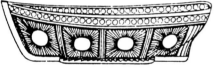

1921
6 Inch.

1874
4½ Inch.
4 Sizes.

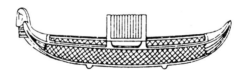

1972
Moulded, 8 and 10 Inch.
Two Sizes, no Cabin to Largest Size.

From Sowerby's Pattern Book 1880s.

39414

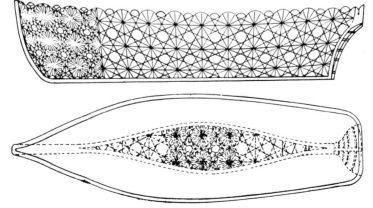

Edward Bolton 11 December 1885.

The best known of the registered glass boats.

TRADE MARKS.

EARTHENWARE.

WALLIS GIMSON & Co.,
FENTON, STOKE-ON-TRENT.

CHINA AND EARTHENWARE.

POWELL, BISHOP, & STONIER,
HANLEY, STAFF.

CHINA.

MINTONS LIMITED,
STOKE-ON-TRENT.

CHINA & EARTHENWARE.

E. J. D. BODLEY,
BURSLEM, STAFF.

EARTHENWARE.

BUCKLEY, HEATH, & CO.,
BURSLEM, STAFF.

CANDLES AND LAMPS.
CLASS 13, 15, 16, 47.

SAMUEL CLARKE,
CHILD'S HILL, LONDON, N.W.

CANDLES AND LAMPS.
CLASS 13, 15, 16, 47.

"FAIRY."

SAMUEL CLARKE,
CHILD'S HILL, LONDON, N.W.

CHINA.

WORCESTER ROYAL
PORCELAIN CO.,
LIMITED,
WORCESTER.

CHINA.

Trade Mark.
DERBY CROWN
PORCELAIN CO.,
LIMITED,
DERBY.

CHINA AND EARTHENWARE.

WM. A.
ADDERLEY & CO.,
LONGTON,
STAFF.

EARTHENWARE.

F & H
FORESTER & HULME,
SUTHERLAND POTTERY,
FENTON,
STOKE-ON-TRENT.

PRESSED GLASS.

TRADE MARK.

GEORGE DAVIDSON & Co.,
TEAMS GLASS WORKS, GATESHEAD.

GLASS.

SOWERBY, LIMITED.
GATESHEAD.

FRENCH CRYSTAL
(FLINT GLASS).

TRADE MARK.

CRISTALLERIES DE BACCARAT.
LONDON: 48, HATTON GARDEN, E.C.

Pottery Gazette advertisement of 1 May 1889, showing the trade marks of
Sowerby & Co. with George Davidson & Co. in the company of such firms as
Worcester Royal Porcelain Co. Ltd. and Mintons Ltd.

SOWERBY & CO. GATESHEAD-ON-TYNE.

Vitro-Porcelain.

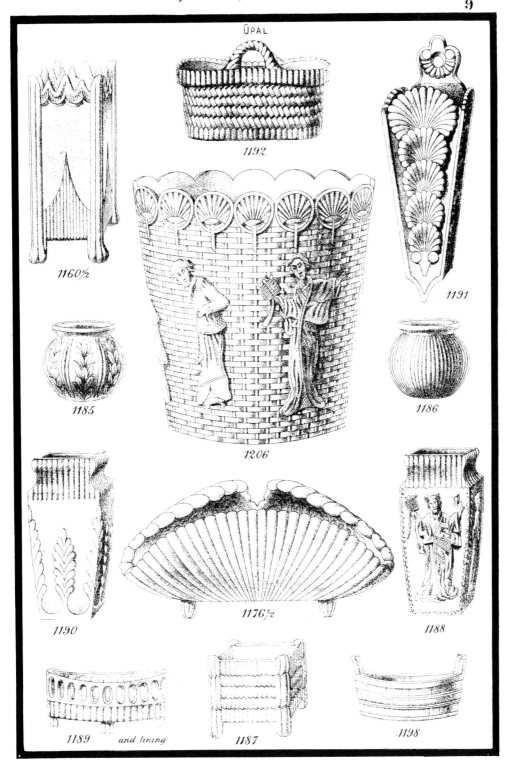

OPAL

1192

1160½

1191

1185

1206

1186

1190

1176½

1188

1189   and lining

1187

1198

TRADE MARK

Pattern Book c1879.

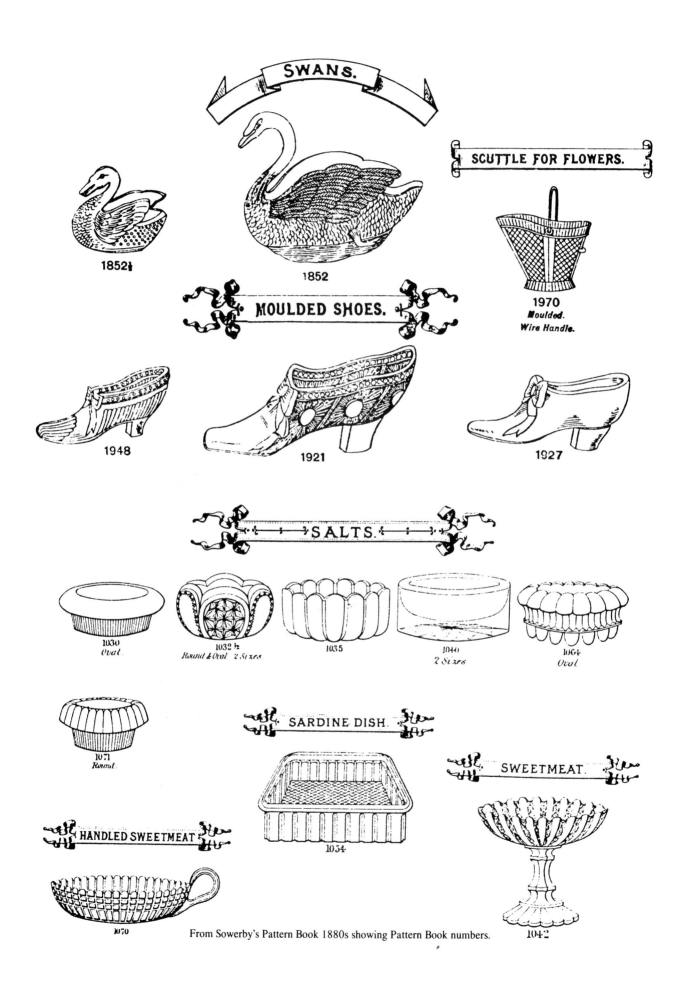

SWANS.

1852½

1852

SCUTTLE FOR FLOWERS.

1970
Moulded.
Wire Handle.

MOULDED SHOES.

1948

1921

1927

SALTS.

1030
Oval

1032½
Round & Oval 2 Sizes

1035

1040
2 Sizes

1064
Oval

1071
Round.

SARDINE DISH

1054

SWEETMEAT.

HANDLED SWEETMEAT

1070

From Sowerby's Pattern Book 1880s showing Pattern Book numbers.

1042

28

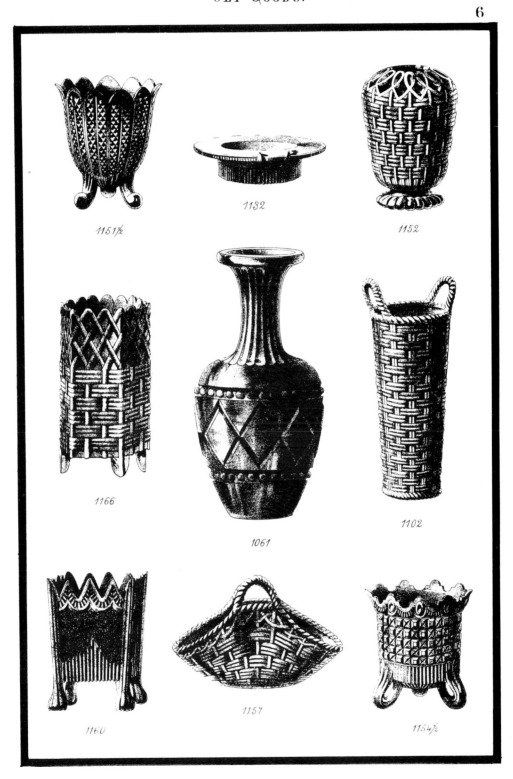

1151½

1132

1152

1166

1061

1102

1160

1157

1154½

TRADE MARK

Pattern Book c1879.

260404

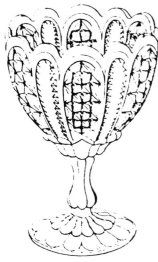

308776

308876

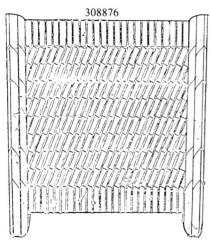

Registration for Ice Bowl. The pattern is the
same as for 13 February 1877.

Sowerby & Co., Ellison Glass Works, Gateshead-on-Tyne. Registrations

Registration No.	Date	Year	Parcel No.	Design
260183 to 86	2 February	1872	1	(Covered dish, decanters and bowl)
260404/5	12 February		6	(Sugars)
260802	29 February		5	(Butter)
267742/3	7 November		7	
273866	20 June	1873	13	Plate
274743	31 July		5	
279876	15 January	1874	6	(Sugar)
281933	22 April		8	(Sugar)
282663/4	1 June		8	(Ice plate and Plate)
284431	17 August		5	(Dish and cover)
285016	10 September		6	(Tumbler shape)
288210	1 January	1875	2	
290778	19 April		5	(Basket)
291873/4	5 June		9	Butter dish and Ice Pail
294376 to 79	10 September		6	78 (Bowl) 79 (Dish and cover)
295444	28 October		4	Dish
297041/2	17 December		16	Sugar and sweetmeat. Suite of glass (rope handle)
298870 to 76	6 March	1876	3	72 (Elaborate sugar) 73 (Bowl) 74 (Covered dish) 75 (Pail) 76 (Jug)
299050 to 54	9 March		7	51 and 52 (Covered dish) 53 and 54 (Sugars)
299424 to 26	27 March		13	24 and 25 (Vases) 26 (Covered dish)
299473	28 March		7	(Handled vase)
300419/20	8 May		6	19 (Vase) 20 (Basket)
300748	24 May		5	Basket (woven effect)
300940	29 May		19	
301312	20 June		1	Flower trough
301326/7	21 June		1	(Covered dish and vase)
302114/5	24 July		13	Glass butter middle and glass butter
302804/5	18 August		10	Plate and Celery vase
304363 to 66	16 October		8	63-65 Vases 66 Plate
305209	15 November		4	(Vase)
306887	16 January	1877	11	Salt
307686 to 96	13 February		8	86 (Finger plate or small vase) 87 and 89 (Bowls) 90 and 91 (Covered vase shapes) 92 and 94 (Bowls) 93 (Vase) 95 and 96 (Sugars)
307957/8	23 February		8	(Candlestick and fluted bowl)
308122/3	1 March		5	(Straight handled bowl and dish)
308414	13 March		10	(Spill vase, basket effect)
308495	15 March		1	(Vase similar to above)
308644	19 March		5	Flower pot (figures and fans)
308713 to 15	22 March		12	(Bullrush motif)
308776	23 March		7	(Vase woven effect)
308876	29 March		4	Glass Ice Bowl
310595 to 97	31 May		9	95 and 96 (Angular bar shape handles)
314265 to 85	18 September		7	65-82 Vases 83 and 84 Baskets (83 Gladstone Bag shape)

Sowerby & Co. (continued)

Registration No.	Date	Year	Parcel No.	Design
315664 to 74	29 October	1877	6	64 Bowl 65-70 Vases 71 Sugar basin 72 Handled vase 73 Basket
316490 to 92	20 November		4	90 Glass plate 91 and 92 Baskets
317233/4	17 December		12	33 Candlestick 34 Jug
317277 to 80	19 December		1	77 Candlestick 78 Sugar basin 79 and 80 Butters
318789 to 95	20 February	1878	3	89 Covered sugar 90 Candlestick 91 Butter 92 Inkstand 93 Sugar 94 Stand 95 Covered sugar
319585 to 89	20 March		7	85 Vase 86 Biscuit jar 87 Glass plate 88 Two-handled basket 89 Round vase
319619/20	22 March		8	Vase and Basket
321368 to 79	14 May		9	68 Butter 69 Sugar box 70 Butter with sunk handle 71 Basket 72 and 73 Vases 74 Two-handled basket 75-8 Vases 79 Basket
322819 to 25	25 June		10	19 Sugar basin 20 Butter 21 Salt 22 Vase 23 Vase 24 Butter 25 Salt
323400	8 July		9	Basket
324321/2	29 July		4	(Vases)
324929 to 32	12 August		6	29 Flower vase 30 Round salt 31 Round vase 32 Four-footed dish
325096 to 101	16 August		11	96 Butter 97 Three-footed salver 98 Round sugar 99 Round trinket stand 100 Round vase 101 Round vase
325534	30 August		16	Comport
328740 to 51	4 November		10	40 Biscuit box 41 Vase 42 Sugar 43 Sugar 44 Vase 45 Vase 46 Basket 47 Jug 48 Water Bottle 49 Round sugar 50 Butter 51 Round dish

314283

18 September 1877

319589

321371

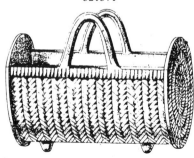

These drawings are taken from the Pattern Book in lieu of the representations.

335972

"New bowl". Most often seen in Patent Ivory Queen's Ware with raised decoration of blossoms.

338296

Sowerby & Co. (continued)

Registration No.	Date	Year	Parcel No.	Design
328919	7 November	1878	17	Candlestick
329376	20 November		11	Candlestick
330348 to 52	13 December		16	48 Double vase
				49 Dish
				50 Dish
				51 Candlestick
				52 Double vase
330604	23 December		2	New pattern vase
330964	8 January	1879	10	Round handled sweetmeat
332051 to 54	8 February		8	51 Round vase on four feet
				52 Three-square vase
				53 Butter
				54 Dish
332195	12 February		17	Dish
333167 to 73	10 March		9	67 Plate and butter dish
				68 Round sugar and cover
				69 Round butter with two handles
				70 Mustard and cover
				71 Basket
				72 Vase
				73 Tea caddy
333424 to 29	17 March		11	24 Butter
				25 Dish on feet
				26 Plate
				27 Trinket stand
				28 Vase
				29 Vase (trinket)
334634 to 43	28 April		7	34 Plate (new design geese & scalloped edge)
				35 Round vase
				36-42 Vases
				43 Mustard
335969 to 72	6 June		10	69 New vase
				70 Butter
				71 Flower pot
				72 New bowl (sometimes found decorated to simulate carved ivory)
336594/5	30 June		14	94 Plate
				95 Double vase
337409 to 15	22 July		6	09 Carafe
				10 Square plate
				11 Plate
				12 Hanging vase
				13 Two handled bowl
				14 Double vase
				15 Vase
337623 to 27	29 July		13	23-25 Vases
				26 Handled sweetmeat
				27 Sugar
338294 to 98	14 August		15	94 Sugar
				95 Basket
				96 Vase, three swans
				97 Basket
				98 Double hanging vase
339194 to 200	4 September		7	94 Sugar and cover
				95 Sugar (three feet)
				96 Dish
				97 Basket
				98 Vase
				99 Square dish on four feet
				200 Candlestick with perforations

Sowerby & Co. (continued)

Registration No.	Date	Year	Parcel No.	Design
339498 to 502	12 September	1879	13	498 Butter and cover 499 Sugar 500 Butter and cover 501 Celery vase 502 Jelly dish
340002 to 06	18 September		13	02 Basket 03 Bowl 04 Sugar 05 Square vase 06 Handled jelly
340254	23 September		13	New decoration for pressed glass
343724 to 31	2 December		21	24 Round butter and cover 25 Butter 26 Two handled plate 27-31 Vases
345042 to 44	9 January	1880	11	42 Round vase 43 Square trinket 44 Square sugar
350083 to 93	24 May		8	83 Bowl 84 Sugar 85 Vase 86 Dish 87 Handled dish 88 Basket 89-90 Bowls 91-92 (Trinkets or similar with handles) 93 Butter
352133 to 37	13 July		11	(Vases)
352840 to 45	26 July		10	40-41 New sugar 42 New butter 43 New shape dish 44 New shape basket 45 New shape sugar
355154 to 58	14 September		1	54 Candlestick (bedroom shape) 55 Butter 56-58 Dishes
355627 to 29	24 September		9	27 Butter 28 Sugar 29 Vase
362734 to 44	11 March	1881	2	34-36 Sugars (36 upright churn shape) 37 Round salt 38 Mustard 39 Sugar 40 Salt 41 Candlestick 42 Dish 43 Butter 44 Sugar
363048/9	19 March		11	48 Basket 49 Sweetmeat
364167	20 April		9	Butter
365165	19 May		9	Sugar
370370 to 79	21 September		16	70-71 Sugars 72 and 75 Butters with hollow for ice 73 and 74 Butters (round) 76 Celery vase 77 and 79 Sugars (not on stems, bowl shape) 78 Sweetmeat (has handles, scalloped rim)

352844

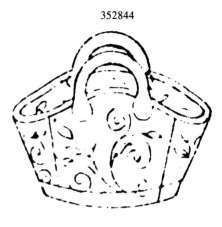

"Dolphin Bowl". In Sowerby Pattern Book of 1882, trade marked but not registered.

6481

19937

48909

Registration No.	Date	Year	Parcel No.	Design
374682 to 86	14 December	1881	6	82 Comport
				83 Dish (square)
				84 Sugar
				85 and 86 Salts
374774 to 78	15 December		10	74 Toast Rack
				75 and 77 Sugars
				76 and 78 Salts

Sowerby's Ellison Glass Works Limited.

Registration No.	Date	Year	Parcel No.	Design
376905	9 February	1882	20	Glass picture frame
380132 to 34	28 April		13	32 Dish
				33 and 34 Sugars
384453 to 55	9 August		14	53 Bowl
				54 Sugar
				55 Photo frame
385624/5	29 August		13	24 Butter
				25 Sugar
388896	25 October		16	Dish
393638 to 43	3 February	1883	11	38 Cheese stand (pyramid shape)
				39 and 41 Sugars (41 not on stem)
				40 Pillar butter & cover
				42 Bowl
				43 Butter

Registration No.	Date	Year	Design
4833	7 April	1884	Pattern
5849	29 April		Pattern and shape
6481	8 May		Pattern and shape of flower vase (twig handles with flowers on twig)
7978/9	5 June		Butter dish and cover, shape and pattern (78 vertical all over ribbing, 79 horizontal ribbing)
10966/7	11 August		66 Pattern and shape
			67 Sugar basin, shape and ornamentation
13563	19 September		Handle of jug made at the side instead of at the back opposite the lip
13792	24 September		Shape of glass post pillar money-box manufacturered in one piece
19937	6 January	1885	Pattern of sugar basin
20775	21 January		Pattern of water jug (middle band of imit. cut)
21284	31 January		Pattern of glass dish
24953	13 April		Shape of butter dish
30244	22 July		Pattern of a sugar
32253	27 August		Pattern of dish (imit. cut)
37110/11	4 November		10 Shape of sugar
			11 Pattern of sugar (fruit pattern)
39062 to 64	3 December		Pattern of sugar (62 not on stem)
42947	10 February	1886	Pattern of dish
44659	11 March		Shape of dish
45759	25 March		Pattern of sugar (scroll band in middle)
47514	21 April		Pattern and shape of pressed glass fan picture frame
48228	4 May		Pattern and shape of butter (fan shaped lid)
48909/10	11 May		09 Shape of celery (scalloped top and feet)
			10 Shape of sweetmeat (shell shape on shell feet)
50071	1 June		Pattern of butter
52434	13 July		Pattern and shape of boat stand

Sowerby's Ellison Glass Works Ltd. (continued)

56962

Registration No.	Date	Year	Design
54314 to 16	18 August	1886	14 Shape and design of moulded glass sugar basin (star burst pattern with plain glass bands criss-crossing) 15 and 16 Shape of moulded glass jelly dish
56961 to 66	23 September		Shape and pattern of sugar. 61 (with stem) 62 (stemless, basket weave pattern) 63 (with stem, imit. cut)
64086	22 December		Pattern of sugar (sun pattern)
64106	23 December		Pattern of butter (with vertical ribbing)
68846	1 March	1887	Pattern of dish (similarities to 64086)
77881	2 August		Pattern and shape of butter (leaf pattern)
77967	3 August		Pattern and shape of biscuit (imit. cut with flutes)
78084	3 August		Pattern and shape of sugar and cover (free pattern with dots)
78551	11 August		Pattern of sugar (free pattern with dots)
78704	13 August		Pattern of sugar (imit. cut)
80530	10 September		Pattern of sugar basin in glass (imit. cut)
83777	7 October		Pattern and shape of an advertising plate in pressed glass
84001	15 October		Pattern of sugar (imit. cut in squares bordered by plain glass)
84218	18 October		Pattern of dish (imit. cut)
84747	21 October		Pattern of butter (vine pattern)
85870	1 November		Shape of comportier and dish (shown with leaf pattern to dish)
87058	15 November		Pattern and shape of shoe (with bow, fluted side and toe)
87776/7	24 November		76 Pattern of sugar (gadroons on base) 77 Pattern of salt (hexagonal with mitres)
91431/2	14 January	1888	31 Pattern of dish (imit. cut) 32 Pattern of sugar (imit. cut and mitres)
95300	7 March		(Gondola shape with imit. cut)
95894	16 March		
98215/6	18 April		(Imit. cut coal bucket and an anvil)
99715	9 May		(Elaborate imit. cut)
106892	30 August		(Vase and pattern)
106938	31 August		(Elaborate imit. cut)
111269/70	17 October		69 (All pillars star shaped) 70 (Flower shape with six petals)
113560	13 November		(Imit. cut. Engraved?)
114044	17 November		(Candle holder)
117569	17 January	1889	
120229	23 February		(Cup)
122393	30 March		(Swan sitting on bowl)
126940	11 June		(Elaborate imit. cut)
133053	11 September		(Jug shape)
133909	24 September		(Jug shape)
139808	6 December		
141080	27 December		(Imit. cut flower shapes)
142675	22 January	1890	(Basket shape)
165559	30 January	1891	
173059	18 June		(Mostly imit. cut)(Sowerby & Co., Lemington Glass Works, Newcastle-on-Tyne)

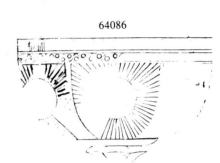

64086

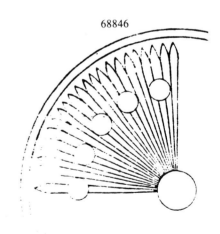

68846

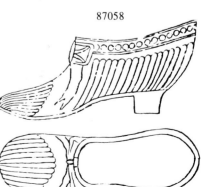

87058

87776

24 November 1887
Gadroons similar to Edward Moore.

Sowerby's Ellison Glass Works Ltd. (continued)

Registration No.	Date	Year	Design
189324	16 March	1892	(Imit. cut)
215082	15 July	1893	(Angular, tumbler design)
217199	25 August		(Angular, dish)
238352	23 August	1894	(Tumbler with twisted pillar base)

George Sowerby Ltd, Lemington Glassworks, Newcastle-upon-Tyne

358727	13 June	1900	(Tumbler shape)
363130	8 September		(Similar)
374792	1 June	1901	

99715

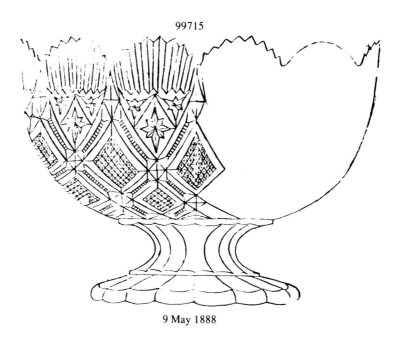

9 May 1888

141080

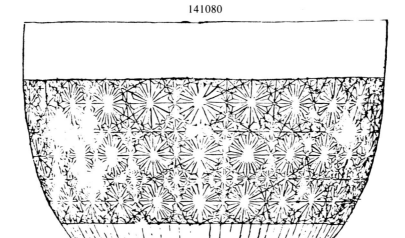

27 December 1889
Not unlike pattern of G. Davidson & Co. of August 1891.

Burtles, Tate & Co., Poland Street, Manchester.

Burtles, Tate & Co., Poland Street first registered in 1870 a design for ornamenting glass. The second registration in October 1871 was of a hand, registered as a chimney piece ornament. There is not much between then and 1885 when there were several registrations of flower stands and holders. The best known in pressed glass are January 8th 1885, a swan flower holder, not unlike the one in Sowerby's pattern book, June 29th, a flower boat and on December 28th 1886, an elephant flower holder. All three can be found in opal glass and remind one very much of Sowerby pieces. In 1887 there is a shoe flower holder, which again can be compared to one of Sowerby's of about that time. At the end of the century the electric light shade patterns are pretty, but the best pieces were definitely mid-1880s because of their resemblance to Sowerby.

64234

28 December 1886

65455

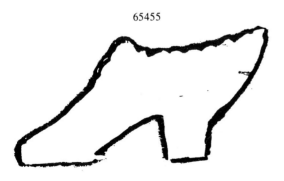

17 January 1887

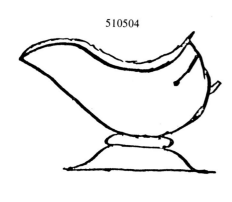

475286

501822

510504

Burtles, Tate & Co., Poland Street Glass Works, Manchester. Registrations

Registration No.	Date	Year	Parcel No.	Design
239136	24 February	1870	9	Design for ornamenting glass (vertical columns)
256336	3 October	1871	4	Design for Chimney Piece ornament (hand)
262193	23 April	1872	5	Ornamental glass
351062	17 June	1880	19	(Crimped edge: glass vessel)
399313	12 June	1883	14	(Glass vase and stand)
3613/4	14 March	1884		Ornamental design applicable for patterns
20085/6	8 January	1885		85 Design for glass flower holder or bracket
				86 Design for glass flower holder (swan)
20972	24 January			Shape and pattern of flower stand
21108 to 10	28 January			Pattern and shape of flower stand (crimped edge)
21326/7	2 February			Shape and pattern of flower stand (similar)
21328/9				Shape and pattern of flower stand (29 slender stem - turned over crimped top)
24100	20 March			Shape and pattern of flower stand
26480	7 May			Shape of glass shell
29106	29 June			Pattern of flower boat
34196	26 September			Pattern and shape of glass flower vase
39807	18 December			Pattern and shape of flower bracket
44445	8 March	1886		Pattern and shape of flower boat
64234	28 December			Pattern and shape of flower holder (elephant)
65455	17 January	1887		Pattern and shape of new flower holder (shoe)
98578	23 April	1888		Design for a glass sugar basin (imit. cut)
109531	1 October			
117556/7	14 January	1889		Design for flower vase (56 naturalistic tree trunk shape)
120808	4 March			Design for flower vase (ostrich shape)
142985	28 January	1890		Design for electric light globe
148661	30 April			Whisky vase
166178	10 February	1891		(Triple flower vase on short stem)
216088	3 August	1893		Design for glass dish (simple imit. cut)
316413	24 March	1898		
336261	6 April	1899		Design for electric light shade (leaf pattern)
339343	8 June			Design for electric light shade (oak leaves and acorns)
351372	5 January	1900		Design for electric light shade (shell pattern)
386616/7	3 February	1902		(Spiral rods)
388857	20 March			(Elab. patterned vase)
391814	3 June			Design for a perforated division of a dish
403657	17 January	1903		Design for electric shade
406300	5 March			Design for cover for bird glass
427524	25 February	1904		Design for arm of flower stand (spiral rod shape)
474329	20 February	1906		Design for railway carriage lamp glass (classical leaf motifs)
475286	7 March			Design for salad bowl (imit. cut)
501821/2	11 May	1907		Designs for salt cellar and ink-pot (as if set in a book for the base)
502044	15 May			Design for flower vase
510504	29 August			Design for salt cellar - (scuttle shape)

James Derbyshire & Brother, Hulme, Manchester.

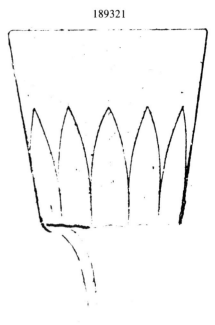

189321

The fourth Manchester firm, James Derbyshire & Brother of Hulme, registered thirteen items between 1864 and 1869, namely five goblets, two butter coolers, pressed basin moons (the description given in the register), a gas moon, a celery stand, a plain barrel shaped tumbler, a dish imitating cut glass and ornamental designs for a set, to consist of sugar basin, cream jug and butter dish, equally imitating cut glass. The designs of 1865 for the celery stand and gas moon have the Greek key pattern like the Molineux & Webb comport of 1864, though the James Derbyshire celery is more elaborate and heavy looking.

25 August 1865

In 1870 the firm registered as J.J. & T. Derbyshire. Both in 1870 and 1872 there are ornamental designs for a Breakfast set. The 1868 design for a set of sugar basin, cream jug and butter dish is an elaborate one imitating cut glass with faceted diamond shapes, set in petal swags. The pattern is continuous around the bowl. The dish which follows in the records is similar. The Breakfast set pattern for sugar basin, butter dish, cream jug and vase of 1870 has a scroll border with a diamond shaped pattern spaced at equal distance round the bowl of the sugar basin and butter dish cover. For the butter lid there are four diamond cartouches round the centre of the domed lid. The pattern is much simpler than that of 1868, though there is a resemblance. The 1872 set consists of designs for sugar basin, cream jug, butter dish and cover, flower vase and celery, round and oval dishes and a comport. The design is classical and different with star centres and vertical lines to give the impression of columns. There is a scroll border and a fine ribbed edge to the pieces. Most of these James Derbyshire sets were of the highest quality and sadly are difficult to find. In 1872 too, there are such diverse registrations as a hand, quite plain with a jewelled wrist, a Roman vase, and a dolphin comport, which is a couple of years earlier than the Percival, Vicker's dolphin stand. The dolphins form the base of the comport. The dish top has a most attractive shell pattern. By 1876 the firm became James Derbyshire & Sons. These early Derbyshire registrations set a standard by which later registrations should be judged.

242570

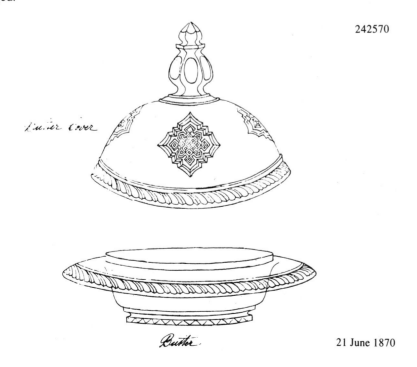

Butter Cover

Butter.

21 June 1870

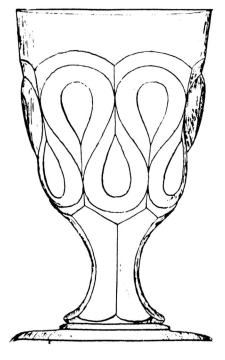

198277

James Derbyshire & Brother, Hulme, Manchester. Registrations

Registration No.	Date	Year	Parcel No.	Design
175421	14 June	1864	4	Goblet
180699	2 November		4	Butter cooler
182248	10 December		7	Pressed basin moons
186847	16 May	1865	4	Celery stand
189066	15 August		4	Gas moon
189321	25 August		6	Goblet
189705	12 September		2	Goblet
193419	14 December		5	Plain barrel shape tumbler
198277	16 June	1866	4	Goblet
206304	25 February	1867	5	Butter cooler
218988	29 May	1868	11	Ornamental designs for set; sugar basin, cream jug and butter dish
227410	22 February	1869	12	Ornamental design dish (imit. cut)
228612	13 April		7	Goblet

J.J. & T. Derbyshire

242570	21 June	1870	3	Ornamental design for a breakfast set
251012	15 March	1871	9	(Ornamental design)
261445	25 March	1872	5	Bridgewater & British Union Glass Works, Manchester. (Pattern)
262680	11 May		9	(Hand)
267727	6 November		11	Roman vase
268739	11 December		4	The dolphin comport
268810	14 December		8	Breakfast set

James Derbyshire & Sons, Trentham Street, Chester Road, Hulme

305541	28 November	1876	10

186847

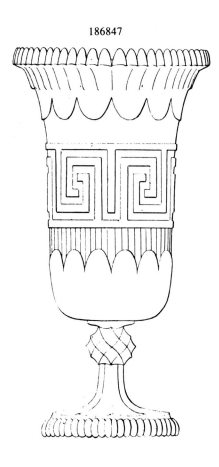

218988

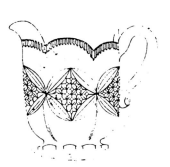

John Derbyshire, Regent Road Flint Glass Works, Salford, Manchester.

In 1873 John Derbyshire produced a fine "sugar, cream and service in glass" in the pineapple pattern. Between the oval shaped diamond pattern, like the body of a pineapple, are leaf shapes similar to the top of the fruit. At that time too, he registered a couple of goblets with an oval figure of eight pattern. They are somewhat similar to those registered in 1866 when the firm was James Derbyshire & Brother. In 1874 came the now best known registrations; a glass hand holding a naturalistic vase with bullrushes; the most sought after of all, the lion paperweight after Landseer; a greyhound for "paperweight and jar cover" and the figure of Britannia. About a year later John Derbyshire produced two more figures in the shape of Punch and Judy. These were marked with his trademark and can be found in both frosted and clear glass. In 1875 also there was a Conservatory vase and "Lady's Boot" spill holder. This is one of the earliest shoe shapes, Sowerby's was over ten years later. Glass shoes with streamers, bows or buckles, like the boat troughs and swan shapes were a popular theme. In 1876 John Derbyshire registered a winged sphinx paperweight (Molineaux, Webb & Co did a sphinx in 1875) a swan vase, "spell" glass, and finally a tobacco jar with lid. The lion, greyhound and Britannia paperweights all have a distinctive ridged plinth as do some of the Newfoundland dog paperweights (which are mostly unmarked) that are attributed to John Derbyshire. The dog in question is similar to the one that was painted by Landseer in a painting known as "A Distinguished Member of the Humane Society", and then used as a model for porcelain plaques and such like. The plinth for the winged sphinx is completely different and has a pattern of scroll motifs. The last registration in 1877 is in the name of "The Regent Flint Glass Co." Apart from the patents John Derbyshire marked some of his glass with an anchor and his initials, the lion for instance has both registration and personal mark. A. Ruch & Co., of 12 Lawrence Pountney Lane, London, also used an anchor as a trademark in the 1890s and therefore if the pieces were registered they have a set of numbers to identify them, whereas Derbyshire pieces are prior to the 1884 registered numbers and have the diamond shaped mark.

The whole point of the Patent Office design registrations is that if the letters and numbers are clear in the diamond shaped marks up to 1884, a definite day, month, year and parcel number can be given for the item registered. So often the marks are indistinct and it is no good hazarding a guess at the unformed letter or number without checking the item's description against the possibilities and eliminating the unlikely ones. The parcel number is very important as an added clue if the marks are not clear, and there are also registered drawings of the objects so it should be possible to say what factory it cannot be, even if it is difficult to ascertain the exact date of the piece. The same applies to the numbers given after 1884. As with jigsaws, there is only one answer, but when the pieces fit together it is very satisfying and rewarding and for the collector the search for certain colours, pieces and patterns, is very special.

280197

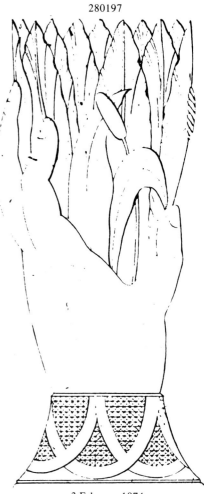

3 February 1874

300300

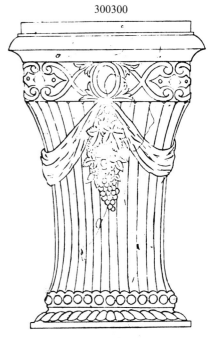

28 April 1876

274962

John Derbyshire, Regent Road Flint Glass Works, Salford

Registration No.	Date	Year	Parcel No.	Design
274961 to 63	8 August	1873	7	61 Sugar, cream and service in glass (pineapple pattern) 62 and 63 Goblet and service in glass (oval pattern)
275756	2 September		9	Piano foot
279532	6 January	1874	6	Sugar basin and cream ewer
280197	3 February		5	Glass hand and vase
282260	12 May		6	Piano foot
283406	3 July		4	Lion after Landseer for a paperweight
285175	11 September		5	Greyhound
287495	26 November		5	Britannia - same figure but different sides
293356	5 August	1875	8	Conservatory vase
296643	6 December		7	Lady's boot. Spill holder
299022/3	9 March	1876	4	22 Winged sphinx. Paperweight 23 Swan vase
300300	28 April		2	Spell glass
300655	17 May		9	Tobacco jar with lid

Regent Flint Glass Co., Regent Road

308667	21 March	1877	4	Preserve jar
309902	4 May		4	Bull's head piano foot

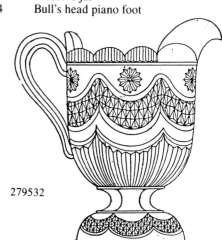

279532

299022

Molineux & Co., Manchester

186462

The second area to be considered for pressed glass firms is that of Manchester. Molineux & Co. of Manchester registered their first design on 7 December 1846 for a decanter — they were one of the earliest of the main firms to register. The firm as Molineux & Webb (then Molineaux, Webb & Co. from 1864 to 1890) registered some sixty designs, but it was not until 1865 that the spelling changed to Molineaux. It was in 1864 that they registered a comport, or raised dish, with the well known Greek key pattern. It is interesting to compare the celery glass of 1865, which equally has the Greek key pattern with that of the heavier James Derbyshire celery glass for the same year. The pattern is carried through into 1866 with a cream jug. The domestic items of the 1860s and 1870s are of a certain quality; simple and in good taste. In 1870 some of the designs have a look of Davidson with panelled designs of plain glass next to diamond ones and there is a butter with the Greek key motif back again. In 1874 and 1875 there are some mundane registrations for railway carriage glass roof lamps, but later in 1875 there is an unusual pressed glass sphinx which is worth comparing with the year later, winged sphinx of John Derbyshire. They also did a pressed glass 'dolphin' pillar that year which was one of the earliest although Percival, Vickers & Co. Limited registered a naturalistic flower holder in 1874 with a dolphin stand. In 1882 W.H. Heppell did their dolphin series; in 1884 Davidson showed a dolphin base candlestick in their pattern book and Sowerby's made a dolphin bowl. This bowl has blossom decoration on it and has three dolphins for feet. The bowl is found in many colours and is very striking to look at. It is illustrated in the Sowerby pattern book of 1882, but the bowls were made for many years after, and into the twentieth century, so it is not always easy to date them. Dolphins were a popular theme in Victorian glassware, along with swans and the more aesthetic peacock.

1 May 1865
Celery glass can be compared with that registered by James Derbyshire & Brother.

Molineaux, Webb & Co., unlike Davidson and Greener, registered only a few designs imitating cut glass early on, but their pattern books show that they produced many other types of glass. Not all is for pressed glass, but for high quality cut and engraved glass, normally associated with Stourbridge. There are pages of claret jugs and thin fine wine glasses. The largest section of the designs is of decanters, followed by sugar basins and cream jugs, carafes and tumblers, water jugs, goblets and celeries with smaller sections on butters, marmalades, comports and so on. Some of these patterns were for moulded glass in imitation of cut glass as shown in the advertisements of the early 1880s in the Pottery Gazette. In the 1890s there are two interesting registrations, one in 1895 showing a service of glass with a scale design and in 1896 a typical Art Nouveau design similar to the Greener one.

293100

26 July 1875
Glass Sphinx. Again comparisons may be made with the later "Winged Sphinx" of John Derbyshire.

178045

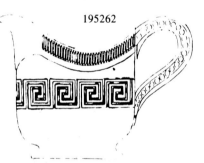

178046

Both the above have the same registration lozenge.

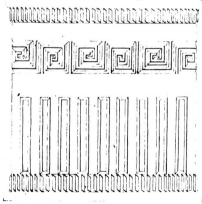

195262

209086

Molineux & Co., Manchester. Registrations

Registration No.	Date	Year	Parcel No.	Design
38643	7 December	1846	2	Decanter

Molineux & Webb, Kirby Street, Manchester

178045/6	27 August	1864	4	Comport or raised dish

Molineaux, Webb & Co.

182483	22 December	1864	6	Dish
186462/3	1 May	1865	8	62 Celery glass 63 Sugar basin
186808	12 May		6	Dish
187182/3	29 May		8	Cream jug & dish
190755 to 58	4 October		4	55 Cover of butter dish 56 Stand of butter dish 57 Butter dish 58 Cover of butter dish
191555	31 October		8	Glass dish
194616 to 18	18 January	1866	6	16 Basin 17 Cream jug 18 Celery
194685	20 January		2	Marmalade
194825	30 January		7	Marmalade
195262	15 February		2	Cream jug
209086	24 June	1867	3	Ornamental design for a glass biscuit jar
210199	10 August		3	Dish — ornamental design
210484	26 August		5	Ornamental design for a basin or butter cover
210941/2	10 September		4	Cream jug and basin, ornamental design
215734	13 January	1868	1	Ornamental design for a comport or elevated dish
216348	31 January		9	Ornamental design for a comport or elevated dish
216632	8 February		4	Ornamental design for an inkstand and cover
219769	11 July		4	Ornamental design for a celery glass
220898/9	20 August		6	Ornamental designs for a cream glass and basin glass
220900	20 August		6	Ornamental design for a sardine glass
226916/7	1 February	1869	12	Ornamental designs for a dish and celery glass
228202	27 March		1	Ornamental design for a butter
237741	3 January	1870	3	Ornamental design for a dish
239084	22 February		4	Ornamental design for a glass tumbler
240217	2 April		4	Ornamental design for a butter
241961	26 May		6	Ornamental design for a comport
242968 to 70	6 July		2	Ornamental designs for two butters and a biscuit jar
247463/4	18 November		2	Butter dishes
249600	17 January	1871	7	Dish
249808 to 10	24 January		3	08 Butter dish 09 Cream jug 10 Basin
280493 to 95	14 February	1874	10	Glass railway carriage roof lamps
289283	12 February	1875	9	Roof lamp for railway carriages
289645 to 47	26 February		4	Butters
293100	26 July		3	A pressed glass sphinx
295133	16 October		10	A pressed glass dolphin pillar

Registered as Molineux, Webb & Co.

Molineaux, Webb & Co., (continued)

Registration No.	Date	Year	Parcel No.	Design
315429	17 October	1877	2	Pressed glass dish
316776	3 December		2	Pressed glass dish
316862	6 December		3	Pressed glass dish
340206	23 September	1879	2	A pressed glass dish
344911	5 January	1880	2	Design for a pressed glass butter
344960	7 January		2	Design for a pressed glass basin (star on foot of bowl and base)
345166 to 68	14 January		2	Pressed butter dishes
370618/9	28 September	1881	3	18 Cream jug (star on base) 19 Basin (star on foot)
371262	12 October		5	A pressed glass pickle dish
375281	2 January	1882	1	Pressed glass dish (star on base)

23040/1	5 March	1885		Pattern and shape
23333 to 38	10 March			Pattern and shape
23378	11 March			Pattern and shape
29780/1	14 July			Pattern and shape
31844	21 August			Shape and pattern
70422	23 March	1887		Shape
71528	6 April			Pattern
134908	5 October	1889		(Imit. cut)

Molineaux, Webb & Co. Ltd.

143153	28 January	1890		(Imit. cut)
144779	25 February			(Free pattern)
158948	15 October			
164521	12 January	1891		
201225	21 October	1892		(Tumbler)
209414	17 March	1893		(Imit. cut service)
217651	4 September			(Barrel)
220471 to 73	14 October			(Liquor holder)
233768	11 June	1894		(Horse shoe shape)
251393	15 March	1895		(Scale design suite)
269113	15 January	1896		(Vase. Free design - similar to Greener 325194 in 1898)
271700	26 February			(Dish as above)
338590	20 May	1899		
352198	20 January	1900		(Imit. cut with gadroons)
388595	15 March	1902		(Lamp shade imit. cut)
391285	21 May			(Lamp shade imit. cut)

271700

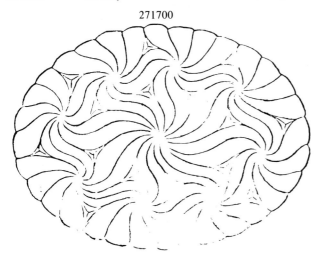

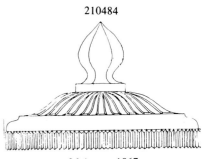

210484

26 August 1867

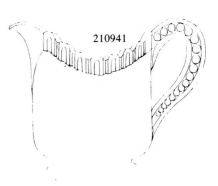

210941

10 September 1867

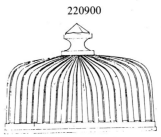

220900

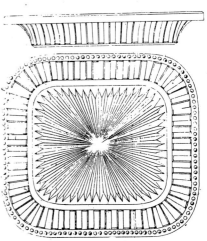

20 August 1868

6658

Elevation

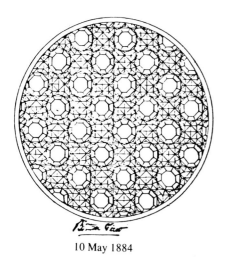

Back Face

10 May 1884

Percival, Yates & Vickers
Jersey Street, Manchester

Percival, Yates & Vickers of Jersey Street, Manchester as Percival & Yates registered their first item in 1847, three months after Molineux & Co., which was for an unexciting bottle. In June and November of that year they registered a salt cellar, a decanter, a match box and dish and in 1848 their first sugar basin. In 1865 there are four domestic items, a sugar and cream jug, comport and butter dish. Nothing is registered in 1866 but from 1867, when the firm became Percival, Vickers & Co. Ltd., there are registrations for every year to 1902 with the exceptions of 1875, 1877, 1879 and 1901. The firm registered a good many goblets and tumblers including in the 1880s all the usual domestic items of butters, cruets, marmalade jars and dishes. In 1884 the design for a round platter was in a pattern very similar to hobnail cutting. It is very like the Davidson registered one of 1890. In the mid 1880s and 1890s there were several patterns imitating cut glass, though one of the earliest pieces is the celery glass of December 1868. One of the best registrations is in 1891 when there was a set of glass with vertical and horizontal parallel mitres and this pattern occurs a few times. Some of the earlier glass had a distinctive frosted look with patterns of clear stars or diamond and leaf shapes. It is good quality colourless pressed glass, and it is relatively easy to find.

13 March 1891

217227

6 March 1868

One of the early leaf patterns (see photograph).

Percival & Yates, The British and Foreign Flint Glass Works, Manchester. Registrations

183353

Registration No.	Date	Year	Parcel No.	Design
42296	25 March	1847	3	Bottle
43655	17 June		1	Bottle
43850	30 June		6	Salt cellar
46788/9	5 November		2	88 Decanter (address given as Jersey St., Manchester)
				89 Match box
47344	27 November		2	Dish
49779	11 February	1848	2	Sugar basin

Percival, Yates & Vickers, Jersey Street, Manchester

183352/3	18 January	1865	1	Sugar and cream (large star pattern grouped round middle)
185030	21 March		6	Comport (similar)
189121/2	18 August		4	Butter dish (sunburst pattern on base, ribbed rim)

Percival, Vickers & Co. Limited

209574

209574/5	16 July	1867	2	(Bowl and oval dish elaborate pattern imit. cut)
217227	6 March	1868	7	(Decoration leaf pattern)
223322	23 October		4	(Goblet pattern of circles)
225440	14 December		6	(Ornamental design tankard)
225673	21 December		4	Celery (imit. cut)
228889	26 April	1869	5	(Pattern imit. cut)
234517	16 October		3	(Goblet imit. cut similar to above)
235821	6 November		3	(Tumbler)
237550	23 December		8	(Tumbler)
240010	26 March	1870	8	(Goblet)
243554	1 August		1	(Flower vase on stem)
253067	7 June	1871	5	(Pattern imit. cut with clear oval vertical bands)
256264	30 September		10	(Pattern - tumbler)
258445	7 December		5	(Pattern - tumbler)
262405	2 May	1872	7	(Goblet)
263032	30 May		7	
263314	11 June		4	Piano foot
269194	23 December		3	(Goblet)
269694	15 January	1873	4	(Tumbler shape)
272685 to 88	7 May		2	(Ornamental designs - plates)
278266	13 November		8	Butter cover
284031	29 July	1874	8	(Naturalistic flower holder. Dolphin stand)
301579	30 June	1876	7	A butter middle
319090	1 March	1878	8	Pressed dish
351024	17 June	1880	3	Glass tumbler
352870	27 July		9	Celery stand. Shape only registered
357730	5 November		5	Piano foot
372018	22 October	1881	15	Finger bowl (triangular)
378495	17 March	1882	4	(Dish and cover concentric ribbing)
381436	25 May		1	Oblong dish
390615	27 November		1	Design for oblong dish in glass (hobnail pattern on base)
394205	14 February	1883	11	Half pint tumbler
397022	17 April		3	(Oblong dish - hobnail pattern on base)
402690	24 August		2	Tumbler
406456	2 November		12	Jelly glass (mould)

284031

225673

Percival, Vickers & Co. Limited

225440

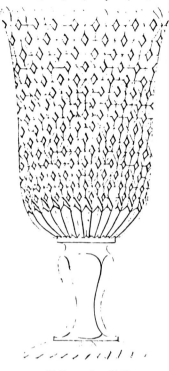

228889

14 December 1868

21 December 1868

26 April 1869

272685

272686

272687

272688

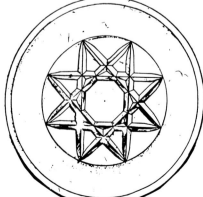

7 May 1873

Percival, Vickers & Co., Ltd. (continued)

45942

Registration No.	Date	Year	Design
1415	7 February	1884	Pattern for pressed glass ware
6658	10 May		Design for round platter in moulded glass (imit. cut similar to hobnail)
15332	18 October		Shape and pattern in pressed glass (imit. cut similar to above)
18749	10 December		Railway and other lamps - pressed scalloped band on glass
20355	14 January	1885	Pattern for pressed butter trencher (imit. cut)
20936	22 January		Design for pressed glass marmalade (imit. cut)
27553	28 May		Pattern for moulded marmalade
29145	1 July		Design for pressed glass butter (imit. cut)
35293	10 October		Design for pressed glass cruets (imit. cut)
40484	1 January	1886	Pressed glass cruet (imit. cut & plain glass)
45942	26 March		Moulded glass marmalade or biscuit jar (imit. cut)
53468	3 August		Moulded glass tumbler
56047	11 September		Pattern for pressed glass dish
60108	29 October		Design for pressed glass pillar or lamp stand (in form of lighthouse)
71869	14 April	1887	Pattern of a moulded cruet
75942	29 June		Pattern for moulded glass marmalade (with vertical mitres)
80632	12 September		Pattern of a pressed glass celery vase (imit. cut)
93905	18 February	1888	(Dish, pattern with octagons and squares)
115077	28 November		(Dish oval and two triangular shaped dishes for jam and marmalade. All have vertical mitres)
126869	8 June	1889	(Imit. cut)
134907	5 October		(Bowls, sugar and cream imit. cut with squares of plain glass)
159189	16 October	1890	Jam dish (plain vertical mitres)
168130	13 March	1891	Set of glass (vertical and horizontal parallel mitres)
173044	18 June		(Imit. cut)
189247	15 March	1892	Marmalade (imit. cut)
189344	16 March		Marmalade
192876	21 May		Improved shape of glass retort
193694/5	9 June		
193821	14 June		(Imit. cut)
194638	27 June		Cruet bottle
196639	10 August		Celery glass (imit. cut with clear glass vertical bands)
211617	3 May	1893	Jam dish (imit. cut)
213381	10 June		(Imit. cut)
233766	11 June	1894	Moulded jam dish (imit. cut base, plain plinth)
254406	7 May	1895	Electric light shade (imit. cut)
268968	13 January	1896	(Imit. cut)
275802	7 May		(Simple imit. cut)
287653	4 November		(Hobnail imit. cut moulded glass dish)
292506	23 January	1897	Moulded glass jam stand (imit. cut round upper half, octagonal shape)
305840	20 September		Moulded glass electric shade (imit. cut)
314494	18 February	1898	Glass spirit jar
319151	19 May		Butter dish, moulded glass (imit. cut)
323997	20 August		
336510	12 April	1899	(Moulded sugar and cream jug elab. imit. cut and classical shape for cream jug)
361366	3 August	1900	Design for electric shade in moulded glass (shade has pattern of over-lapping leaves)
390019	22 April	1902	Design for moulded glass dish (imit. cut upper half of dish)

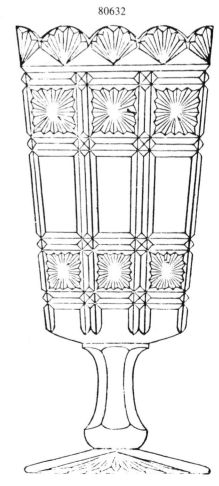

80632

75942

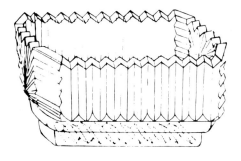

29 June 1887

268968

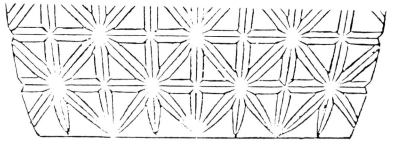

13 January 1896

(See photograph of three celery vases)

305840

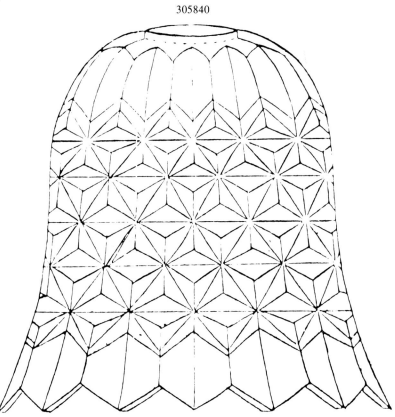

20 September 1897

71869

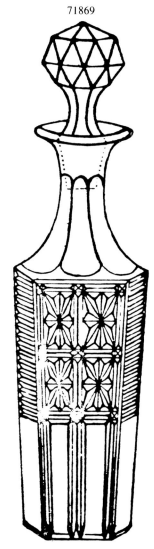

14 April 1887

GOLD MEDAL.

NEWCASTLE EXHIBITION, 1887.

GOLD MEDAL.

NEWCASTLE EXHIBITION, 1887.

SPECIMEN PAGES

OF

1889 Catalogue

OF

PRESSED GLASS

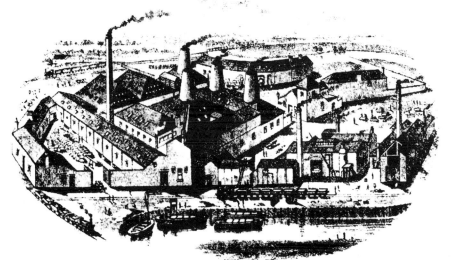

MANUFACTURED BY

GEO. DAVIDSON & CO.,

Teams Glass Works,

GATESHEAD-ON-TYNE.

OFFICES WHERE SAMPLES MAY BE SEEN:—

LONDON:—

23, Thavies Inn, Holborn, E.C.

MANCHESTER:—

15, Booth Street, Piccadilly.

INDEX OF BLACK AND WHITE PHOTOGRAPHS

1. John Derbyshire. 3 July 1874.
   Lion paperweight after Landseer.
   (Trustees of the Victoria & Albert Museum)

2. Henry Greener. 14 June 1881.
3. G. Davidson c1885. In catalogue of 1885.
4. Percival, Vickers & Co. Ltd. 13 January 1896
   2, 3, 4 Celery vases.
   (Trustees of the Victoria & Albert Museum)

5. G. Davidson & Co. 14 July 1903.
   Tea caddy.

6. Sowerby & Co. 13 February 1877.
   Salt cellar. Shows both registration and trade marks.
   Registration for basket weave pattern.

7. Sowerby & Co. 29 October 1877 trade mark on
   lid and bowl.
   Covered sugar. Frosted and plain glass.

8. Angus & Greener. 26 June 1867.
   Sugar basin. Frosted and plain glass.

9. Heavy cut glass bowl on stand to be compared with
   moulded piece by Percival, Vickers & Co., Ltd.
   Probably from a Manchester firm and likely to be
   Percival, Vickers & Co., Ltd.

10. Percival, Vickers & Co. Ltd. 16 July 1867.
    Comport, showing how good imitation cut glass could be.
    (Trustees of the Victoria & Albert Museum)

11. Percival, Vickers & Co. Ltd. 26 April 1869.
12. Sowerby & Co. 1 June 1874.
13. George Davidson & Co. c1885.
    Trade Marked.
    Three biscuit barrels.

14. Percival, Vickers & Co. Ltd. 6 March 1868.
    Comport and sugar bowl in frosted and plain glass.
    See registration drawings. (Private Collection)

15. Sowerby & Co. 4 November 1878 and trade mark.
    Cream jug. Patent Ivory Queen's Ware.

16. Sowerby & Co. c1879 trade marked.
    Swan flower holder. Patent Ivory Queen's Ware.

17. Sowerby & Co. 4 November 1878 and trade mark.
    Cream jug. Patent Ivory Queen's Ware. Registration
    was for the four feet and possibly the rim.

18. Sowerby & Co. 6 June 1879. Trade marked.
    "New Bowl". Patent Ivory Queen's Ware.

19. Henry Greener. 31 July 1869.
    Sugar bowl. Lettered "Gladstone for the Million".
    (Private collection)

20. G. Davidson & Co. c1885 trade marked.
    Dish. Daisy pattern and lettering "Give us this day", etc.

21. Edward Moore. 7 October 1886.
    Covered butter.
    (Trustees of the Victoria & Albert Museum)

22. Jane Webb & Joseph Hammond trading as the Executors of
    the late Joseph Webb. 16 April 1873.
    Dish. Frosted with clear shell feet. A piece of Stourbridge
    pressed glass. Edward Moore bought up this firm's moulds
    in 1888.

23. G. Davidson & Co. c1890 trade marked.
    Covered butter. 'Twig' knop similar to basket handle of
    15 August 1891.

24. Molineux, Webb & Co. 1 May 1865.
    Sugar bowl. Frosted and clear glass.
25. Angus & Greener. 26 June 1867.
    Raised dish. Frosted and clear glass.
    (24, 25 Trustees of the Victoria & Albert Museum)

26. Sowerby's Ellison Glass Works Ltd. 15 November 1887
    and trade mark. Shoe.

27. Sowerby's Ellison Glass Works Ltd. c1888 trade marked.
    Shoe.

28. Unmarked c1890.
    Shoe. Probably Sowerby's. Amber glass.

29. Sowerby & Co. c1880 trade marked.
    Opal. "Elizabeth, Elspeth, Betsy and Bess".
30. Opal. "Crosspatch".
31. Turquoise. "Lavender's Blue".
    29, 30, 31 Three vitro-porcelain pieces showing nursery
    rhyme characters from designs by Walter Crane.

32. W. H. Heppell & Co. 6 December 1881.
    Sugar bowl in opal. Shell shape.

33. Sowerby & Co. 17 December 1875.
    Cream jug in jet with "rope" handle.

34. Percival, Yates & Vickers. 18 August 1865.
    Covered butter dish in frosted glass.

35. Greener & Co. 14 December 1888.
    Dish lettered "Peace and Plenty".

36. Sowerby's Ellison Glass Works Ltd. 1 March 1887.
    Dish.
37. Sowerby's Ellison Glass Works Ltd. 22 December 1886.
    Small Boat.
    36, 37 Two similar patterns. Trade marked.

38. Edward Bolton. 11 December 1885.
    Flower trough made as a boat. One of the best known
    of the boat shapes.

39. Sowerby & Co. 20 February 1878 and trade mark.
    Bowl in frosted and plain glass.

40. Sowerby's Ellison Glass Works Ltd. 10 February 1886.
    Boat flower trough.

41. Molineux & Webb. 27 August 1864.
    Comport in frosted glass with clear glass
    "Greek Key" motif.

42. Edward Moore. 7 October 1886.
Comport.

43. Sowerby & Co. c1880 trade marked.
Half-pint tumbler.

44. No mark, manufacturer not known. c 1865.
Tumbler with heavy base.

45. Percival, Yates & Vickers. 18 January 1865.
Sugar bowl in frosted and clear glass.

46. Sowerby's Ellison Glass Works Ltd. 1 March 1887.
Plate incorporating pattern of 22 December 1886.
(Trustees of the Victoria & Albert Museum)

47. Sowerby's Ellison Glass Works Ltd.
Plate for Golden Jubilee of Queen Victoria.
(Trustees of the Victoria & Albert Museum)

48. The Rochester Tumbler Co., Pittsburgh, Pennsylvania, U.S.A.
13 February 1880.
Showing lozenge mark clearly.

49. G. Davidson & Co. c1885 trade marked.
Basket in amber glass.

50. G. Davidson & Co. 15 August 1891.
Two baskets in amber and clear glass with
rustic handles.

51. Sowerby & Co. 20 February 1878.
Inkstand in roughened and clear glass.

52. G. Davidson & Co. c1888 trade marked.
Small comport.

53. Henry Greener. 14 June 1881 and first trade mark.
Comport.

54. Sowerby & Co. 1 June 1874.
Toast rack. Registration appears on other different pieces
and was probably for distinctive "bobble" rim.

55. *Top Row*
Sowerby's Ellison Glass Works Ltd.
3 Custard cups. 1st c1885, 2nd c1890, 3rd registered
11 March 1881. All three trade marked.

Row Two
Sowerby's Ellison Glass Works Ltd.
2 Custard cups registered 23 February 1889 and
11 March 1881. Trade marked.
G. Davidson & Co. c1885.
1 Large tot glass "Only a Thimble Full".

Row Three
Sowerby & Co.
Basket 13 February 1877 and trade mark.
Small tot glass c1880 trade marked.

Row Four
Sowerby & Co. c1880 trade marked.
Hexagonal salt cellar. In pattern book of 1882.

Percival, Vickers & Co. Ltd. 29 June 1887.
Salt cellar.

Bottom Row
G. Davidson & Co. 15 August 1891.
Salt cellar.

Henry Greener. First trade mark c1880
Small salt cellar.

56. Possibly Greener & Co. c1880
Three unmarked small ornamental lions after John
Derbyshire's famous lion paperweight. In clear, amber
and bright blue glass.

57. Greener & Co. 20 September 1893.
Wheelbarrow salt cellar/ornament.

58. W. H. Heppell & Co. 19 June 1880.
Colliery truck salt cellar/ornament.

59. Sowerby's Ellison Glass Works Ltd. c1885 trade marked.
Biscuit barrel with fern decoration.

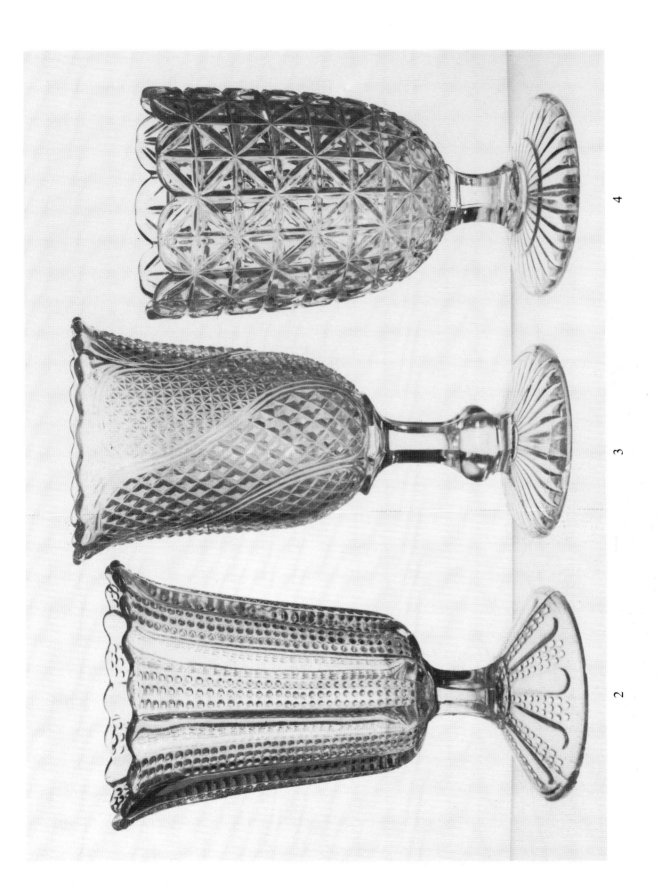

2

3

4

6

5

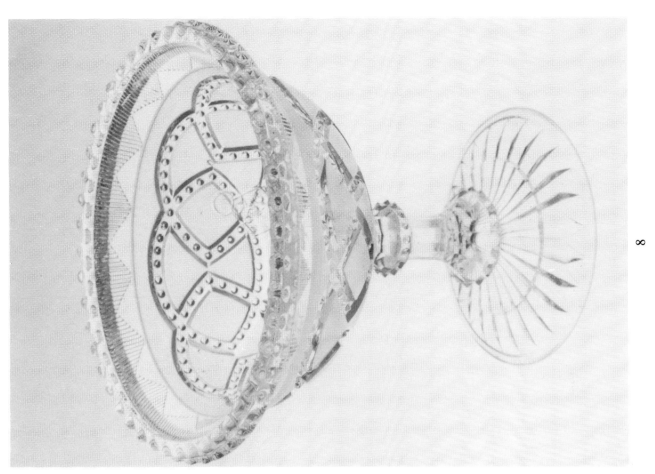

8

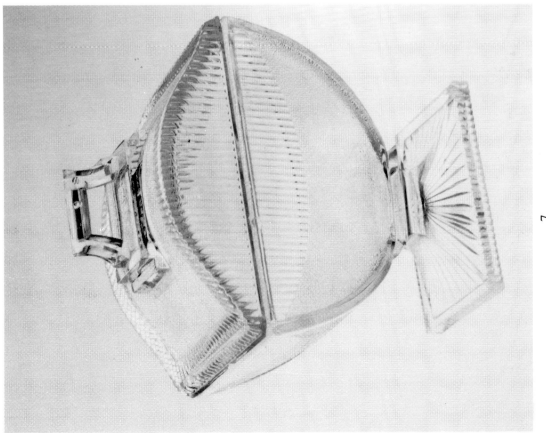

7

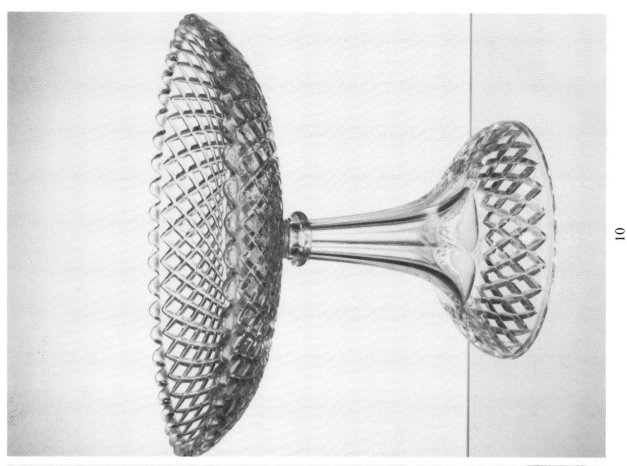

10

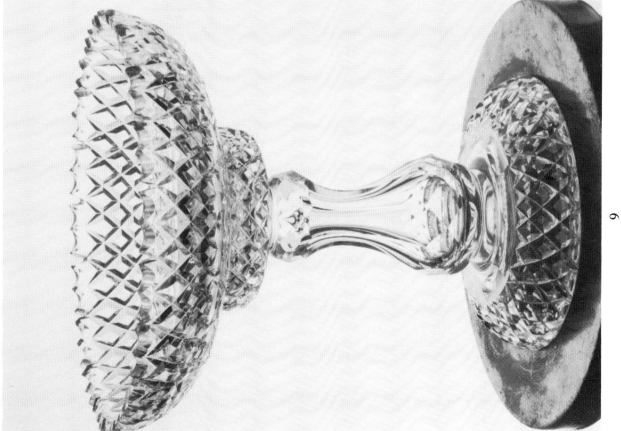

9

58

11   12   13

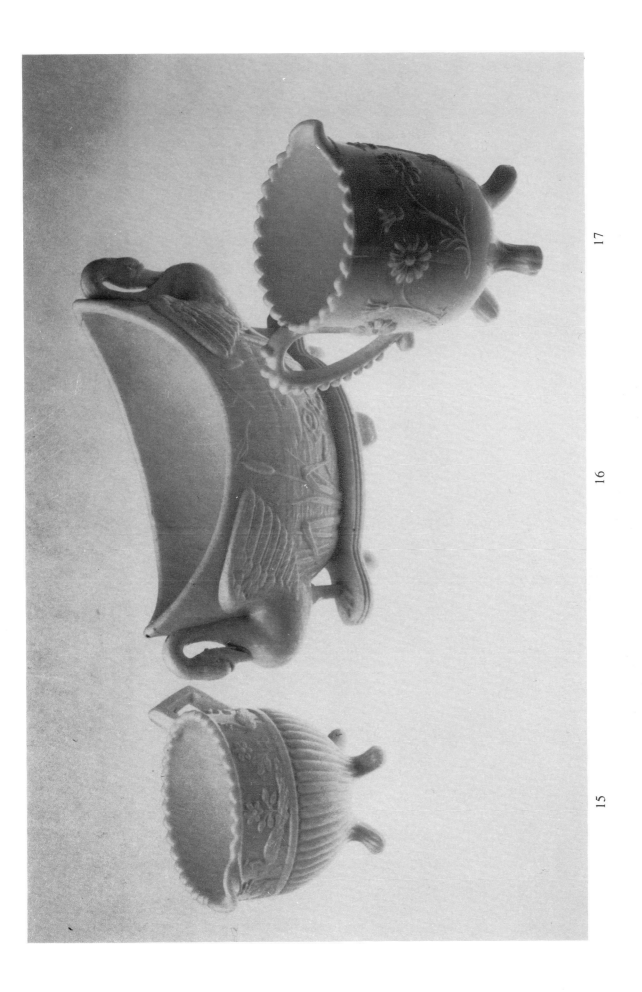

15

16

17

19

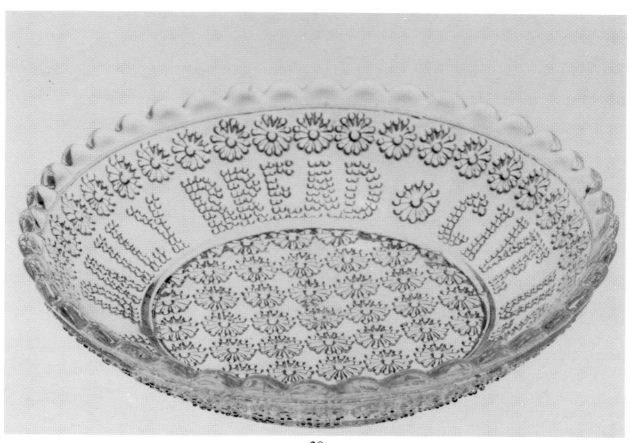

20

21

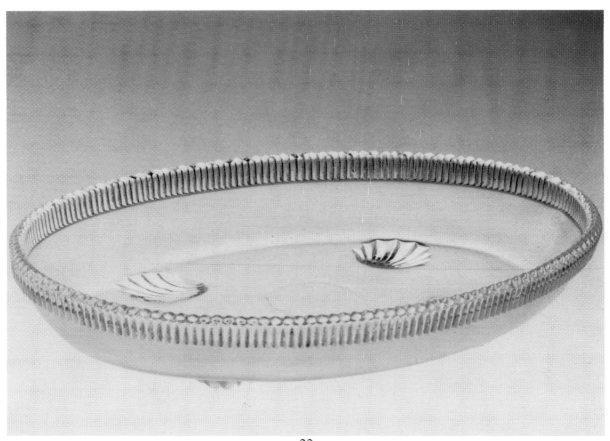

22

23

24   25

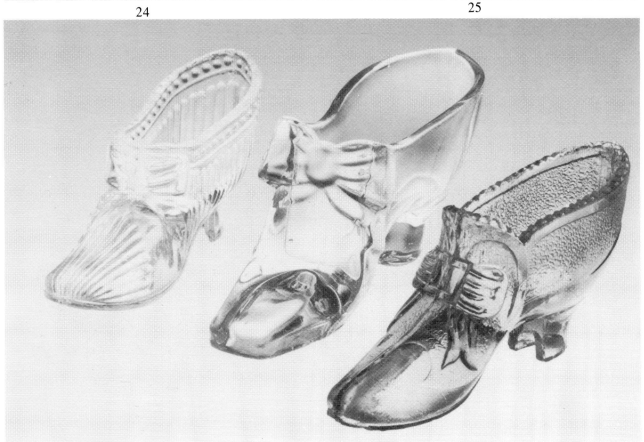

26   27   28

29

30

31

32

33

34

35

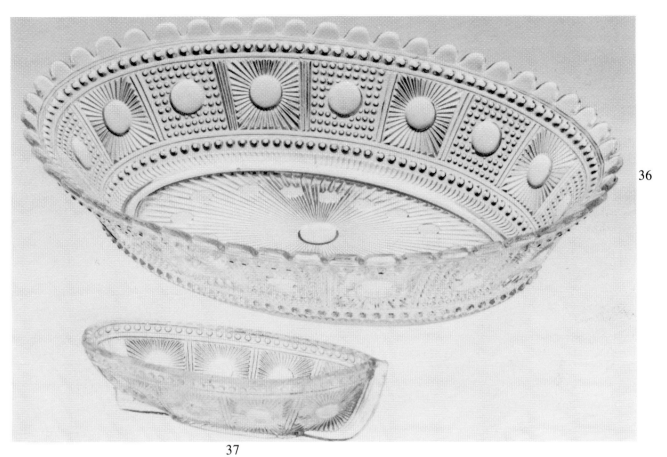

36

37

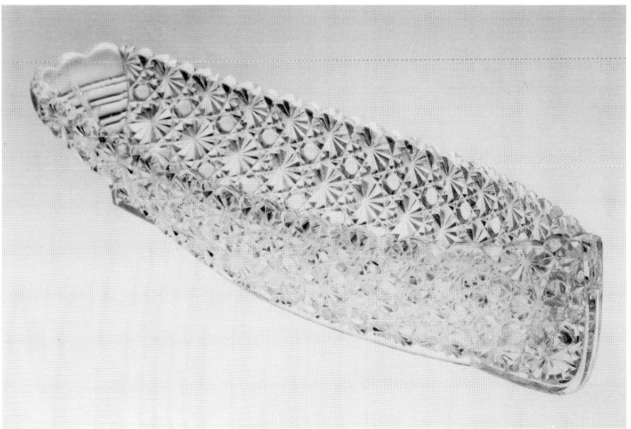

38

39

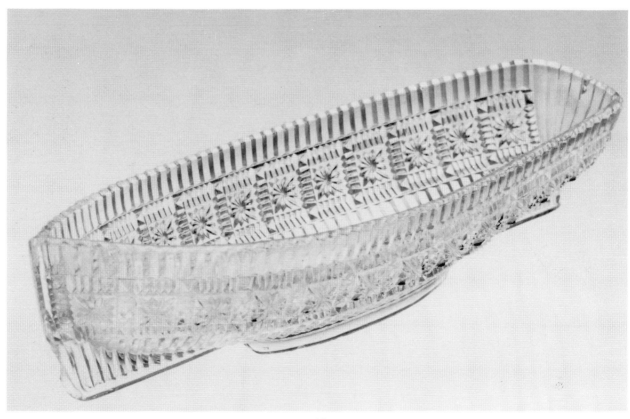

40

41

42

43

44

45

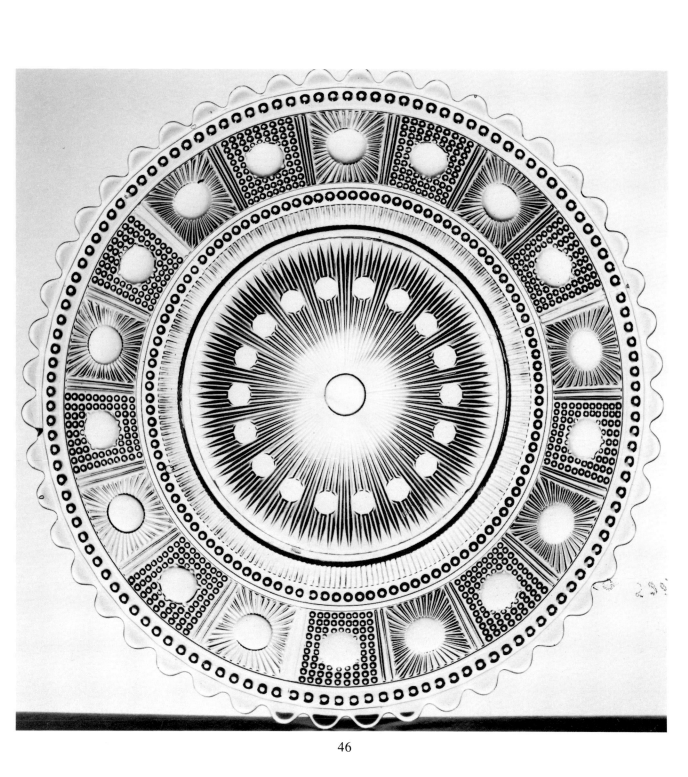

46

47

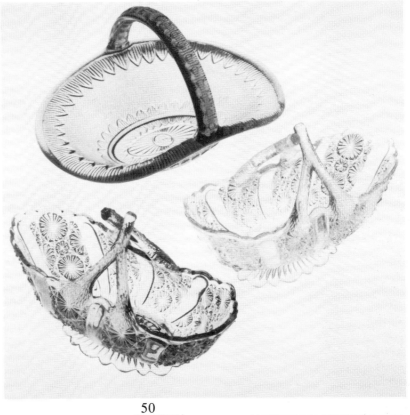

48

50

51

52   53

54

55

56

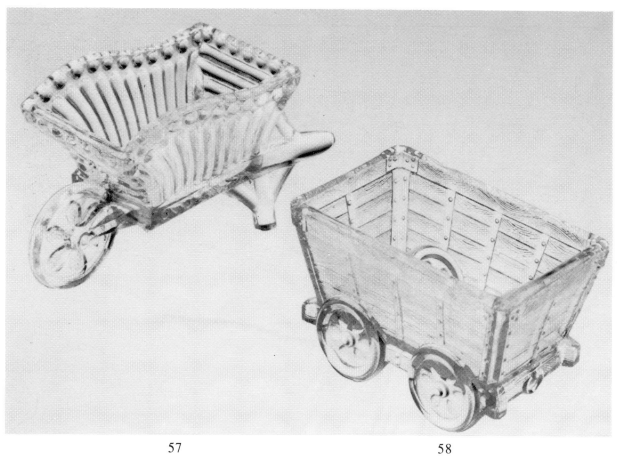

57   58

59

INDEX OF COLOUR PHOTOGRAPHS

1

2   3

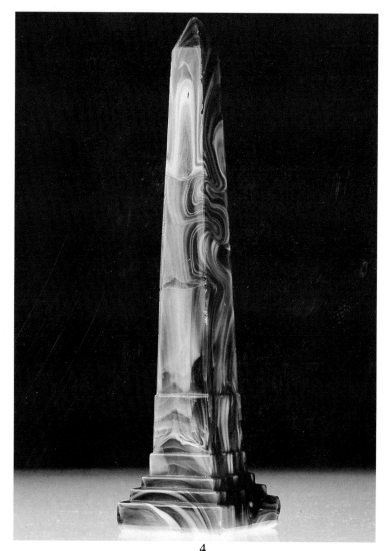

4

5

6   7

8

9

10

11

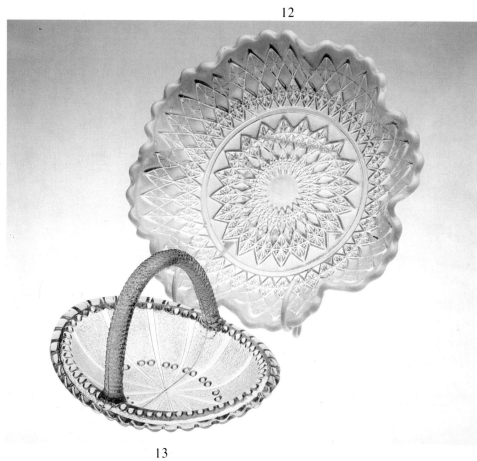

12

13

14

15

16   17

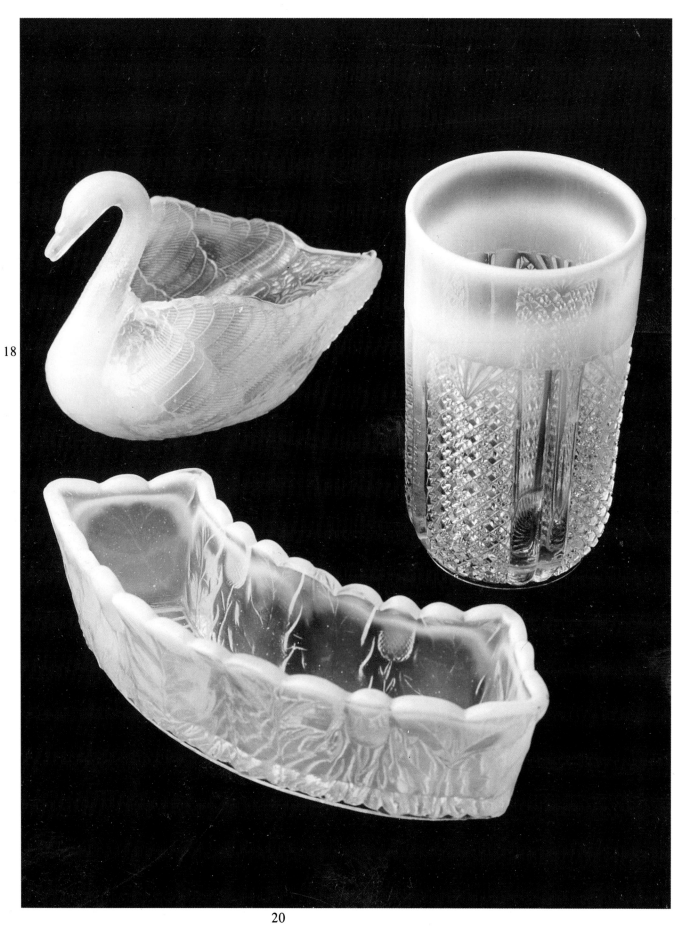

18

19

20

21

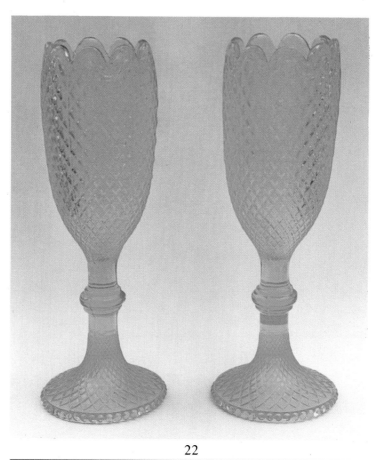

22

23

Designs and Trade Marks:
Registers and Representations

Information from the Public Record Office states:

"Those records of the Patent Office and Industrial Property Department of the Board of Trade which have now been transferred to the Public Record Office include Registers and Representations of Designs and Trade Marks. A Representation of a Design gives a sample, drawing or photograph of the article, whilst the Registers give the registered number, the exact date of registration, type of design and the maker's name and address but not necessarily the name of the designer. Registered designs should carry either a diamond mark or the registered number. Trade Marks also have a registered number."

Ornamental Designs 1842-1883

The Designs Act 1842 created thirteen classes of ornamental designs including all manufactured goods. It gave three years protection to the proprietors of ornamental designs of articles wholly or chiefly made of (1) metal, (2) wood, (3) glass or (4) earthenware, of (5) paper-hangings and (6) carpets, of (8) shawls, if not printed, and of (11) woven and printed fabrics of linen, cotton, wool, silk, hair or mixed material, if they were properly described as "furnitures" and if the repeat of the design was more than 12" x 8".

Nine months protection was given to (7) printed shawls, (9) printed yarns, threads and warps, and to (10) woven and printed fabrics of linen, cotton, wool, silk, hair or mixed material, not covered by the three years protection.

One year's protection was given to (12) woven fabrics not included in the previous two categories, and to (13) lace and any other manufactured ornamental substance or article not included elsewhere.

Records
BT 43: Ornamental Designs Act 1842: Representations
BT 44: Ornamental Designs Act 1842: Registers

The Patents, Designs and Trade Marks Act 1883 amalgamated the previous categories into which designs had been divided and registered the articles, both ornamental and useful, in a single numerical series, extending the protection to five years.

Records
BT 50: Patents Designs and Trade Marks Act 1883: Representations
BT 51: Patents Designs and Trade Marks Act 1883: Registers
BT 82: Representations of Trade Marks (in numerical sequence from
　　　　1876 to 1938)

Before 1884 if a firm registered several items on any one day, each object had the same registration date lozenge, although the Register gave each item an individual number. An example of this is the registration of three lots for 8th August 1873 by John Derbyshire. Both of the designs for the table glass were very different, but items of these designs would have had the same date lozenge, as the designs were entered on the same day.

Registry Marks

Glass objects (particularly pressed glass objects) made between 1842 and 1883 sometimes bear a diamond shaped mark which indicates that they were registered at the Patent Office Design Registry. This mark can be used to determine the exact date of registration and, by consulting official records held by the Public Record Office, the name of the firm or person who registered the design. Glass objects were registered under Class III.

After 1883 a new series of registrations began which are indicated on the object by a serial number. These numerical registrations were not divided into classes but continued in straight sequence irrespective of material. Details of the numbers of the first registration in each year from 1884 to 1908 are given for glass.

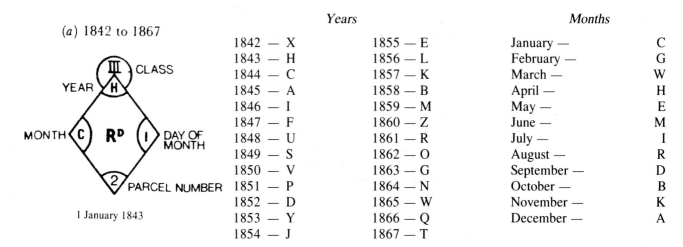

1842-1867

	Years			Months	
1842 — X		1855 — E	January —		C
1843 — H		1856 — L	February —		G
1844 — C		1857 — K	March —		W
1845 — A		1858 — B	April —		H
1846 — I		1859 — M	May —		E
1847 — F		1860 — Z	June —		M
1848 — U		1861 — R	July —		I
1849 — S		1862 — O	August —		R
1850 — V		1863 — G	September —		D
1851 — P		1864 — N	October —		B
1852 — D		1865 — W	November —		K
1853 — Y		1866 — Q	December —		A
1854 — J		1867 — T			

(a) 1842 to 1867

1 January 1843

(R may be found as the month mark for 1—19 September 1857, and K for December 1860).

1868-1883

Years			Months	
1868 — X	1876 — V	January —		C
1869 — H	1877 — P	February —		G
1870 — C	1878 — D	March —		W
1871 — A	1879 — Y	April —		H
1872 — I	1880 — J	May —		E
1873 — F	1881 — E	June —		M
1874 — U	1882 — L	July —		I
1875 — S	1883 — K	August —		R
		September —		D
		October —		B
		November —		K
		December —		A

(b) 1868 to 1883

1 January 1869

(For 1—6 March 1878, G was used for the month and W for the year)

Date of Deposit	No. of Parcel	No. of Design	Name of Proprietor	Address of Proprietor

Date of Deposit	Parcel	Design	Name of Proprietor	Address of Proprietor

Left table:

Date of Deposit	No of Parcel	No of Design	Name of Proprietor	Address of Proprietor
1847				
August 1	1	36445	Rice Harris	Islington Glassworks Birmingham
" 4	"	6	do	do
20	1	36925	Anthony Thatcher	The Yorkshire Bottle Compy Ferry Bridge near Birmingham
25	3	36987	W (Ann) Brunton	Birmingham
7	3	36992	Arthur Smith	Yorkshire Bottle Co Ferry Bridge
8	1	37224	do	do
October 7	4	37676	Griffith Shaw	132 Gt Guildford St Redcliffe
14	2	37706	Samuel Chambers	92 Aston St Birmingham
26	11	38329	George Wells & Co	24 Kings Rd Palmers Rise
Decr 7	2	38643	Stevens & Co	Manchester Rd Leeds Glass Manufacturers
January 2	5	39810	Hammond Turner & Sons	Birmingham
7	2	39960	John Nickolson	Myart Smith Lane Blackfriars London
12	10	42071	The Aire & Calder Bottle Compy Ferry Bridge near Thomas Steel
March 25	3	42296	Percival & Yates	
April 12	3	42601	Vincent Price	33 Waterloo St in the county of Middlesex
16	2	42631	W E & B W Richardson	Wordley near Stourbridge
	5		do	do
May 12	6	43137	William Young & Co	10 Upper Thames Street
14	5	43213	William Young & Co	Leicester Street
31	4	43469	The Aire & Calder Bottle Company	10 Upper Thames St
June 3	3	43655	Alex Soyer	13 Old Bond St London
17	1	43729	John Cliff	Manchester
23	1	43850	Percival & Yates	32 Grosvenor Manchester
30	6	43850		Manchester
July 5	4	43915	John Dobie	City Road St Smith Field
6	2	43924	W H & B & S Richardson	Wordley near Stourbridge
"	"	5	do	do
"	"	6	do	do
"	"	7	do	do

Right table:

Date of Deposit	No of Parcel	No of Design	Name of Proprietor	Address of Proprietor
1847				
July 17	3	44041	Robert Best	Birmingham
29	5	44616	The Aire & Calder Bottle Compy	10 Upper Thames St
October 1	5	46131	F & C Osler	Broad Street Birmingham
12	3	46292	The Aire & Calder Bottle Compy	10 Upper Thames Street
14	6	46306	Charles Lloyd	Birmingham
22	5	46484	Charles Rowley	23 & 24 Methods St Birmingham and 19 Hatton Garden London
28	3	46519	F & C Osler	
23	2	46523	John Field Christy & Co	
28	1	46662	Alexis Soyer	
November 2	1	46748	F & C Osler	
5	2	46788	Percival & Yates	Jersey Street Manchester
			do	do
27	2	47344	do	do
December 9	5	47532	Edmund Crofe & Thomas Blackwell	21 Soho Square
11	1	47601	do	
1848				
January 6	5	48516	Edmund Crofe and Thomas Blackwell	
6	5	48718	Joseph Barlow	120 Long Acre London
11	3	48858	R H Wingfield	Birmingham
17	5	49021	John Davis	near Stourbridge London Well
26	2	49205	The Yorkshire Bottle Company	
February 7	5	49700	Complect Regnal and John Woolwood	73 Lambs Conduit Street
14	2	49779	Percival & Yates	Jersey Street Manchester
22	7	50271	John Combe & Son	11 Bush Lane
26	3	50369	The Yorkshire Bottle Company	London Wall
"	6	50378	The Aire & Calder Bottle Compy	10 Upper Thames Street
March 2	4	50413	Crofe & Blackwell	Soho Square
29	6	50463	Edmund Regnal & John Woolwood	73 Lambs Conduit London
2	4	50520	The Aire & Calder Bottle Compy	10 Upper Thames St
18	4	50912	Jonas Defries	Houndsditch
"	"	3		do

Date of Deposit	No. of Parcel	No. of Design	Name of Proprietor	Address of Proprietor
1849				
March 18,	24	50944	Isaac Defries	Wolverhampton
" 20,	5	50988	Henry Bethune	Birmingham
" 27,	10	51199	William Bennison	do
" 30,	2	51213	Joseph Musgrave & Co	80 St Paul's Church Yard
May 10,	5	51882	Jonas Defries	Kidderminster
" 23,	1	52126	Alexis Soyer	The Reform Club, P.C. Mall
" 31,	1	52150	W. H. & J. F. Richardson	Sundry, Brettleburgy, Worcester
" "	9	52160	do	do
June 1,	6	52179	do	do
" 13,	4	52328	do	Worsley, Worcester
" "	9	52534	{ Anthony Thatcher & The Yorkshire Metal Company }	Leary, Derby Yorkshire
July 31,	2	53121	Rev. Bigott	4 New Park Place
" 21,	4	53633	{ ... }	27 Bucklersbury
Aug.			do	do
" 7,	2	53601	do	do
" 30,	3	54128	do	do
" "	9	54130	do	do
" "	1		do	do
Sept. 17,	3	54973	George & Robert Andrew	137 Aldersgate Street
" 11,		54974	Joseph Green	73 Bishopsgate
" 23,	5	55552	Peter & Everton	6 ... Manchester Streets
Oct. 2,	1	54614	Joseph Green	Birmingham
" 28,	2	55052	Westwood & Moore	The Crystal Works, Mill Lane, Crosby Hill
1849				
January 4,	6	57024	do	do
" 12,	5	57319	S. Musgrave & Co	80 St Paul's Church Yard
Feb. 28,	5	58596	Westwood & Moore	Bradley Lane, Staffordshire
March 12,	1	58852	David Wilkinson	Manchester
April 2,	7	59335	Crofe & Blackwell	21 Soho Square, London
" 18,	1	59584	Thomas Gammon	Birmingham

Date of Deposit	No. of Parcel	No. of Design	Name of Proprietor	Address of Proprietor
1849				
April 24,	3	59686	W. H. & J. F. Richardson	Worsley near Stourbridge, Worcester
May 8,	2	59872	W. H. Winfield	Birmingham
" 22,	2	60072	Thomas Gammon	Birmingham
June 6,	8	60692	John Davis	Bartlet Lane, Staffordshire
July 31,	1	61115	W. & C. Osler	44 Broad St, London & Broad St, Birmingham
" 5,	6	61144	R. W. Mansfield	Birmingham
" 18,	11	61273	David Wilkinson	Manchester
	1,3	62716	John Cliff Penner	33 Chelsea
	6	62918	Thomas Gammon	Birmingham
	2	62923	W. H. & J. F. Richardson	Worsley near Stourbridge, Worcester
	6	62989	Westwood & Moore	
	6	63116	Henry Venner	
	5	64111	Wheat Bro.	Sheffield
	6	64172	Bishops Birkett & Co	Chester
	3	64376	{ ... }	
	3	64456	{ ... }	Stratford Birmingham
	5	64359	Crofe & Blackwell	21 Soho Square

Date of Deposit	No of Parcel	No. of Design	Name of Proprietor	Address of Proprietor
1850				
January 31	4	66954 / 5	William Rowe	12 New Wharf Whitefriars
Feby 6	9	67167	Henry Grinder	75 Watling Street
13	8	67467 / 8	Sherwood & Co	Eccleston Flint Glass Works Nr St Helens Lancashire
27	2	67781	Rees, Henry Napoleon Price	32 Lombard Street
March 4	3	67831 / 2	William Kidd	Saunders Cottage, New Road, Hammersmith
11	11	68066	Anthony Thatcher of the Yorkshire Bottle Company	London Wall
12	6	68073	John R. Isaac	Liverpool
April 16	2	68834	Price John McManus	11 Holcomb Street Belgrave Square
19	8	69046	Wm Hancock & Rd Brown & R. Davies	10 Cross St. Islington; 72 Old Broad St. City
May 23	4	69516 / 17	George Sherwood & Co	Eccleston Flint Glass Works near St. Helens Lancashire
30	2	69601	John Kilner	Dewsbury
31	4	69607	John Cliff Quince	32 Cheapside London
June 29	3	70042	Joseph Henry Stone	High Street, Southwark
July 11	3	70296	F & C Osler	44 Oxford St. London & Broad St. Birmingham
17	4	70377	Badger Brothers	Dudley
19	5	70447	Thomas Yates	34 Vere Place, Liverpool
23	3	70609	George Mosley	Paragon Row, George Rd. Birmingham
24	7	70627	George J. Green	Broad Street, Birmingham
August 7	5	71064	Henry Pershouse	Birmingham
16	3	71179	John Kilner	Brick Hill Lane, Upper Thames Street
17	3	71202	do	do
Sept 18	3	71983	do	Brick Hill Lane London
Octr 9	3	72397	William Haden & Benjamin Jonathan Richardson	Wordsley, Stourbridge, Worcestershire
15	4	72500	Crosse & Blackwell	Soho Square
25	6	73130	J. H. Brown	4 South Street, Finsbury, Lond.
November 5	3	73334	Thomas Gammon	Birmingham
[illegible] 9	2	73428	Thomas Bragg	Birmingham

Date of Deposit	No of Parcel	No. of Design	Name of Proprietor	Address of Proprietor
1850				
Nov 29	4	73917	Jonas Defries	Houndsditch
Dec 11	2	74530	John Cliff Quince	132 Cheapside London
1851				
Jany 11	3	75174 / 5	W. H. B and J. Richardson	73 Lambs Conduit Street and Wordsley Glass Works Stourbridge Worcester
13	15	75738	Eugene Rimmel	39 Gerrard Street, Soho, London
20	5	75875	John Cliff Quince	32 Cheapside, London
22	8	75988	Eliezer Edwards	Birmingham
Feby 14	9	76783	George Lloyd & Thomas Summerfield	Park Glass Works Birmingham
March 29	6	77954	Isaac Aldebert of the Firm of Hallmarke, Aldebert & Hallmarke	57 Long Acre, London
April 1	6	78039	Benjamin Black	49 South Moulton Street
2	3	78049 / 50	Lloyd & Summerfield	Park Glass Works, Spring Hill, Birmingham
17	7	78476	Philip Benjamin	105 Hatton Garden Holborn London
"	8	78477	Lloyd & Summerfield	Park Glass Works Spring Hill Birmingham
June 10	4	79180	Henry David Green Truscott	7 Coburg Road Old Kent Road
July 4	3	79537	Frederic Pellatt	Falcon Glass Works London
21	6	79749	George Jos. Green	Etna Flint Glass Works Birmingham
September 12	2	80554	Davis Greathead & Green	Stourbridge
October 11	3	80929	Joseph Webb	Coalbourn Hill Stourbridge
21	2	81056	Hancock Rixon & Dunt	Cockspur Street, Pall Mall East
24	3	81078	Davis Greathead & Green	Brettell Lane, Staffordshire
"	6	81081	F & C. Osler	Broad St Birmingham; 44 Oxford Street London
31	4	81217	Berens Blumberg & Co	St Pauls Churchyard London

Date of Deposit	No of Parcel	No. of Design		Name of Proprietor	Address of Proprietor
1851					
Novr 18	7	81613	1	W. H. B. & J. Richardson	Wordsley Stourbridge Worcester^e
Decr 26	2	82568	1	Robert Lancaster	Bolton Lancashire
1852					
Jany 10	3	82737	1	Thomas Gammon	Birmingham
Feby 9	1	83700	1	Crosse & Blackwell	Soho Square
14	3	83811	1	George Twigg	Powell Street Birmingham
16	4	83825	1	Westwood and Moore	Glass Works Brierley Hill
March 3	4	84128	2	Hancock Rixon and Dunt	Cockspur Street Pall Mall East
"		9			—
4	4	84136	1	Archibald Henderson Ross and Robert Henderson Ross	Sunderland
"	3	84137	2	Jonas Defries	Houndsditch
"	"	8			
5	4	84155	1	George Twigg	Powell Street Birmingham
10	4	84217	1	Archibald Hilson Ross	Sunderland, Optician
12	4	84228	2	Hancock Rixon and Dunt	Cockspur Street Pall Mall East
"	"	9			
17	4	84264	1	Archibald Hilson Ross, Optician and Robert Henderson, Miner	Sunderland
18	5	84300	1	Joseph Webb	Coalbourn Hill N^r Stourbridge
19	4	84308	1	William Young	34 Queen St. Cheapside
23	1	84386	1	Joseph Webb	Coalbourn Hill Stourbridge
April 6	1	84598	1	John Walsh Walsh	Birmingham
" 14	4	84673	2	John Marten	44 High Street Marylebone
"	"	4		—	—
20	1	84816	1	Twigg & Silvester	Powell Street Birmingham
May 1	2	84947	1	Crosse & Blackwell	Soho Sq^re
11	5	85064	1	A. Marion & Co	Regent Street
June 29	3	85540	1	Jonas Defries	137 Houndsditch
July 21	3	85790	1	J. Bevan & Co	7 Wilderness Row Clerkenwell

Deposit	Parcel	Design		Name of Proprietor	Address of Proprietor
1852					
July 23	5	85806 to 85811	6	William Churcher	28 Thomas Street Oxford Street London
August 30	4	86391	1	Alfred Hely	13^d Cannon Row, Westminster Middlesex
"	"	—			
Novr 3	3	87523	1	William Fentum	Old College Hoxton
13	3	87650	1	Dixley & Son	Stourbridge
16	5	87723	1	Howard Brothers	Woolwich Kent
Decr 9	2	88218	1	King & Co	50 Rupert St Haymarket London
1853					
Jany 28	8	89210	1	Davis Greathead & Green	Stourbridge, Glass Manufacturers
Feby 5	5	89526	1	Dixley & Son	Stourbridge
14	6	89601	1	John Cliffe Quince	10 Upper Thames Street London
April 12	7	90767	1	John Walsh Walsh	Soho & Vesta Glass Works Birmingham Heath Birmingham Warwickshire
"	—	—			
May 17	3	91193	1	Wood & Perkes	Worsbro' Dale near Barnsley, Yorkshire
"	6	91222	1	Stott Walker	10 Upper Thames Street London
31	2	91284	2	do	do do
"	"	5			
June 9	2	91341	1	Hodge & Roberts	London
10	4	91381	1	Robert Best	Birmingham
23	2	91476	1	Joseph Webb	Coalbourn Hill Stourbridge
July 9	1	91634	1	John Walsh Walsh	Soho and Vesta Glass Works, Birmingham Heath, Birmingham Warwickshire
—	—	—		—	
—	—	—		—	
22	1	91764	1	Blackwood & Co	26 Long Acre London
August 19	3	92120	1	Joseph Tylor and Son	Warwick Lane, Newgate Street, London
		—			—

Date of Deposit	No. of Parcel	No. of Design		Name of Proprietor	Address of Proprietor
1854					
August 30	1	96720	2	Geo. Norris	95ᵃ Regent St. London
"			1		
Sept 21	3	96848	1	Jones Defries & Sons	147 Houndsditch
Oct 7	7	97145	2	Wm Reichenbach	33 Borough Road Southwark
			6		
Nov 3	3	97161	1	F. Thwaitt & Co.	Hampton Wick, Middlesex
"		97190	1	Shee James	Redditch
Dec 14	6	97191	1	Davis, Greathead & Green	Flint Glass Works Stourbridge
		97249	1	Jones Defries and Sons	147 Houndsditch
	17	5	97346	6	Benjamin Richardson	Wordsley Hill Stourbridge
Nov 16	2	97770	1	do	do
	11	4	98201	1	Joseph Webb	Coalbourn Hill Glass Works Stourbridge
	23	1	98238	1	Wm Reichenbach	33 Borough Road Southwark
1855					
Jan 29	7	99102	2	Prices Patent Candle Comp.	Belmont Vauxhall
February 10	7	99344	1	Clifton and Blackwell	Colne Lynn
	22	5	99466	1	Prices Patent Candle Co.	Belmont Vauxhall
March 3	6	99572	1	Charles Williams	Vauxhall Road, London
	11	3	99639	1	Davis Greathead & Green	Stourbridge
April 10	4	99823	1	John McLachlan	Williams Street High Street Lambeth
	12	4	99882	1	John Walch Walsh	Jetsea Vista Glass Works Birmingham
June 9	5	99883	1	Joseph Lane	Town Hall Buildings Manchester
			100296	1	F. & C. Osler	44 Oxford St London & Broad St Birmingham
August 14	2	100452	1	Hodge & Roberts	London
	23	3	100549	1	do	do
		100997	2	James Lyon Nokes	Endswell, Derbyshire
	3	100998	1	Davis Greathead & Green	Flint Glass Works Stourbridge

---

Date of Deposit	No. of Parcel	No. of Design		Name of Proprietor	Address of Proprietor
1853					
Oct 3	4	93422	6	Thomas Bichers & Co.	Flint Glass Works near Birmingham
		93422	6		
Nov 13	4	92922	1	H. Richardt	33 Borough Road Southwark
Nov 3	4	93185	1	Defries & Sons	147 Houndsditch
	11	3	93321	1	John Richardt	Manchester
Dec 14	6	93615	1	Prices Patent Candle Comp.	Belmont Vauxhall
	17	1	93626	1	Joseph Webb	Coalbourn Hill Stourbridge
1854					
Jan 9	5	94308	1	Still Mullins	Flourshm Wharf Upper Thames Worcestershire
	7	1	95065	1	Wm Reichenbach	Stent
Feb	21	4	94121	1	Davis Greathead & Green	Stourbridge Worcestershire
	22	2	94906	1	B. Reichenbach	33 Borough Road Southwark
	14	3	95056	1	Benjamin Richardson	Wordsley near Stourbridge
	17	1	95065	1	Wm Reichenbach	33 & 34 Borough Road Southwark
March	22	6	95155	1	William Blumner Tah.	Liverpool Street Greenock Street
	23	2	95237	1	Thomas Forbes	Stangveaye Manchester
May	15	5	95145	1	Blackwood & Co.	Long Acre
	24	3	95928	1	John J. Willway	24 Aguthaves Road Bristol
June 3	3	96004	1	Benjamin Richardson	Wordsley Glass Works near Stourbridge
	15	2	96056	1	Joseph Webb	Coalbourn Hill Stourbridge
July 27	2	96491	1	George Norris	95ᵃ Regent Quadrant London
			to		
		96493			
August 2	3	96543	1	Jones Defries & Son	Houndsditch
	3	1	96544	1	Joseph Webb	Coalbourn Hill Stourbridge
	22	1	96657	1	George Norris	95ᵃ Regent St London
	26	2	96703	1	Benjamin Richardson	Wordsley nr Stourbridge

Date of Deposit	No. of Parcel	No. of Design	Name of Proprietor	Address of Proprietor
1855				
August 28 / 1	101235	George Emell & Co	Romney Row
Novr 22 / 4	102292	John Pinkerton	75 Lambs Conduit Street
		George Bell & Co	2 Wellington Street, Hyde Park
Novr 9 / 3	102519	Alfred Zett	14 Murray Park City
10 / 4	102537 / 1	William Richenbach	33 Bow Road, Southwark
12 / 3	102543 / 1	Samuel Flewten	8 Temple Chambers, Whitefriars
			Sheffield
17 / 2	102701 / 1	Henry New	16 New Castle Street, Shoreditch
21 / 3	102720 / 1	Aubin Chapman	65 Flat Lands, St Mary le Strand

Date of Deposit	No. of Parcel	No. of Design	Name of Proprietor	Address of Proprietor
1855				
Decr			William England	St Fleet St, London
	18 / 4	108055 / 1	Arthur Brandish	Birmingham

Date of Deposit	No. of Parcel	No. of Design	Name of Proprietor	Address of Proprietor
1856				
Feby. 9 / 3	103724 / 1	Benjamin Richardson	Wordsley near Stourbridge
11 / 4	103731 / 1	Crofse and Blackwell	21 Soho Square
13 / 4	103734 / 1	James Defries & Sons	Houndsditch
March 25 / 6	104212 / 1	Benjamin Richardson	Wordsley near Stourbridge
				Flint Glass Manufactory
April 55 / 3	104307 / 1	William Richerbach	33 Bow Road, Southwark
7 / 3	104579 / 1	Elizer Edwards	Birmingham
May 1 / 4	104614 / 1	John Filmer	Booth Warehouse 48 Upper Thames
14 / 1	104728 / 1	Wm Young	Queen Street, Cheapside
June 23 / 2	105196 / 1	Peter Robinson	Warrington, Lancashire
			Edward Bolen	
Septr 8 / 3	106216 / 1	Benjamin Richardson	Wordsley, Stourbridge
20 / 3	106366 / 1	do	do
Octr 1 / 6	106452 / 1	William Bird	University Street
7 / 4	106534 / 1	Solomon Marr	Aldersgate Street, London
8 / 4	106559 / 4	Louis Grane and Charles	9 Park Road, Dalston
	to		Francis Hayward	
		106562		

Date of Deposit	No. of Parcel	No. of Design	Name of Proprietor	Address of Proprietor
1856				
Octr 2 9 / 2	106571 / 1		6 Charles Terrace Asylum Road Old Kent Road
Novr 5 / 2	106915 / 1		1 Helmet Row, Old Street
15 / 2	107079 / 1		St Lukes, London
18 / 1	107516 / 1		6 Bartletts Buildings, Holborn, London
				9 Southampton Street, Strand
1857				
January 5 / 2	107485 / 2	Owen Parry	Cranbourn Hill, Stourbridge
16 XIII / 3			Birmingham
14. 5	108575 / 1	James Joseph Barton	Tonlowitz
30 / 4	108985 / 1	James Inns	Birmingham
Feby 10 / 8	108985 / 1	B. Ferwitz	Tonlowitz
March 21 / 3	109434 / 1	Joseph Webb	21 Soho Square
April 30 / 4	109830 / 1	Elizer Edwards	Wordsley near Stourbridge
Nov 14 / 3	109641 / 1	Jonas Defries & Sons	
June 9 / 3	109943 / 1	Crofse and Blackwell	Parade Works, Birmingham
July 2 / 1	110109 / 1	Benjamin Richardson	City Glass Works, Glasgow
August 20 / 2	110942 / 2	Powell & Horton	
		3	James Couper Sons	44 Oxford St, London &
24 / 1	111017 / 1	F. C. Osler	Broad St, Birmingham

Date of Deposit	No. of Parcel	No. of Design	Name of Proprietor	Address of Proprietor
1857				
Sept. 12	2	112281	Frederick Simpson	Red Hill Surrey
Nov. 6	3	112878	Benjamin Richardson	Wordsley near Stourbridge
" 7	4	112901	George Brown	York
" 7	2	112917	Hodges & Reed	101 Hatton Garden London
Dec. 17	3	112421	James Couper & Sons	City Glass Works Glasgow
19	4	112467	Andrew Reid	Lenerith
21	1	112469		
"	6	112470	R. Winfield & Son	Birmingham

Date of Deposit	Parcel	Design	Name of Proprietor	Address of Proprietor
1858				
August 28	2	114999	Joseph Webb	Coalbourne Hill Glass Works Stourbridge
Sept. 16	3	115551	Henry Emery	58 Cheapside London EC
"	"	to		
"	"	115553		
Oct. 27	2	116444	David Jacobs	33 Haymarket London
Dec. 10	3	117336	Edward Ashton	37 Newman Street Oxford Street
"	3	117501	Angus Greener	Wear Flint Glass Works Sunderland

Date of Deposit	No. of Parcel	No. of Design	Name of Proprietor	Address of Proprietor
1858				
Feb. 24	7	113105	Anne Harriet Bufford	Birmingham
"	"	"		
"	"	113107		
Mar. 9	9	113179	Victor Hunt	Birmingham
"	4	113236	John Henry Watson and Elizabeth	166 High Street Kensington London
			Trading under the title of Weston & Gent	
"	"		H. A. Rosenback	339.34 Bore Road Southwark
Mar. 20	5	113960	George Edward Ashton	8 Wardley Street Oxford St
April 13	3	113410	James Goodchild	77 High Street, Borough
"	1	113422	John Fox Long	Count of Surrey 463 Bridge Road Liverpool
May 10	4	113685	John Tanning Fox & Co	of Liverpool
"	3	113720	Peerless and Richards	Bristol
June 2	2	113907	F. & C. Osler	Broad St Birmingham and 44 Oxford St London
23	5	114047	William Blamire Tate	Sunderland & Gateshead
21	3	114071	Benjamin Richardson	Wordsley Flint Glass Works near Stourbridge
29	2	114082	Mathew Wheelton	Leith Eastern Agricultural Glass Cutter

Date of Deposit	Parcel	Design	Name of Proprietor	Address of Proprietor
1859				
Jan. 1	2	117763	Bower & Arrol	16 Dixon Street Glasgow
"	5	117209	Joseph Tutchin	22 Colchester Liverpool
Feb. 11	5	118406	Joseph Sedger	3 Grosvenor Terrace Rotherhithe with Laundry of Surrey
"	"	118630	Mrs Eliza Hunt	113 Aldersgate St Barbican House Fisher
March 14	5	118204	Robert Logan	4 Red Lion Square
May 20	6	119975	Davis Pritchard & Green	94 Flint Glass Works Lambeth
"	4	119906	Finch Hill & Paraire	15 Southland Lane Pay Williamston
June 14	7	120532	James Cripps	26 Kirby Street Hatton Garden
July 8	2	120613	Thomas 6 Dawkins	Little Warner Street Clerkenwell London
September 22	5	122349	William Lyggatt Gilbert	St Pauls Square Birmingham
"	4	122368	Trustee and son	
Oct. 26	6	123370	J & F Lloyd & Co	170 Strand
Nov. 25	1	124208	Clarke & Timmins	77 Snow Hill London Birmingham

Register (left):

Date of Deposit	No of Parcel	No of Design	Name of Proprietor	Address of Proprietor
1860				
Jan 19 /5		123806 1	Weston Grant & Symons	16 Great Warrington Butts and 13 Mil Fall Street, Hill St Pauls & C
Feby 4 /7		126202 1	James Lombster	41 Clayton Street, Caledonian Road Islington London
28 /3		126804 1	Peter Peel	Birmingham
April 14 /4		128002 1	Frances Madan	Colwell Road
14 /5		128066 1	James Hinks	Birmingham
Septr 5 /1		132703 1	Winston Powell	Parade Works, Birmingham
23 /3		133418 1	Frances Speak	144 Oxford Street W
Nov 10 /7		135384 1	Geo. Booton of Birmingham trading under the Firm of Booton & Hone	6 Bartletts Buildings and 66 Oxford Street
23 /6		136029 1	James Lewis	
1861				
Jany 3 /2		137154 1	James Tyson Nobbs	31 High & Fleet Birmingham
26 /2		137646 1	James Hinks	Birmingham
Feby 12 /4		138254 1	George Matheson	126 Bothwell St Glasgow
March 6 /10		138724 1	Ward Brennan and Robert Brown	Union St Glasgow
/1		138947 1	James Hinks	Birmingham
26 /10		139073 2	J & Dyfrus & Son	Houndsditch
/5		139076		
28 /4		139266 1	Weston Grant & Co	16 Gt Street Warrington Butts
Classes IV 30 /1		139286 5 to 139290	J & JD Cook	5th Wellington Street, Glasgow
April 8 /6		139493 1	A W Winfield & Son	Birmingham
24 /2		140188 1	Prudence Lewis	67 Fleet Street Dublin
May 23 /1		140932 1	Edward Mercir	Castle Street Reading

Register (right):

Date of Deposit	No of Parcel	No of Design	Name of Proprietor	Address of Proprietor
1861				
June 5 /7		141261 2 / 2	Dobson & Pearce	19 St James's Street London
27 /1		141573 1	Edward Moore & Corby	The Tyne Flint Glass Works South Shields
29 /4		141642 1	Edwd Moore & Co	Tyne Flint Glass Works South Shields
August 5 /3		142371 1	Pearce & Corby	9 Brooke Street, Holborn
21 /3		142014 2 / 14 2815	Prudence Lewis	6 Fleet Street Quicklime
Dec 12 /5		142545 1	Edwin Martin Thornton	6 Brooke Street Holborn
19 /4		142792 1	David H Keats	66 Queen St Finsbury Square
1862				
Jany 13 /5		148562 1	Robert Hennell & Sons	14 Northumberland Street
Feby 12 /5		149306 1	Henry Shatwin	30 Queen Street Birmingham
22 /7		149522 2 / 149522	Grace Barras	44 Cambridge Street Birmingham
24 /6		149561 1	James Dyson & Kirks	Upper Hockley St Birmingham L
March 3 /9		149946 1	Elegie & Blackwell	2 and 21 Soho Square
April 7 /10		150512 2 / 150513	Cusp & Blackwell	2 and 21 Soho Square
8 /6		150526 1	William Johnston	49 Mitchell Street Glasgow
11 /6		150809 1	Mercer Hampton Sopransino	Birmingham
28 /6		151261 5 to 151265	Dobson & Pearce	19 St James's Street S.W.
May 1 /1		151468 1	Robinson Donald & Co	Bothwell Lane McCampbell St Glasgow
Classes III-IV 9 /10		151570 3 / 151572	A W Winfield & Son	Birmingham

Date of Deposit	No of Parcel	No of Design	Name of Proprietor	Address of Proprietor
1862				
May 20 / 5		157915 / 1	Dobson & Pearce	19 St James Street
„ / 6		157416 / 1	Thomas March	Lord Chamberlain Office, St James Palace
June 12 / 6		157426 / 1	A. W. N. Pugin & Co	8 Church Passage, London the Manufacturer
25 / 3		157722 / 1	Alfred Dunn of the firm of Naylor & Co	7 Princes Street, Cavendish
Augt 16 / 6		157822	Mabrige & Sons	Birmingham
Septr 9 / 6		157589 / 1	Robert Wards	6 Angel & Gate Court Golden Lane, Saint Lukes
Feby 1 / 3		157557 / 1	Major Edwards	Birmingham
„ 16 / 5		157670 / 3 ... 157672	Alfred Dunn of the firm J. Naylor & Co / J. Naylor & Co Saint Cavendish (agent)	
23 / 3		157672 / 12	Johnston, Frazer & Co	78 Gordon Street Glasgow
„ / 9		157678 / 1	George Kenny Type	107 Great Charles Street Birmingham
Novr 11 / 4		157823 / 1	James Heath & Son	Birmingham
13 / 4		157800 / 2	Defries & Sons	Houndsditch, London
„ / 7		157802 / 1	S. Mordan & Co	22 City Road London EC
1863				
March 26 / 5		160895 / 1	B. Mordan	Albion Works City Road London
April 8 / 7		161282 / 1	Napoleon Price	158 New Bond Street London
May 12 / 3		162269 / 1	Dobson & Pearce	19 St James St S.W.
June 9 / 2		163192 / 1	Isaac Braun	19 St James Street Birmingham
16 / 5		163531 / 1	Dobson & Pearce	19 St James Street
July 1 / 4		163900 / 1	Isaac Baines	Birmingham
8 / 8		162119 / 1	Bewley & Draper	23 Mary St Dublin

Date of Deposit	No of Parcel	No of Design	Name of Proprietor	Address of Proprietor
1863				
July 9 / 8		164138 / 1	B. Edwards	Birmingham
Octbr 16 / 5		164365 / 2	Alfred Dunn of the firm of the	7 Princes Street, Cavendish Square, London
		164366 / 8	firm of Naylor & Co	same, London
Novr 4 / 8		168109 / 1	Nicolas Jacquot	3 Rue de la Paix Paris
5 / 5		168202 / 1	Hodd & Linley	31 Hatton Garden
25 / 6		169480 / 1	Hodd & Linley	31 Hatton Garden
Decr 8 / 6		169906 / 1	Septimus Pugh	2 New Bond Street
24 / 6		170523 / 2 ... 4	J Defries & Sons	147 Houndsditch
26 / 1		170526 / 2	J Defries & Sons	147 Houndsditch
1864				
Jany 11 / 11		170914	The Tuttbury Glass Company	Tutbury, Staffordshire & 190 High Holborn London
Feby 6 / 6		171516 / 2	Alfred Dunn of the firm / Naylor & Co / 2	7 Princes Street Cavendish Square London
March 8 / 1		172348 / 5		
„ „		„ 9		
„ „		172350 / 2	Dobson & Pearce	19 St James Street Piccadilly
„ „		„ 2		
18 / 11		172611 / 1	James Lees	6 Bartletts Buildings Holborn London
May 11 / 6		174479 / 1	Frederic Lewis	6 Fleet Street Dublin
Chrism 25 / 4		174854 / 1	Emily Temple	104 Wynd Street
June 8 / 5		175314 / 1	Swan & Co	19 St James St S.W.
14 / 4		175421 / 1	James Derbyshire & Bro	4 Skinner Place Lee London
15 / 3		175494 / 1	Samuel & Charles Bashall	Flint Glass Works St Helens Lancashire

Deposit — Parcel — Design — Name of Proprietor — Address of Proprietor

Date of Deposit — No. of Parcel — No. of Design — Name of Proprietor — Address of Proprietor

1865

1864

Date of Deposit	No. of Parcel	No. of Design	Name of Proprietor	Address of Proprietor
Jany 18	6	194616 to 194618	3. Molineaux Webb & Co	Manchester
"	"	194685	1. Molineaux Webb & Co	Manchester
20	2	194825	1. Molineaux Webb & Co	Manchester
30	1	194814	1. William Brooke	Leeds Yorkshire Glass Works
31	8	194871	1. H. B. Tate	4 Seward Street E C
Feby 1	9	194958	1. J. Nesbitt & Co	33 High Holborn W C
2	6	194958	1. J. Nesbitt & Co	Manchester
15	2	195262	1. Molineaux Webb & Co	Manchester
17	1	195272	Robinson & Bolton	33 Haymarket London
March 21	5	195623	1. Kenny & Brown	Sheffield
"	10	195639	1. Notson & Ware	4 Pall Mall
16	6	195956	1. J. C. Bishop & Co	Frith Lancashire
7	1	196244	James Green	35 Upper Thames Street London
April 6	2	196366 to 196368	3 James Maynard MacKay	6 Belcombe Street, Belgrave Square London
"	"	196368		
7	6	196419	2 Alfred Arculus	Birmingham
21	5	196694	1. Richard Gent	7 Old Hackney Road
May 2	2	197022	1. Richard Gent	7 Old Hackney Road London
"	6	197006	1. James Carter Marsh	Aldersgate Street House Place
8	2	197154	1. Eliezer Edwards	4 Paul Square Birmingham
10	4	197248	1. McDermott Connolly & Co	Percy de Glasbow-on-Tyne
22	17	197656	2 Thomas Charles Marsh	Annapolis Coal Perfumes Palace
"	"	197657		
24	1	197703	2 Angell & Greener	Wear Flint Glass Works Sunderland
"	"	197704		

Date of Deposit	No. of Parcel	No. of Design	Name of Proprietor	Address of Proprietor
1866				
March 14, 9	16, 9	206745, 1	Sidney Brown	5 Blackfriars Road S.
" "	16, 3	206845, 1	Charles March	Thornagh Palace
April 4, 10	11, 5	207202, 1	Sidney Brown	5 Blackfriars Road S.
" "	11, 5	207447, 1	Mohr & Smith	Birmingham
" "	16, 7	207561, 1	James Lewis	Bartletts Buildings Holborn, London
May 21, 4	1, 2	207471, 1	Anthony Gent	...Birmingham
" "	1, 2	208419, 2	James Hinks & Son	Birmingham
" "		208420		
" "	3	208421, 1	Richard Gent	7 Edward Hartney Lane
" 22, 10		200435, 1	W. L. Bishop & Co.	St Helens, Lancashire
" 23, 5		200519, 1	James Fallis & Son	Birmingham
June 7, 7		200779, 1	Samuel Chandler & Son	110 Brook Street Lambeth
" 24, 3		200086, 1	Molineaux Webb & Co.	Kirby Street Manchester
" 26, 8		200161, 1	Angus & Greener	Flint Glass Works Sunderland
" 29, 4		200722, 1	John Whitehouse & Sons	8 Birshall Hill Birmingham
July 2, 4		200332, 1	J. M. Johnson & Sons	3 Castle Street Holborn and 56 Hatton Garden London
" "	16, 2	209594, 7	Edward Vickers & Co. (limited)	Manchester
" "		209595		
August 10, 3		210199, 1	Molineaux Webb & Co.	Manchester
" "	16, 5	210325, 2	William Warner Tate	47 Leonard Street Tabernacle Street, London
" "	26, 5	210484, 1	Molineaux Webb & Co.	Manchester
" "	30, 3	210619, 2	Napoleon Montanari	12 Langford Road, Herbert Town, W. West Batignolles, Paris. Manchester
Sept 10, 4		210941, 2	Molineaux Webb & Co.	
" "		210942		
Oct 18, 4		212432, 1	John Robinson & Bolton	Farrington

Date of Deposit	No. of Parcel	No. of Design	Name of Proprietor	Address of Proprietor
1866				
June 16, 4		198277, 1	James Derbyshire & Brother	Bridgewater Flint-Glass Works, Hulme, Manchester
" 5, 6		198278, 1	Rowbotham & Woodall	Birmingham
August 13, 8		199959, 1	George Arthur Feagle & Edwin Martin	John Street, Cotswold Road, Lambeth S.
" 23, 6		200233, 1	Angus & Greener	Flint Glass Works, Sunderland
Sept 22, 5		201546, 1	Eugene Rimmel	96 Strand
" 26, 5		201705, 1	George Fisher	87 Murray Street, Kent Road London
Feb 12, 1		202342, 1	Eugene Rimmel	96 Strand at Strand
Nov 2, 10, 6		203523, 1	F & C Bishop & Co.	Ashton, Lancashire
" 28, 5		204182, 1	Michael & James Beck	Stockport
June 22, 3		215210, 1	Holgate, Richardson & Dougton	Waterloo, near Stockport
" 29, 1		205220, 1	Pellatt & Co.	25 Baker Street Portman Square
1867				
Aug 5, 6		205330, 1	Pellatt & Co.	25 Baker Street
" 11, 0		205711, 1	James Green	Fenton Potteries James Street London
Feb 26, 4		205812, 1	Angus & Greener	Wearsight Glass Works Sunderland
Feb 1, 1		205852, 2	Pellatt & Co.	25 Baker Street Portman Square
" "		205853		
" 8, 7		205997, 1	John Robson	19 Princess Street
" 23, 9		206280, 1	H. P. Downing	Plainer Glass Works Helena State Bowling Row
" 25, 5		206304, 1	James Derbyshire & Brother	Bridgewater Flint-Glass Works Hulme Manchester

Left page

Date of Deposit	No. of Parcel	No. of Design	Name of Proprietor	Address of Proprietor
1867				
Oct 19	4	212674 to 212677	Thomas Webb & Sons	Stourbridge Glass Works Stourbridge
Nov 14	5	213851	Richardson & Smith	Stourbridge
25	6	214321	Frederick Adey	Ruskall Heat Birmingham
26	9	214357-2 214358	Angus & Greener	Wear Flint Glass Work Sunderland
Feby 2	4	214594	Edward Webb	Fordley Stourbridge
21	6	214750	Edward Rickens Holloredge	Wordsley near Stourbridge
1868				
Jany 4/3	1	215734	Molineaux Webb & Co	Manchester
7	11	215917	Francis Riordan	Albion Works City Road London
31	9	216348	Molineaux Webb & Co	Manchester
13		216361-2 216362	J & C Bullop & Co	Manchester
Feby 8	4	216632	Molineaux Webb & Co	Manchester
21	4	216996-2 216997	J Defries & Sons	Houndsditch London
27	6	217101 217103	Gustav Böhm The Falkny Glass Company	Ferback Germany 39-4 Wilmington London Falkny Staffordshire
28	4	217107 to 217109		
Mch 5	11	217207	Edward Moore & Co	Tyne Flint Glass Work South Shields
6	7	217224	Percival Vickers & Co (Limited)	Manchester

Right page

Date of Deposit	No. of Parcel	No. of Design	Name of Proprietor	Address of Proprietor
1867				
March 2	6	212676	Phillips & Pearce	35 Old Bond Street London
30	7	212715	Rappoll & Co	1st Sarrophest Sund London
April 1	7	212724	Angus & Greener	near Flint Glass Sunderland
24	7	214486	Herr Webb & Co	Stourbridge Flint Glass Works Stourbridge
May 4	6	214561	Angus & Greener	Wear Flint Glass Work Sunderland
Aug 21	11	218866	Berman and Field	Birmingham Wilmington & Co
29	8	218984	Frederick Curtby	Newhall Street Birmingham
	11	218985	James Longshaw & Brothers	Bretock Works Melene Manchester
1868				
June 6	2	219163-3 to 219165	Berman & Field	39-4 Wilmington London
11	6	219303	S & C Bullop & Co	St Helens Lancashire
July 11	14	219769	Molineaux Webb & Co	Kirby Street Manchester
Aug 20	1	220050	Henry Thiranlin	77 Dale Street Liverpool
18	1	220230	Edward Jones	3rd Rivers East Coswell Road
6	8	220317	Richard Gent	7 Oral Hackney Road London
20	6	220093 220900	Molineaux Webb & Co	
Sept 4	7	221220	S & C Bishop & Co	St Helens Lancashire
10	8	221497	Herr Webb & Co	Russia Street Glass Works Manchester
29		221498	Boulton & Mills	Audnam Glass Works Stourbridge

Date of Deposit	No of Parcel	No of Design	Name of Proprietor	Address of Proprietor
1888				
Septr 12	7	221520	E. Edwards	49 Frederick Street, Birmingham
13	5	221563	Isidore Kevreux & Co	Flint Glass Works, Sunderland
17	5	221684	Angus & Greener	Wear Flint Glass Works, Sunderland
"		221795	Percival Vickers & Co Limited	Jersey Street, Manchester
19	8			
Octr 13	5	222546	H.V. & L. Lee	Sherwood Street, Hounsditch
21	7	223307	Ashford & Sons	Staffordshire, Manchester
23	4	223322	Percival Vickers & Co Limited	Jersey Street, Manchester
"				
Novr 6	11	224027	James Jacob	Bartlett's Buildings, Holborn, London
Decr 2	7	225010	J. Straw & Son	No 12 Aldersgate Street
4	16	225286	Manchester Hodgson & Co	14-17 Flint Street, Dublin
14	6	225440	Percival Vickers & Co (Limited)	Jersey Street, Manchester
21	14	225673	Percival Vickers & Co (Limited)	Jersey Street, Manchester
30	4	225472	Elijah Atkins	Birmingham
1869				
Jany 1	9	226052	S. & W. Batick & Co	St Helens, Lancashire
20	5	226509	Elijah Atkins	48 Great Hampton Street, Birmingham
		226510		
28	8	226743	Thomas Patmore & Sons	Birmingham
Feby 1	12	226916	Rothevan & Webb & Co	Jersey Street, Manchester
		226917		
11	1	227246	Charles Joseph King	14 Queenhithe, Upper Thames Street, E.C.
8	8	227274	Thomas Wesley	36 Bridge Street, Birmingham
"				
"				

No. of Design	Name of Proprietor	Address of Proprietor
1889		
Feby 22 — 12 227410	1. James Derbyshire & Brother	Helena, Manchester
24 — 4 227429	2. Elijah Atkins	48 Great Hampton Street, Birmingham
227430		
March 24 — 7 228147	J. & C. Bishop & Co	St Helens, Lancashire
7 — 1 228202	1. Rothevan & Webb & Co	St Helens, Manchester & Sherwood Street
31 — 2 228216	2. H.V. & L. Lee	
228297		
April 5 — 3 228424	1. John Straw	Aldersgate Street, Manchester
13 — 7 228612	2. James Derbyshire & Brother	Helena Manchester
20 — 9 228762	1. Angus & Greener	Wear Flint Glass Works, Sunderland
26 — 5 228850	1. Percival Vickers & Co	Jersey Street, Manchester
May 20 — 7 229522	1. C. & F. Meyer & Co	Schoenbull Street, London C.C.
June 8 — 6 229581	M.S. & G. Phillips & Pearce	153 New Bond Street, London
July 1 — 6 230096	1. New Webb & Co	Vine & Mill Works, Manchester
2 — 6 230631	1. Lovenstahl & Hope	110 Portland Street, Manchester
5 — 3 230716	1. Edward Bolton	Orford Lane Glassworks, Warrington
6 — 9 230802	1. William Thomas Longue	Wolverhampton
31 — 8 231430	1. Henry Greener	Wear Flint Glass Works, Sunderland
August 12 — 8 231927	1. Henry Greener	Wear Flint Glass Works, Sunderland
Septr 4 — 3 232243	1. Sidney Brown	9 Blackfriars Road, L.C.
9 — 6 232893	3. Insell & Baker	Birmingham
13 — 0 233022	3. Henry Staverichter & Co	12 Allen Street, Goswell Street, E.C.
" — " to 233024		

Date of Deposit	No. of Parcel	No. of Design	Name of Proprietor	Address of Proprietor	Date of Deposit	Parcel	Design	Name of Proprietor	Address of Proprietor
1869					**1870**				
Sept 15	3	233092	Sidney Brown	8 Blackfriars Road SE	Sep 14	11	238105	Henry Greener	Sear Flint Glass Works Sunderland
27	6	233716	Henry Brauwichter & Co	12 Alben Place Parcell Street E.C.	15/10		238145	Edward Bolton	Farringdon Manchester Star manufacturer
Octr 16	3	234517	Percival Vickers & Co Limited	Lersey Street Manchester					
19	5	234489	Eugene Rimmel	Portland London	11		238151	S. A. Hicks	8 Hatton Garden London
28	1	235782	F Fletcher	6 Charles Street Commercial Road Peckham	18	6	238431	Edward Bolton	Birmingham manufacturer
					Feby 3	12	238593	Britton & Mills	Aldnam Glass Works Stourbridge
							238594		
Nov 2	1	235568	Richard Gent	24 West Railway Road	4	11	238637	William Romer Hamblet	Alpheus Bakersham London
3	11	235690	A Kenyon	Holt Town Glass Works	8	9	238653	Mr Tyke	Goalhard Kent E
4	9	235710	James Lewis	Geen Street Manchester	16	7	238716	James Halesby	Birmingham
		235711			21	7	239056	Wm Felce & Son	Finsbrook Fitzroy Square
6	3	235821	Percival Vickers & Co Limited	Manchester	22	4	239084	Antonius Kirk & Co	
					24	9	239136	Buttler & Co	
10	6	236001	R Gent	27 Oval Hackney Road Hackney	28	8	239244	Hodgetts Richardson	Wordsley Glass Works Stourbridge
		236002	Ker Webb & Co	Ruffin Street Glass Works Manchester			239242	Pargeter	
16	13	236235	Henry Brown	8 Blackfriars Road SE	March 22	3	239748	Joseph Gatcliffe & Co	Manchester
Nov 7	7	236921	Henry Greener	Sear Flint Glass Works Sunderland	26	9	240010	Percival Vickers & Co	Manchester
14	3	237141	James Couper & Sons	City Flint Glass Works Glasgow	April 2	4	240217	Antonius Gratton	
15	4	237158	Lloyd & Summerfield	Birmingham	29	7	241052	William Henry Gratton	
18	1	237228	Christor Fran & Co	Morbox Road Glasgow	May 5	11	241063	Lambroch & Co	Birmingham
23	8	237560	Percival Vickers & Co Limited				241259	Alfred Arculus	Birmingham
					19	11	241590	Isaac Rick Carton	30 Northumberland Place Plymouth
1870					26	6	241964	Antonius Webb & Co	Kirby Street Ancoat Manchester
Jany 3	3	237741	Molineaux Webb & Co	Kirby Street Ancrots Manchester	8	8	241963	Gustav Boehm	3 & 4 Aldermanbury London
7	4	237893	L R Docens	13 Smithy Door Manchester			241964		
12	8	238052	Hodgetts Richardson & Pargeter	Wordsley Glass Works Stourbridge	27	10	242010	Gustav Boehm	304 Aldermanbury London

Date of Deposit	No of Parcel	No of Design	Name of Proprietor	Address of Proprietor
1870				
June 10	4	244248. 1	Frederick Oldby	165 Great Nichol West Birmingham
21	3	244250. 1	J & J Berkshire	Milne Brandcester
23	2	244262. 1	James Hickson	75 Southgate Road, London
July 1	2	244268 3 to 244270	Molineux Webb & Co	Kirby Street, Manchester
			James Bond	Fenchurch Road, London
18	4	244267. 1	Ernest Vickers & Morse	Broad Street, Manchester
19	7	244354. 1	Lowenthal & Morse	Blunt Glass Works
Sept 1	6	244491. 1 W Gammon & Co	Birmingham
13	8	244871. 1	Allen & Baker	Bishopsgate Within Birmingham
22	7	245051. 2	Edward Hand Jeffery	Matlock Kirk Sheffield
		245052		
Dec 6	1	245568. 1	Frederic Impey	15 Woolstock Street
			John Bury Quaitt	Great Street W
12	5	245730. 1	J Barrett	23 Faston Street North London & C District
22	6	246163. 1	Hodgetts Richardson	Wordsley Glass Works
			& Brazier	Stourbridge
Nov 24	8	246394. 1	Richard Young	24 Mad Faskur Street
1	5	246500. 1	Glover & Mullin	Westminster Birmingham
4	7	246924. 1	J W & J Lee	St Saward Street Sevenn
10	11	247051. 1	Henry Greener	Foran Flint Glass Works, Sunderland
14	10	247322. 1	James Lewis	6 Burlett Buildings Holborn
18	2	247163. 2	Robinson Tibbs & Co	Kirby Street Manchester
		247464		
22	4	247945. 1	Henry Tucker & Co	New Street Square E C
23	6	247983. 1	Fader Thornhill	44 New Bond Street
Feb 9	9	248459. 1	Saml C Bishop & Co	St Helens Lancashire

Date of Deposit	No of Parcel	No of Design	Name of Proprietor	Address of Proprietor
1870				
Dec 23	1	249039. 1	Alex Sullivan	17 Welby & Co
24	10	249099. 1	E & C Bishops and Co	Flint Glass Work St Helens Lancashire
1871				
Jany 17	7	249600. 1	Molineux Webb & Co	State Molineux Webb
24	3	249808. 3 to 249810	Molineux Webb & Co	Kirby Street Manchester
25	8	249882. 1	Boulton & Mills	Autumn Glass Works Stourbridge
26	4	249890. 6 to 249893	Apsley Pellatt Hanemann	15 Greenwich Street
				Corporation Street, Manchester
28	11	249969. 1	Boulton & Mills	Bostman Glass Works, Stourbridge
Feb 16	2	250430. 1	Brockwood & Co	18 Woodstock Hill City E C
24	8	250600. 1	Blackwood & Co	
1	14	250678. 1	Boulton & Mills	Autumn Glass Works, Stourbridge
2	8	250921. 1		
8	5	250835. 1	Boulton & Mills	
13	9	251012. 1		Autumn Glass Works, Stourbridge
16	8	251034. 1	John Sims & Mary Pieper	
22	3	251131. 3 to 251133	Stuart & Mills	Autumn Glass Works, Stourbridge
April 7	9	252159. 1	Edward Bolton	Corporation Glass Work
Aug 25	12	252823. 1	John Mary Wood	25 Baker Street Portman Square W

Deposit	Parcel	Design	Name of Proprietor	Address of Proprietor
1871				
June 7, 5		253067, 1	Aerial Vickers & Limited	Manchester
21, 6		253471, 1	N. Ainsworth	32 Brook Street Holborn
July 17, 1		254050, 1	Boulton & Mills	Audnam Glassworks Stourbridge
18, 3		254058, 1	Phillips & Pearce	155 New Bond Street N
August 3, 7		254464, 1	Thomas Nat Wickens	6 Gutter Lane Cheapside
17, 4		254464, 4	Philip Pargeter	Red House Glassworks Stourbridge
22, 4		254993, 1	William Henry Hewitt	Birmingham
Sept 2, 2		255351	Chance & Sullivan	Spon Lane Works, Smethwick near Birmingham
"				Birmingham
6, 7		255383, 1	Rev. Webb & Co	Stourbridge
8, 8		255459	Michael Alexander Ditz	17, 19 & 21 Garden Lane in the City of London
" "			trading as Ditz & Co	the City of London
30, 10		256264	Percival Vickers & Co Limited	Jersey Street Manchester
Oct 3, 4		256336, 1	Brutton, Tate & Co	Poland Street Manchester
13, 9		256680, 1	James Barnes	Birmingham
Nov 6, 9		257563 & 1	Rosenthal & Sons	Smethwick, London &c
24, 10		257929, 1	H. Barth Binko	Westgate Glass Works London
Dec 7, 5		258445, 1	Percival Vickers & Co Limited	Jersey Street Manchester
1872				
Jany 5, 6		259270, 1	James Lewis	Bartletts Buildings Holborn London
10, 8		259391, 1	James Buckley	9 Livingston Street Birmingham
27, 12		260051, 1	M. Kuhn	3 Rue Scribe Paris
29, 11		260064, 2	Akerman Korrall & Phillips	18 Rydal Street Portsville N
Feby 2, 1		260183, 4	Sowerby & Co	Ellison Glass Works Gateshead-on-Tyne
" "		to 260186		

Deposit	Parcel	Design	Name of Proprietor	Address of Proprietor
1872				
Feby 12, 1		260397, 1	Woodall Keen & Woodall	Birmingham
"	6	260404, 2	Sowerby & Co	Ellison Glass Works Gateshead-on-Tyne
"		260405		
15, 8		260472, 1	Gustav Boehm	344 Aldermanbury London
22, 6		260643	Hodgetts, Richardson & Co	Wordsley Glassworks, Stourbridge
"		to 260650		
29, 5		260802	Sowerby & Co	Ellison Glass Works Gateshead-on-Tyne
March 2, 12		260854	The Crewe Refinery Company	40 Jermyn Street N
14, 2		261123, 3	Hodgetts, Richardson & Son	Wordsley Glass Works Stourbridge
"		to 261172		
15, 8		261182	Akerman Korrall & Phillips	18 Rydal Street Portsville N
19, 6		261264, 1	H. W. Hickins	Gutter Lane Cheapside
25, 5		261445, 3	S. & F. Derbyshire	Bridgewater near Salford near Manchester, Birmingham
27, 7		261532, 1	N. F. Copeland & Son	160 New Bond Street
April 6, 8		261950, 1	Stan. Frederic Cooke	105 Cannon Street London
19, 3		262010, 1	Horton & White	99 Great Charles Street Birmingham
23, 5		262198, 1	Brutton, Tate & Co	Poland Street Hulme near Road Manchester
May 2, 7		262405, 1	Percival Vickers & Co Limited	Manchester
11, 9		262680, 1	S. & F. Derbyshire	Bridgewater Glass Works Manchester

Date of Deposit	No. of Parcel	No. of Design	Name of Proprietor	Address of Proprietor
1872				
Aug 30. 7		263032	1. Pearsall Vickers & Co. Limited	Manchester
June 11. 4		263311/4	1. Pearsall Vickers & Co. Limited	Manchester
13. 3		263362	1. Rev. Webb & Co.	Prussia Street Glass Works Manchester
June I.18. 2		263395	1. Anne & Mrs Fussell	45 Woodcock St. Birmingham
21. 6		263540	1. Jane Webb & Joseph Hammond — trading as the executors of the late Joseph Webb	Stourbridge
22. 1		263543	1. E.T. Rippingille	Holborn Hill London
July 5. 7		263929	1. F. Osler (Pearce) Glass	329.33 Red Lion Street Holborn W.C.
18. 6		264288	1. Robert Sallmann Auguste	6 Liverpool Road London
August 28. 2		265528	1. John Hanbury	Woodywood Road Birmingham
Oct. 2/8		266734	1. S. Mordan & Co.	41 City Road London
Nov. 6. 11		267327	1. J.S & T. Derbyshire	Fulham Manchester
7. 7		267442	2. Scovcroy & Co.	Calcutta
" "		267443		
19. 5		267900	1. Boissière & Ch. Auguste	La Verrerie du Sast (Pire) France
21. 12		268074	3. William Singleton	10 Parkers Hill Sheffield
" "		268076		
Dec. 12. 7		268325	1. Akerman Norrall & Phillips	6 Regent Street Portonville
10. 7		268734	1. Henry Turner	West Flint Glass Works Sunderland
11. 4		268739	1. J.S & T. Derbyshire	Milne Manchester
13. 7		268786	1. Chappin & Webb	76 & 78 Oxford Street & Royal Cutlery Works Sheffield

Date of Deposit	No. of Parcel	No. of Design	Name of Proprietor	Address of Proprietor
1872				
Dec 14. 8		268810	1. J.S & T. Derbyshire & Co.	Milne Manchester
19. 13		268883	2. Jane Webb and Joseph Hammond trading as the executors	
" "		268864	3. the late Joseph Webb of Stourbridge. Glass Manufacturers	
23. 3		269474	1. Pearsall Vickers & Co. (Limited)	Manchester
1873				
June 3. 4		269476	1. Rev. Webb & Co.	Prussia Street Glass Works Manchester
10. 4		269593	1. Charles Joseph King	7 Holborn Bars E.C.
15. 4		269694	1. Pearsall Vickers & Co. Limited	Jersey Street Manchester
Feb. 1. 10		270083	1. William Burrows	City
12. 1		270351	1. Samuel Pearce	North Birmingham
17. 8		270525	1. Henry Herbert	2 Charterhouse Buildings London E.C.
March 5. 7		271027	1. Akerman & Norrall	(Regent St) Portonville
7. 6		271070	3. D. Beck & Co.	12 Holborn Birmingham
" "		271072	to 271072	
12. 1		271146	1. W & F. Mortlock	19 & James Street London
April 5. 2		271867	1. Anne Barnes	44 Summer Lane Birmingham
10. 15		272048	1. Akerman & Norrall	6 Regent Street Portonville
16. 14		272132	1. Jane Webb & Joseph Hammond trading as the executors of the late Joseph Webb of Stourbridge	
29. 1		272381	2. Samuel Jones	13 Westminster Street London
" "		272382		
" "		272424	1. Daniel Pearce	North End Works North End Hammersmith
May 3. 9		272649	1. Z.H. Atkins & Co.	62 Fleet Street London W.C.

109

Date of Deposit	No. of Parcel	No. of Design	Name of Proprietor	Address of Proprietor

1873

Date of Deposit	No. of Parcel	No. of Design	Name of Proprietor	Address of Proprietor
May 2		272685 to 272688	Percival Vickers & Co Limited	Manchester
16.4		272981	Philip Pargeter	Redhouse Glass Works, Wordesley, Stourbridge
26.12		273190	Edward Bolton	Oxford Lane Glass Works, Warrington
24.5		273177	Boulton & Mills	Audnam Glass Work, Stourbridge
6		273178	Jos. Webb & Co	Stanna... Flint Glass Works, Manchester
June 14.5		273730	Lloyd & Summerfield	Park Glass Works, Birmingham
20.13		273866	Sowerby & Co	Ellison Glass Work, Gateshead on Tyne
July 31.5		274743	Sowerby & Co	Ellison Flint Glass Works, Gateshead
August 6.10		274906 to 274910	S H Barrett	2 Bredwork Road, Snedes Road
8.7		274961 to 274963	John Derbyshire	Regent Road Flint Glass Works, Salford
9		274965	Howes & Burley	Birmingham
Sept 2.9		275575	John Derbyshire	Regent Road Flint Glass Works, Salford
6.2		275836	Hodgetts & Richardson &c	Wordsley Flint Glass Works, Stourbridge
25.12		276524 to 276525	James Bromwich	Victoria Building, Venice

1873

Date of Deposit	No. of Parcel	No. of Design	Name of Proprietor	Address of Proprietor
Oct 13.1		277750	Hughes &c	London
14.5		277158	Thomas Riddell	Mason 90, Mare, London; Fields, Hackney
21.8		277328	George Busby	was Birmingham
28.5		277629	Thomas Riddell	Union Place, Mare... Hackney
4		277630		
11.12		277834	Daniel Pearce	York Sud Villa
Nov 4 3.13		277869	Ackman & Form...	...
13.8		278266	...	...
11.5		278372	E A Davis	...
20.9		278481	Benjamin Hulwell	59 Bennett Street, Blackfriars Road
24.6		278772	Edwin Bennen &c	Villa Street EC
Dec 10.11		279179	Eno Webb and Joseph Hammond	Greenborough
			late Joseph Webb	Stourbridge
15.7		279245	La Baronne Gabrielle de Felcherscham	to Percy, Near Bedford
20.5		279374	Edward Bermann Hesdrade Street EC	Same London

1874

Date of Deposit	No. of Parcel	No. of Design	Name of Proprietor	Address of Proprietor
Jany 6.6		279532	John Derbyshire	Regent Road Flint Glass Works, Salford
9		279535	Wm Henry Beck	4 Aldesgate Street
15.6		279876	Sowerby & Co	Ellison Glass Work, Gateshead on Tyne
20.5		279940	Daughters & Crawford	Ludgate East Cherbey, Surrey
Feby 3.5		280147	John Derbyshire	Regent Road Glass Works; Salford Manchester

Deposit	Parcel	Design	Name of Proprietor	Address of Proprietor
1874				
Feb 14.	10	280473. 3	Molineaux Webb & Co	Kirby Street Manchester
" . "		280475. to		
18.	3	280566. 1	Henry Manton junior	108 Great Charles Street Birmingham
13.	2	280660. 1	Thomas Seago & Benjamin Johnson	16 Yorkshire Street Birmingham
March 13.	1	281092. 1	Mawson & Thompson	Aldersgate Street
" .	10	281119. 1	Isaac Barnes	58 Broad Street Birmingham
28.	8	281435. 2	Pellatt & Wood	25 Baker Street Portman Square, W.
		281436.		
April 9.	3	281670. 6	Samuel Evans	Wordesley Stourbridge near Birmingham
" . "		281675. to		
11.	6	281767. 1	Franz Ewert	Broad Weir Street Bristol Germany
13.	3	281771. 1	A. Aronsberg & H. Greiner	Shudehill Manchester S.E.
17.	3	281842. 1	Webb & Co	Ellison Flint Glass Works Manchester
22.	8	281933. 1	Sowerby & Co	Ellison Glass Works Gateshead-on-Tyne
Aug 12.	6	282260. 1	John Derbyshire	Regent Road Salford Glass Works Manchester
15.	10	282371. 1	Miss Pearson	Melton Surrey
20.	10	282476. 1	Philip Pargeter & Stourbridge Glass Manufacturer & Percival Jones of Stourbridge	
			Chance & Hunt Nicholas	Southwark Street S.E.
26.	10	282505. 1	Daniel Pulham & Sons	
29.	2	282648. 1	John Hanbury	38 Lady wood Road Birmingham Warwickshire
1874				
June 1.	8	282663. 2	Sowerby & Co	Ellison Glass Works Gateshead-on-Tyne
		4		
10.	4	282662. 1	Joy & Sones	
15.	1	282961.	Jane Webb & Joseph Hammond Executors of the late Joseph Webb of Stourbridge	Coalbourn Hill Glass Works
24.	4	283214. 1	George Meble & Son	342 Gloucester Street Holborn London
July 3.	4	283406. 1	John Derbyshire	
13.	3	283567. 1	Joy & Sones	387 and ... Birmingham
29.	8	284031. 1	Percival Vickers & Co Limited	Surrey Street Manchester
Aug 10.	8	284291	Percival Jones	15 Westmoreland Street Dublin
17.	5	284431. 1	Sowerby & Co	Ellison Glass Works Gateshead upon Tyne
25.	4	284581. 1	John Short Downing	Craven Works, 1874 Surrey Street Birmingham
26.	5	284672	William Henry Heppell & Co	Newcastle Flint Glassworks
2.	9	284903. 1	Henry Picard	West Flint Glass Works Sunderland 19 Carton Lane, London EC
Sept 11.	0	284903		
10.	6	285010. 1	Sowerby & Co	Ellison Glass Works Gateshead-on-Tyne
11.	3	285175. 1	John Derbyshire	Regent Road Flint Glass Works Manchester
" .	9	285179	Frank Lyon	13 Lorrimer Road Walworth London
24.	6	285632. 1	Walter O Slone	Exeter vacant
Oct 2.	8	285831. 4	R & J Beck	31 Cornhill EC
" . "		285834. to		

Left table

Date of Deposit	No. of Parcel	No. of Design	Name of Proprietor	Address of Proprietor
1874				
Feb 3 . 9		288851 . 4	R & J Beck	31 Cornhill EC
12 . 3		288172 . 1	Thomas Harding	157 Piccadilly SW
13 . 12		286478 . 1	John Dawson Riddell	18 Mark Lane London
26 . 5		286525 . 1	Hodgetts Richardson	Wordsley, Stourbridge
28 . 7		286561 . 1	Edward Bolton	Oxford Lane Glass Works, Warrington
26 . 3		287474 . 1	Charles Joseph Adie	156 Fashion... Birmingham
" . 5		287495 . 1	John Derbyshire	Regent Road Flint Glass Works, Salford
Recd 2 . 5		28961 3 . 1	J G Sarkin & Co	Sheffield
21 . 1		288011 . 1	A Dietrich	4 Coleman Street
" . "		288015 . 1	Jane Webb Joseph Hammond (trading as the executors of the late E.C.) Joseph Webb	Dennhill New Factory EC Stourbridge Flint Glass Manufacturers
" . "		—		
" . "		—		

Right table

Deposit	Parcel	Design	Name of Proprietor	Address of Proprietor
1875				
Feby 4 . 9		289067 . 2	C J Padgett	21 Brewer Street
" . "		289068		Golden Square W
6 . 10		289098 . 2	Thomas Harding	157 Piccadilly SW
" . "		289099		
8 . 11		289165 . 1	Hudson & ...	Southwark Street EC
12 . 9		289203 .	Molineaux Webb & Co	Kirby Street Manchester
15 . 12		289314 . 1	James Lewis	Bartlett Buildings Holborn
22 . 6		287493	Irvingston Kinmond & Co	Kenilworth Street Leamington
26 . 14		28964 5 . 3	Irvingston Kinmond & Co	Leamington
" . "		to	Molineaux Webb & Co	Kirby Street Manchester
" . "		289647		
March 1 . 8		289713 . 1	Henry Defries	147 Houndsditch London
8 . 1		289799 . 1	John Short Downing	Crown Works, 104 Irving Street Birmingham
" . "				Birmingham
9 . 12		289821 . 1	Seago Johnson & Co	George Street Birmingham
13 . 5		289874 . 1	Thomas Lane & Son	Birmingham
24 . 5		289145 . 1	Frank Lyon	32 Aldersgate Street London
30 . 14		290019 . 2	John Short Downing	Crown Works, Irving Street Birmingham
		290192		
April 3 . 10		290263 . 2	G McLea	145 Wigmore Street London
" . "		290264		
19 . 5		290774 . 1	Sowerby & Co	Ellison Glass Works, Gateshead-on-Tyne
23 . 14		290890 . 1	Hodgetts Richardson & Son	Wordsley Glass Works, Stourbridge
26 . 14		290913 . 2	Baxter Bros & Co	Telegraph Lane London &C
May 14 . 9		291347 . 1	Daniel Pearce	North End Villa, North End Road Hammersmith

Second left table

Date of Deposit	No. of Parcel	No. of Design	Name of Proprietor	Address of Proprietor
1875				
May 1 . 2		288210 . 1	Sowerby & Co	Ellison Glass Works Gateshead
" . "			" " Tyne	
7 . 8		288295 . 1	Thomas Lane & Son	Birmingham
16 . 7		288498 . 3	Seago Johnson & Co	23 George Street Birmingham
" . "		to		
" . "		288500		
28 . 11		288838 . 3	Robinson Son & Skinner	Mersey Glass Work Warrington
29 . 12		288806 . 3	John Short Downing	Crown Works, 104 Irving Street Birmingham
" . "		—		
" . 9		288089 . 1	J G Hicks	Hatton Garden

Register of Designs — page 113

Right-hand section

Date of Deposit	No. of Parcel	No. of Design	Name of Proprietor	Address of Proprietor
1875				
Oct. 23, 3	295362	1	William Henry Heppell	Newcastle-on-Tyne
28.14	295444	1	Sowerby & Co	Ellison Glassworks Gateshead-on-Tyne
Nov. 13, 4	295919	1	William Henry Heppell & Co	Newcastle-upon-Tyne
"	295943	1	A. J. Bishop	30 Northumberland Street Strand
25 "	296342	1	John Perkins	23 East Paradise Street ... Robin Hood Street, Nottingham
Dec. 3, 15	296556	1	Edward Webb and John Lewis Gwozdzick	11 & 31 Brooke Street Holborn EC
6 " 5	296644	1	Thomas Webb & Son	Stourbridge
" 7	296643	1	John Derbyshire & Co	Salford, Manchester
17 " 16	297041	1	Sowerby & Co	Wilson Glass Works Gateshead-on-Tyne
"	297042			
22 " 5	297157	1	Thomas Webb & Son	William Road Flint Glass Works, Kirby Street, Manchester
1876				
Jan 4, 5	297683	1	Gage & Co	20 George Street Parade Birmingham
" 6	297634	1	Thomas Webb & Sons	Stourbridge & Charterhouse Street, Holborn Circus London
Feb 2, 1	298055 to 298057	3	G. V. De Luca	5 Guildhall Chambers Basinghall Street London EC
11, 1	298209	1	James Lewis	6 Bartlett's Buildings Holborn Circus London EC
19, 1	298448	4	Whittingham & Percival	Flint Glass Works Pendleton, near Manchester
25, 8	290609	1	William Ford trading under the name of John Ford	Holyrood Glass Works Edinburgh

Left-hand section

Deposit	Parcel	Design	Name of Proprietor	Address of Proprietor
1875				
May 24, 5	294499	3	J. Beet & Co	Hall Street, Birmingham
"	to 294501			
" 14	291532	1	Daniel Pearce	
June 5, 9	294873	2	Sowerby & Co	Ellison Glass Works, Gateshead-on-Tyne
"	294874			
12, 9	294010	2	Hodgetts Richardson & Son	Wordsley Glass Works
"	294041			
16, 6	294113	1	Thomas Gray & Co	Sunderland-on-Tyne
21, 7	294201	1	Ortner & Houle	3 St James's Street SW
July 13, 7	294783	1	Footall & Son	10 Southampton Street, Birmingham
19, 2	294980	1	Benjamin Nathan & Company	Slade Hill Street Sheffield
26, 3	293100	1	Molineaux Webb & Co	Kirby Street, Manchester
August 5, 8	293356	1	John Derbyshire & Co	Regent Road Salford
23, 5	293890	1	James Scott	West Bromwich
" 6		2	John Benson ...	
24, 6	293942	1	Hyde & Co	Saint Bride Street London
September 8, 4	294315 to 294318	4	William Richards & Son	38 Tonbridge Street North, Birmingham
10, 6	294376 to 294379	4	Sowerby & Co	Wilson Glass Works Gateshead-on-Tyne
14, 16	294522	1	Joseph Polak	59 Francis Road Aston Birmingham
15, 1	294523	1	Charles Louis N Roderick Jones	38 Howard Street, Birmingham
18, 4	294595	1	Hodgetts, Richardson & Son	Wordsley Glass Works, Stourbridge
23, 6	294653	2	Edward Bolton	Orford Lane Glass Works, Warrington
"	294654			
Oct 16, 10	295133	1	Molineaux Webb & Co	Kirby Street, Manchester

Left portion:

Date of Deposit	No. of Parcel	No. of Design	Name of Proprietor	Address of Proprietor
1876				
Feb. 26	9	298626 } 298627	Thomas Webb & Sons	Stourbridge and (Charterhouse Street Hatton Circus, London)
March 6	3	298890 to 298896	Sowerby & Co	—
" 9	4	299022 to 299023	John Derbyshire & Co	Regent Road Manchester
" 7	7	299050 to 299054	Sowerby & Co	Ellison Glass Works Gateshead on Tyne
11	10	299158	Hodgetts, Richardson & Son	Stourbridge
18	7	299251 to 299252	J. C. Oston	145 Oxford Street London W
22	3	299305	Charles Thiel	42 Augusta Street Birmingham
27	13	299424 to 299426	Sowerby & Co	Ellison Glassworks Gateshead on Tyne
28	1	299427	Hodgetts, Richardson & Son	Wordsley near Stourbridge
" 7	7	299473	Sowerby & Co	Ellison Glass Works Gateshead on Tyne
April 4	7	299697	Joseph Benson	Cut Glass Works Charles Street Sheffield
11	10	299826	Daniel Pearce	Frith Glass Works York Road
28	2	300300	John Derbyshire & Co	Regent Road Flint Glass Works Manchester
May 3	11	300371	Boulton & Mills	Audnam Glass Works Stourbridge

Right portion:

Date of Deposit	No. of Parcel	No. of Design	Name of Proprietor	Address of Proprietor
1876				
May 8	6	300419 to 300420	Sowerby & Co	Ellison Glass Works Gateshead on Tyne
9	10	300456	F. A. Atkins & Co	62 Great Hampton Street Birmingham
11	6	300487	Henry Manton junior	108 Great Hampton Row Hockley Birmingham
13	3	300619	Charles Harris	Frithville Road Flint Glass Works
17	9	300655	John Derbyshire & Co	Royal Road Manchester / Salford Manchester
20	2	300672	Wykes, Brierley & Co	Hair Glassworks Castleford Yorkshire
24	5	300748	Sowerby & Co	Ellison Glass Works Castleford Yorkshire
29	19	300940	Sowerby & Co	Ellison Glass Works Gateshead on Tyne
June 6	2	301058 to 301067	Whittingham & Percival	Birchfields Flint Glass Works Manchester
" 2	2	301236 to 301363	Whittingham & Percival	Whit Lane, Pendleton Manchester
15	8	301238	John Short Downing	Greenworks Commercial Street Birmingham
17	3	301298	Boulton & Mills	Audnam Glass Works Stourbridge
20	1	301312	Sowerby & Co	Ellison Glass Works Gateshead on Tyne
21	1	301326 / 301327	Sowerby & Co	Ellison Glass Works Gateshead on Tyne
" 5	5	301331	Henry Pether	25 Cripplegate London
30	7	301579	Percival Vickers & Co Limited	Jersey Street Ancoats Manchester
July 14	8	301951	Pittman & Roff	42 Great Marlborough Street Regent Street W

Date of Deposit	No. of Parcel	No. of Design	Name of Proprietor	Address of Proprietor
1876				
Nov 30	8	305579 . 1	Aston & Marlow	79 & 80 Newtown Row, Birmingham
Dec 5	9	305705 . 1	William S. Ramsey	83 & 84 Spring...Newtown, E.C.
8	3	305778 . 1	James Aston	Newtown Row, Birmingham
11	4	305839 . 1	Frederick Winston	19 Bridge...Blandford...
18	2	306083 . 1	Sykes Macauy & Co	Albert Glass Works, Castleford, Yorkshire
19.16		306149 . 1	Andrew Stern	The Prussian Steel Glass Works, Pelham Road, Manchester / Birmingham
20	8	306185 . 1	Lloyd & Summerfield	Birmingham
22.17	18	306884 . 1	George Davidson & Co	Teams Flint Glass Works, Gateshead-on-Tyne
	11	306882 . 1	Sowerby & Co	Ellison Glass Works, Gateshead-on-Tyne
22	7	307126 . 1	Thomas Tullis	Beaconsfield Terrace, Harrington
31	11	307426 . 1	Henry Brett & Co	26 High Holborn...
1	1	307433 . 4	Winston, Beck & Co	4 Rawford Place...
12	9	307671 . 1	Stael & Brownlaw	Canning Works, Hulme, Manchester
13	8	307686 . 11	Sowerby & Co	Ellison Glass Works, Gateshead-on-Tyne
		to		
		307696		
17	1	307869 . 1	James Aston	Steel Town Row, Birmingham
21.10		307910 . 1	J. T. Crawford	Sullivan Street, Soho, Harrington, B.
23	8	307957 . 2	Sowerby & Co	Ellison Glass Works, Gateshead-on-Tyne
		307958		
28.15		308104 . 1	George Davidson & Co	Teams Flint Glass Works, Gateshead-on-Tyne

Date of Deposit	No. of Parcel	No. of Design	Name of Proprietor	Address of Proprietor
1876				
July 19	6	301999 . 1	E Cetti & Co	119 & 31 Brooke Street, Holborn and Hatton, London
24. 13		302114 . 2	Sowerby & Co	Ellison Glass Works, Gateshead-on-Tyne
		302115		
20	6	302199 . 1	Henry Greener	Teams Flint Glass Works, Sunderland
8		302201 . 1	Gustave Marquot	Bagel sur Bar-sur-Aube, France
Aug 16	7	302625 . 1	Barrow & Co	Glass Works, Smethwick, Square Birmingham
19. 10		302804 . 2	Sowerby & Co	Ellison Glass Works, Gateshead-on-Tyne
		302805		
26. 14		302912 . 1	Joseph Kidd	Hulme Flint Glass Works, Manchester
Sept 1	3	303199 . 1	Albert Bradbrook	39 Newgate Street, London E.C.
7	9	303379 . 1	Sykes Macauy & Co	Castleford, Yorkshire
25	1	303830 . 1	Barrow & Co	Glass Works, Smethwick, Square, Birmingham
Oct 2	2	303996 . 1	Hugo & Co	Bridge Street, Parade, Birmingham Road
11	5	304306 . 1	Winston, Beck	
16	8	304363 . 1	Sowerby & Co	Ellison Glass Works, Gateshead-on-Tyne
		to		
		304366		
17	6	304376 . 3		Sheffield
		to		
		304380		
Nov 15	4	305209 . 1	Benjamin Meacham & Co	Sheffield
		305207 . 1		
17	7	305727 . 1	Isaac Barnes & Co	Ellison Glass Works, Gateshead-on-Tyne
28. 10		305541 . 1	James Derbyshire & Sons	30 Broad Street, Birmingham / Greenheys, Manchester Road, Hulme, Manchester

Date of Deposit	No of Parcel	No of Design	Name of Proprietor	Address of Proprietor
1871				
March 1. 5		308192	2 Sowerby & Co	Ellison Glass Works Gateshead on Tyne
" "		306123		
7. 11		308257	2 F & C Osler	Birmingham
" "		308258		
8. 13		308328	1 Bran...son & Robinson	11 Aldersgate Street London E C
13. 10		308444	Sowerby & Co	Ellison Glass Works Gateshead on Tyne
15. 1		308495	1 Sowerby & Co	Ellison Glass Works Gateshead on Tyne
19. 5		308544	1 Sowerby & Co	Ellison Glass Works Gateshead on Tyne
21. 11		308667	1 The Regent Flint Glass Co.	Regent Flint Glass Works Gateshead on Tyne
22. 12		308713	3 Sowerby & Co	Ellison Glass Works Gateshead-on-Tyne
" "		308714	Sowerby & Co	
" "		308715		
23. 7		308776	1 Sowerby & Co	
29. 4		308776	1 Sowerby & Co	
April 18. 3		309484	12 Teago & Co	23 George Street Birmingham
		309485		
19. 5		309542	1 John Davis & Co	...Harbour Stourbridge
" 6		309543	1 Boulton & Mills	Stourbridge
23. 7		309621	1 Crosse & Blackwell	21 Soho Square W
26. 6		309695	1 Max Sugar	5 Blackfriars Road SE
28. 12		309765	1 Max Sugar	5 Blackfriars Road SE
May 4. 4		309902	1 The "Regent" Flint Glass Co.	Gateshead-on-Tyne
12. 10		310037	4 Charles Green	
22. 14		310358	1 Ellis Allen & Co	Fort Harbour Tunstall Road Glasgow
" "		310446	1 H. Lester	48 Crown Street Soho
24. 6				

Date of Deposit	No of Parcel	No of Design	Name of Proprietor	Address of Proprietor
1877				
May 24. 10		310450	2 G. F. De Luca	5 Guildhall Chambers Basinghall Street London E C
		310451		
31. 9		310595	5 Sowerby & Co	Ellison Glass Works Gateshead-on-Tyne
" "		310596		
" "		310597		
June 14. 14		310657	1 Bolton... & Wood	Oxford Lane Glass Works Warrington
21. 10		311138	1 James Lewis	6 Bartlett Buildings Holborn
July 20. 6		312061	1 Ernest August Thomson	Thornton Street Strangeways Manchester
"	12.	312070	2 Sheldon & Pavey	Back of 83 New John Street West Birmingham
		312071		
" 21. 2		312121	1 Eugene Valade	12 Rue Lorrain Paris
August 2. 6		342457	1 William Kesler	48 Eyre Street Hill
" 9. 1		312701	1 Schrada... A. Rhodes	Britannia Works Howard Street Sheffield
Sept 4. 3		313701	1 James Henry Stone	4 St Paul's Square Birmingham
17. 2		314156	2 Wilhmann & Rosh	42 Great Marlborough Street
" "		314157		
18. 17		314265	21	Ellison Glass Works Gateshead-on-Tyne
" "		314285	Sowerby & Co	
Oct 2. 6/12		314482	1 Samuel Crask	116 Leopold Street Birmingham
13. 12		314938	1 Samuel H. Martin & Co	16 Great Marlborough Street
13. 12		315269	1 F V. De Luca	Guildhall Chambers Basinghall Street London EC
17. 2		315429	1 Molineaux Webb & Co	Kirby Road Manchester
29. 6		315664		Sowerby & Co
to				
" "		315674		
30. 6		315683	1 ...Spirit Aging Company	67 Farringdon Road Glasgow

Date of Deposit	No. of Parcel	No. of Design	Name of Proprietor	Address of Proprietor
1877				
Nov 15.	5	316299. 1	Jehinda D Rhodes	Britannia Works, Howard Street, Sheffield
" 15.	"			
20.	4	316403	Sowerby & Co	Ellison Glass Works, Gateshead-on-Tyne
"	"	316491		
"	"	316492		
24.10		316623. 1	R. Hodges	279 High Street, Camden Town NW
Dec 31. 2		316776. 1	Molineaux Webb & Co	Kirby Street, Manchester
"	6. 23	316862. 1	Molineaux Webb & Co	Kirby Street, Manchester
"	17.12	317233. 2	Sowerby & Co	Ellison Glass Works, Gateshead-on-Tyne
"	-	317234		
"	19. 1	317277. 4	Sowerby & Co	Ellison Glass Works, Gateshead-on-Tyne
"		317276		
"		317279		
"		317280		
1878				
Janⁿ 5.	1	317583 3. 2	Archibald Hodge & Co	58 Bridge Street, Port Dundas, Glasgow
"		317584		
" 18.	2	317822. 1	Frederick William Brownen	Gummy Works, Hulme, Manchester
Feb 4	14	318371. 1	Eugene Bon-Rougier	Vraignolaine France
"	9	318467. 1	Widmore Hyatt	5 Newhall Street, Dudley
"	5	318468. 1	James Henry Shore	45 St Paul's Square, Birmingham
"	20.	3	318489	Sowerby & Co	Ellison Glass Works, Gateshead-on-Tyne
"		318490	"	
"		318791	"	
"		318792	"	
"		318793	"	
"		318794	"	
"		318795	"	

Date of Deposit	No. of Parcel	No. of Design	Name of Proprietor	Address of Proprietor
1878				
Mar 1. ⅓	8	319090. 1	Percival Vickers & Co	Jersey Street, Manchester
"	14. 10	319141. 1	H & J Milne	Caledonian Glassworks, Edinburgh
"	16. 0	319353.	E Kenry Brontin & Co	Catherine de Lignerolles Pontllac
"	19. 6	319355. 1	Samuel Rockhouse	London Pottery Works, Vauxhall Street, Fishstall Road, Nine Elms
"	20. 7	319585 5.	Sowerby & Co	Ellison Glass Works, Gateshead-on-Tyne
"		319586		
"		319587		
"		319586		
"		319589		
"	21. 6	319599. 1	W? & L Dee	8 Sherwood Street
"	22. 8	319619. 2	Sowerby & Co	Ellison Glass Works, Gateshead-on-Tyne
"	"	319620		
April 19. 10		320276. 1	W Napier & Sons	114 Houndsditch, City, London
" 18. 1		320330. 1	Brittans Farmer & Williams	3 & 5 Lime Windmill Street, Soho Square
May 11. 8		321308. 1	Samuel Jones	Bark Row, Frenmore in the county of Chester
" 11. 9		321340. 1	Sam Tryzuch	Wood Lodge, Abbeydale, Suffolk
"		321368. 12.		
"		321369.		
"		321370		
"		321371		
"		321372	Sowerby & Co	Ellison Glass Works, Gateshead-on-Tyne
"		321373		
"		321374		
"		321375		
"		321378		
"		321379. 14		

117

Date of Deposit	No. of Parcel	No. of Design	Name of Proprietor	Address of Proprietor
1878				
Mar 27	22	322009	1. Vve Jardin Roux Bazin & Co	Agreement department of the Charente France [illegible]
" 30	16	322080	1. Hooker's Cream Milk Co. Limited	5 Midland Railway Station [illegible]
June 8	11	322393	1. Henry Greener	Wear Flint Glass Works, Sunderland
" 25	16	322819 322820 322821 322822 322823 322824 322825	Sowerby & Co	Ellison Glass Works Gateshead on Tyne
" 2[illegible]	10	322947	1. H[illegible] & L. Lee	8 [illegible] Street
July 8	9	323400	1. Sowerby & Co	Ellison Glass Works Gateshead on Tyne
" [illegible]	5	323711	1. W. H. Britton	7 Holland Street [illegible] Birmingham
" 2[illegible]	15	324317	1. [illegible]	Birmingham
29	4	324321 324322	2. Sowerby & Co	Ellison Glass Works Gateshead-on-Tyne
Augt 2	12	324501	1. J Barnes & Co	30 [illegible] Birmingham
" 1[illegible]	6	324929 324930 324931 324932	4 Sowerby & Co	Ellison Glass Works, Gateshead on Tyne
" 16	11	325096 to 325101	6. Sowerby & Co	Ellison Glass Works Gateshead on Tyne
" 28	4	325439	1 Joseph Wilson Holtzer	Birmingham
" 30	16	325534	1 Sowerby & Co 13	Ellison Glass Works Gateshead on Tyne

Date of Deposit	No. of Parcel	No. of Design	Name of Proprietor	Address of Proprietor
1878				
August 31	8	325347	1 Henry Greener	Wear Flint Glass Works Sunderland
Septr 5	14	325702	1 F & C. Osler	Birmingham
" 7	2	325876	1 Robert Gourlay	Bishopbriggs near Glasgow
" 23	6	326775 326776	2. George Davidson & Co	Teams Glass Works Gateshead on Tyne
Oct 15	4	327641 327642	2. Jane Webb, Joseph Hammond & Henry Fitzroy Webb trading as the Executors of the late Joseph Webb of Stourbridge	
" 19	3	327771	1. J Gill & E. Rawlinson	2 Dunn Street, Every Street Ancoats Manchester
" 26	12	328347	1. William Boyd & Co	Blythswood Foundry Glasgow
	14	328349	1. Oscar Braunmüller	[illegible]
Nov 4	[illegible]	328740/2 328741 328742 328743 328744 328745 328746 328747 328748 328749 328750 328751	Sowerby & Co	Ellison Glass Works Gateshead on Tyne
7	17	328919	1. Sowerby & Co	Ellison Glass Works Gateshead-on-Tyne
12	6	329010	1. Francis Thomas Bond M.D.	Barton [illegible] in the City of Gloucester
20	11	329376	1. Sowerby & Co	Ellison Glass Works Gateshead-on-Tyne

Date of Deposit	No. of Parcel	No. of Design	Name of Proprietor	Address of Proprietor

1878

Nov. 4. 21. 12. 329408 1. First Two Rivers, [illegible]

Date of Deposit	No. of Parcel	No. of Design	Name of Proprietor	Address of Proprietor

1879

Date of Deposit	No. of Parcel	No. of Design	Name of Proprietor	Address of Proprietor
1874				
July 29	7	337572	Coalburn Ale Glass Work.	
		337573 }	John Webb, Joseph Hammond and Mary Fitzroy Webb of Stourbridge	
		337574 }		
		337575 }		
(B)	13	337623	} Sowerby & Co	Ellison Glass Works, Gateshead-on-Tyne
		to		
		337627		
Aug. 6	1	337775	Shorden & Co	Albion Works, City Road, London
8	12	338015	Henry Greener	Wear Flint Glass Works, Millfield, Sunderland
11	7	338093	Matthew Turnbull	Cornhill Glass Works, Southwick Sunderland
14	12	338286	H. H. Heppell & Co	York Street, Newcastle-on-Tyne
		338287 }		
15		338294 }		Ellison Glass Works Gateshead-on-Tyne
		338295	} Sowerby & Co	
		338296		
		338297		
		338298		
26	14	338734	Davies & Lewis	British Pottery
	1	339194	} Sowerby & Co	Ellison Glass Works Gateshead-on-Tyne
		339195		
		339196		
		339197		
		339198		
		339199		
		339200		
	12	339494	John Jackson Wheeler, 189 Fulham Road in the County of Middlesex	

Date of Deposit	No. of Parcel	No. of Design	Name of Proprietor	Address of Proprietor
1879				
Sep 12	12	13 339499 5	Sowerby & Co.	Ellison Glass Works Gateshead on Tyne
"	"	339500		
"	"	339501		
"	"	339502		
"	"	339503		
"	13	13 340002 5	Sowerby & Co.	
"	"	4		
"	"	340006		
"	14	19 340004	Henry Greener	Wear Flint Glass Works (Gateshead)
"		2 340206	Molineaux Webb & Co	Kirby Street, Manchester
23	"	13 340254	Sowerby & Co	Ellison Glass Works Gateshead on Tyne
"	"			
24	15	340369	George W W Edwards	Wolverhampton Kirkwood Street
Nov 17	7	340241	Sowerby & Co	
Dec 3	21	343724 8	E V De Luca	Ellison Glass Works Gateshead on Tyne
31	"	343725		
"	"	343726		
"	"	343727		
"	"	343728		
"	"	343729		
"	"	343730		
"	"	343731		
15	9	344251	E V De Luca	21 Jewin Crescent, Aldersgate Street E C
1880				
Jany 5	2	344911 1	Molineaux Webb & Co	Kirby Street, Manchester
"	7	2 344960 1	Molineaux West & Co	Kirby Street, Manchester

Date of Deposit	No. of Parcel	No. of Design	Name of Proprietor	Address of Proprietor
1880				
Jan 1/9	11	345042 2	Sowerby & Co	Ellison Glass Works Gateshead on Tyne
"	"	345043		
"	"	345044		
"	12	3 345071	W Lister Smith	Kirby Street Birmingham
"	14	2 345166 3		
"		345167	Molineaux Webb & Co	Kirby Street Manchester
"		345168		
20	14	345451 1	Abraham Zittau	3 John Street, Cheetham Hill, Manchester
July 4	13	346020 2	Rochester Tumbler Co	Pittsburgh Penn USA
"		346021		
"	13	346369 1	The Rochester Tumbler Co	Pittsburgh Penn USA
"	16	346585 1	Mina Perez	Charlotte Street, Fitzroy Square W
"	17	346587		New Cross
March 11		347165 1		Millwall
4	"	347241		
"	10	347240 1		
23	12	347895 1	E V De Luca	21 Mary Crescent, Harrogate Street E C
"	3	348165 1		
"	9	348166		
"	11	348191		East Lothian Road
May 5	2	348657 1		
"	10	16 349740 1	William Smith & Co	Birmingham
"	11	13 349749 1	William Hall	
"	14	5 349749 1	Hugh Coulman	
"	21	3 350028 1	William Smith & Co	Birmingham
"	22	1 350065 1	Daniel Pearce	North End Hammersmith

Date of Deposit	No of Parcel	No of Design	Name of Proprietor	Address of Proprietor
1880				
May 24	8	350083 (11)	Sowerby &co	Ellison Glass Works, Gateshead on Tyne
		350084		
		350085		
		350086		
		350087		
		350088		
		350089		
		350090		
		350091		
		350092		
		350093		
" 21	11	350211	1. Geo Macro & Co	Filho Glass Works, Castleford Yorkshire
"	15	350281	C.H. Wortling M.D.	11 West Margaret Street W.
" 31	15	350246	S. Williamson & Sons	90 Caledonian Road, Galloway
June 8	6	350146	Ferdinand Brechens	Fabrica of 1870, Siebengasse Cologne
"	3	350244	1. Israel Verner & Co	124 Neal Street
"	14	350252	1. Bristo Co & Co	Stamf... Liverpool
"	16	351191	1. W.H. Kappel & Co	
"	5	351352	German William Building	ex Good Crocker Street, Liverpool
"	2	351455	4. Robert Brierne	L. ..., Birmingham
July 1	8	351728 (Repd) Architects	Glass Works, 376 Broad Street, Birmingham
Vol 1	11	351966	1. Richard & Brun	Bristol Hill, Staffordshire
"	10	351961	1. ... W. Walton	4 Pall Mall

Date of Deposit	No of Parcel	No of Design	Name of Proprietor	Address of Proprietor
1880				
July 13	11	350133 (5)	Swerby & Co	Ellison Glass Works, Gateshead on Tyne (Entered in ... Errors)
		350134		
"	11	352108	1. William Faraday Perry	Bass Mead, Essex
"	14	350291	Eckson Father & Sons	14 Harricke Esplanade, Southampton (Entd on... King of Glasgow)
"	16	350240	6. Swerby & Co	Filho Glass Works, Gateshead on Tyne (Entered on one)
"	"	350845		Sussex Street, Manchester
"	"	350816	1. Percival, Veekson & Co	
August 14	14	350746	1. R.D. Brundage	880 Broadway, New York City U.S.A.
"	16	354071	1. Merrill.... & Fisher	Shropshire (Warwickshire), Birmingham
Septr 10	1	352935	1. W.H. Kappel & Co	Newcastle on Tyne
"	11	353154	6. Swerby & Co	Filho Glass Works, Gateshead on Tyne
"	"	353158		
"	4	354607	3.	
"	"	354620	1. Swerby & Co	Ellison Glass Works, Gateshead on Tyne
"	"	354629		
"	16	354979	1. Young's Paraffin Light	& Mineral Oil Co., Bishops Road
Octr 3	1	356011	1. James Pargeter Richardson	Monteith, Sapperton
"	5	356515	Carolina Amelia Elizabeth Swallow	9 Burrell Place, ...
			1. Henry Broughton	Lower Broughton Road, Manchester
"	18	356807	14. Robt, Robt Walter	Soho Vista Glass Work, Birmingham

Date of Deposit	No. of Parcel	No. of Design	Name of Proprietor	Address of Proprietor
1878				
Feb 4	8	4 361535	John Shaw & Sons	Latimer Works, 52 Eyre Lane, Sheffield
		361536		
"	16	361810	Chubb & Son	
"	28	362243	James William Hughes	
"	"	362518	Glass Flower	
"	10	362525	Henry Greener	Wear Flint Glass Works, Sunderland
"	11	362453	Augustus Richardson	
"	11	2 362734		
		362735		
		362736		
		362737		
		362738	Sowerby & Co	Ellison Glass Works, Gateshead-on-Tyne
		362739		
		362740		
		362741		
		362742		
		362743		
		362744		
"	19	11 363048	Sowerby & Co	Ellison Glass Works, Gateshead-on-Tyne
"	"	363049		
"	23	9 363194	Young's Paraffin Light & Mineral Oil Co Limited	Birmingham
"	"	363203		
"	30	8 363454	William Thomas Clegg	Vincent Street Westminster
"	"	363456		
"	4	6 363448	William Pratt	134 Steelhouse Lane, Birmingham
"	9	363795	John Gough	12, Parade, Birmingham
"	20	364167	Sowerby & Co	Ellison Glass Works, Gateshead-on-Tyne

Date of Deposit	No of Parcel	No. of Design	Name of Proprietor	Address of Proprietor
1881		3		
April 21	13	364187	Henry Greener	Near Flint Glass Works, Sunderland
30	17	364574	Samuel Elijah Culver	2 Pipson Crescent, Clerkenwell
May 19	9	365,1657	Sowerby & Co	Ellison Glass Works, Gateshead-on-Tyne 1871
31	6	365634	Thomas Wimberry	72 Bellevue Road, Leeds
June 14	9	366032	Henry Greener	Millfield, Sunderland
22	11	366273	R.A.C. Wilson	15 Wilton Street, Grays, Glen Road
24	10	366408	Henry Greener	Near Flint Glass Works, Sunderland
July 16	9	367237	Brasier & Carver	45 Rathbone Place, W
"	"	to 370379		
	15	368636	J. Defries & Sons	147 Houndsditch
September 2	23	369463	Robert Gardner & Co	8 Brooke Street, Holborn
Oct 19	9	370198	Alfred Augustus Daly	6 Landowne Gardens, South Lambeth SE
"	"	370199		
21	16	370370	Sowerby & Co	Ellison Glass Works, Field Houndsditch Typo
"	"	to 370379		
23	20	370469	J. Defries & Sons	147 Houndsditch, Viscount Bow Lynn
26	1	370524	W. B. Kilminster & Co	
26	3	370616	Molineaux Webb & Co	Kirby Street, Manchester
"	"	370619		
Feb 12	5	371262	Molineaux Webb & Co	Kirby Street, Manchester
14	2	371343	William Bartlett & Sons	Abbey Mills, Redditch
22	15	372078	Percival Vickers & Co Limited	Jersey Street, Manchester
Nov 7	3	372860	W. H. Heppell & Co	Newcastle on Tyne
6	10	372967	Max Sugar	6 Market Avenue, Holborn Viaduct EC
Class 15	15	373268	A. Dullmann	37 Monkwell Street EC
7 Class IV 5		373295		

Date of Deposit	No of Parcel	No. of Design	Name of Proprietor	Address of Proprietor
1881				
November 26	6	378918	William Legg & ...	Vincent Works, Westminster
December	8	378432	J. Defries & Son	147 Houndsditch
"	13	378437	W. H. Heppell & Co	Newcastle on Tyne
"	11	378475	Henry Greener	Near Flint Glass Works, Sunderland
8	8	378497	Harwood Son & Harren	187 Newhall Street, Birmingham
31	12	378629	McLeod Hawkes	Bromsgrove Street, Birmingham
		378631		Ellison Glass Works, Gateshead-on-Tyne
14	6	378682	Sowerby & Co	147 Houndsditch
"	"	to 378686		
July 16	9	378773	J. Defries & Sons	
	10	378774		
	"	378775	Sowerby & Co	Ellison Glass Works, Gateshead-on-Tyne
	"	378776		
	"	378777		
	"	378778		
23	1	375013	2. Hawkesford & Booth	7 Bath Street, & 2s Great Hampton Row, Birmingham
		375014		
28	7	375151	PP Verity & Sons	31 King Street, Covent Garden WC
	"	to 375155		
1882				
January 2	1	375281	Molineaux Webb & Co	Kirby Street, Ancoats, Manchester
24	7	375360	George Whybrow	48-49 Wellclose Square, London E
26	8	376428	Angus Richardson & Son	Stourbridge
February 9	20	376905	Sowerby; Ellison Glass Works Limited	Gateshead-on-Tyne
16	19	377222	R. W. Winfield & Co	Birmingham

Date of Export	No. of Parcel	No. of Design	Name of Proprietor	Address of Proprietor
1882				
March 4	10	378022	Henry Greener	Near Flint Glass Works, Sunderland
"	1	378023	2.	} Near Flint Glass Works, Sunderland
"	15	378063	3. Samuel Prentice Jun.	Alfred Street, Manchester
"			}	}
Aug	9, 14	384453	Percival Vickers & Co Limited	Jersey Street & Ardwick, Manchester
"	8	384455	Richard Bick	Bradley Works, Birmingham
" 28	19	378972	Defries & Sons	147 Houndsditch
April 8	10	379366	John William Webb & Robert Michael Sinclair	75 Fore Lane Market, Flint Glass &
"	16	385736	Henry Arthur Richardson	Wordsley, Stourbridge
12	7	379463	John Ford Dowsing	Brown Works, Commercial Street, Birmingham
24	2	379826		Street, Birmingham
28	1	380077	James Bryan & Sons	Grimsby Place, Sheffield
"	13	380132	3	
"	1	380133	Townley's Albion Glass Works Limited	Gateshead-on-Tyne
"	"	380134	Edward Edwards	Park Road, Wollaston, Near Stourbridge
May 25	1	361436	Percival Vickers & Co Limited	Percy Street, Manchester
" 12	1	361481	Henry Greener	Wear Flint Glass Works, Sunderland
30	1	381672	3 William Skye & Co Limited	Vincent Street, Westminster
"		381678		
July	1	382831	Sidney Brown	Blackfriars Road SE
"	12	382858	Defries & Sons	147 Houndsditch

Register of Designs — two sub-tables (page rotated).

Right-hand column group

Date of Deposit	No. of Parcel	No. of Design	Name of Proprietor	Address of Proprietor
1882				
Nov. 24	17	390584 3	Henry Greener	Wear Flint Glass Works, Sunderland
"	6	6 390586	W. E. Tappell & Co	Jersey Street
27	14 11	394205	Percival Vickers & Co Limited	Manchester
"	16 10	394320	Jonas & ...	... Buildings
"	" 2	394680	Henry Burwell	119 ... Street ...
March 17	1	395417	Young's Paraffin Light Mineral Oil Co Limited	Elizabeth Lamp Works, Birmingham
"	2	395418		
11	6	395786 1	Henry G Richardson	Wordsley Flint Glass Works, Stourbridge
27	5	396091	G. Boulter & Mill	... Glass Works, ...
31	9	396305	Henry Greener	Flint Glass Works, Sunderland
April 6	1	396530	Buckley & Co	Stourbridge
12	22	396833	Rudolf Edward Frank	Red Post Part ... City of London
17	3	397022	Percival Vickers & Schmidt	Jersey Street, Manchester
21	5	397473	Josiah Lane	41 to 43 Hampton Street Glass Works, Birmingham
May 1	16	397604	Henry Greener	Wear Flint Glass Core, Sunderland
8	4	397827	John Castle	87 Edward Street, Parade, Birmingham
"	5	397828	Henry Bethey Richardson	Wordsley Flint Glass Works near Stourbridge
16	2	398241	Edmund Foale	Amesbury House near Bexley, Kent

Left-hand column group

Date of Deposit	No. of Parcel	No. of Design	Name of Proprietor	Address of Proprietor
	18	2 391302	H. ...	Regent Street, London
13	15	391669 1	Walton & Co	West Lancashire Flint Glass Works, ...
Class III 1-19		18 392093	Walter Thornhill & Co	144 & 145 New Bond Street, ...
1883				
January 6	5	392521 3	William James	201 Broad Street, Birmingham
	to	392523		
25	20	393243 2	John Walsh Walsh	The Vesta Glass Works, Birmingham
	"	393244		
February 3	11	393638 6	Sowerby's Ellison Glass Works Limited	Gateshead-on-Tyne
"	"	393639		
"	"	393640		
"	"	393641		
"	"	393642		
"	"	393643 6		

Date of Deposit	No of Parcel	No of Design	Name of Proprietor	Address of Proprietor
1883				
May 23	6	398435	1 Helegard & Co	43 Union Street, Ryde, Isle of Wight
" 28	18	398610	1 Allen & Hamburgs	Slough Court, Lombard Street E.C.
June 1	11	398825	1 Henry Wm. M. Wetzel	Wilson, Anderson, S.C.
" 6	10	398981	1 Gil de Luca	647 King Lane, Aldersgate Street E.C.
" 7	20	399063	1 Alfred & Sons	147 Houndsditch
"	22	399065	1 Witm & Co & Roth	44 Upper Marlborough Street
" 9	7	399144	1 O'Andaro Company	111 City Road, London S.E.
"	12	14	399313	1 Buckley, Tale & Co	Poland Street, Manchester
Sept.	13	3	399455	1 J. Smith & Son	219 Argyle Street, Glasgow
" 24	14	400089	2 Ammann Schroder &	Glasgow, Germany
"	"	400905	3	
August 2	4	401665	1 Hancox Batchelor & Co	110 Cannon Street, London E.C.
"	11	402039	1 Allen & Hamburgs	Slough Court, Lombard Street E.C.
"	11	402690	1 Percival Vickers & Co Limited	254 Upper Street, Upper Manchester
" 24	2			
" 31	5	403109	1 Birstall & Bingley	Hall Street, Birmingham
September 13	8	403804	1 Thomas Webb & Sons	Dennis Glass Works, Stourbridge
"	15	1	403905	Richard Dendy Sadler	141 Haberdashe in the city of London
Oct	24	13	404322	1 Mr. B. Simmons & Co	80, 82 Kings Cross Road N.O.

Date of Deposit	No of Parcel	No of Design	Name of Proprietor	Address of Proprietor
1883				
October 2	19	404649	1 W. Reynolds & Sons	31 Port Street, Buckfield Street, Bishopsgate
"	6	10	404797	1 James Kiwi & Matthew Lewis	6 Bartlett Buildings, Holborn Circus, London S.C.
"	12	15	405338	1 William Barker and Son	48 & 49 Bishopsgate Street Without E.C.
"	14	405367	1 Yong Hotel Cheshire	Colony Hundred & York, Road City Road & C.
"	15	8	405382	2 Richard Dendy Sadler and William Bagley	141 Water Lane, Tower Street in the City of London
"	"	405383	3	
November 2	12	405456	1 Percival Vickers & Co Limited	189 Fulham Road, London S.W.
"	9	16	406673	1 John J. Wheeler	141 Water Lane, Tower Street in the City of London
"	13	15	406860	2 Richard Dendy Sadler & William Bagley	Stourbridge
"	"	406881	3	
"	14	11	406942	2 Thomas Webb & Sons	Wear Flint Glass Works, Sunderland
"	"	406943	3	
"	"	12	406944	1 Henry Greener	4 Waterloo Place, Sunderland
"	17	11	407253	2 James & Grieve	Grove Passage, Liverpool
"	"	"	407254	3	
Dec.	20	2	407766	1 Thomas Butler & Co	123 & 125, Finsbury
" 12	11	408221	1 Cuthbert Britton	Pavement, London E.C.
"	"			Sloe & Herbert Hutton Sloe & Anthony & Co Batty & Co

GLASS REGISTER 1884 — 1908

First number of each year

675	23rd January	1884
19937	6th January	1885
40484	1st January	1886
64590	1st January	1887
90649	4th January	1888
116710	1st January	1889
141333	1st January	1890
163914	1st January	1891
185803	4th January	1892
205280	3rd January	1893
224765	1st January	1894
247064	2nd January	1895
268508	2nd January	1896
291360	4th January	1897
311691	1st January	1898
331808	4th January	1899
351372	5th January	1900
368272	3rd January	1901
385541	10th January	1902
403012	3rd January	1903
424157	4th January	1904
447615	3rd January	1905
471617	3rd January	1906
493532	2nd January	1907
518475	2nd January	1908

The descriptions against the registrations are as in the registers of 1842—1883 and 1884—1908, or as written on the drawing submitted to the Design Registration office. When the description is within brackets it is taken from looking at the drawing of the original object registered, and is observation.

On pieces of glass prior to 1884, the date of the glass, when it was registered, can be worked out from the diamond shaped registration mark. In the registers, a number was given alongside the date and this number has been included in the lists to provide as much information as possible. However, during and after 1884 articles were stamped with the number that was given at the time of registration, so the number of the pressed glass then coincides with the number given in the register and the date is ascertained by looking up that number in the register. It must be emphasised that this number was only used after the diamond registration mark was disbanded.

The glass register from 1842 to 1884 is as complete as possible. The 1884 onwards register has been edited, due to the large numbers of registered items. It must be made clear that the firms left out are mainly those that are not likely to be encountered in the study of household glass, such as that of 30th January 1885, registered by Thorsten Nordenfelt, Civil Engineer. "Design for bottle with moulded ridge for scraping off excess liquid".

Despite this pruning the list of registrations is more full than any lists hitherto published and includes all types of glass.

Registration No.	Date	Year	Registered Party	Design
675	23 January	1884	Kemp and Taylor, Manchester. Stationers	Improved shape of ink bottle with recess at upper part of bottle to hold pen
1113	31 January		Lawrence Brothers, London. Merchants	Shape of bottle
1415	7 February		Percival, Vickers & Co. Ltd., Manchester. Glass Makers	Pattern for pressed glassware
1627	9 February		Barnes and Company, Birmingham. Glass Maker	Shape of sugar or cream basin; oblong, taper, eight sides
1628			Barnes and Company (see prior)	Shape of a flint jelly dish; oblong, rounded sides
1815	13 February		William Barker & Son, London. Wine Merchant	Shape of bottle
1909	14 February		John Walsh Walsh, (The Soho & Vesta Glass Works), Birmingham. Glass Maker	Arch-topped, rolled over pillar known as the "Queen Anne" and applied to glass
2339	22 February		Edwin William Streeter, London. Diamond Merchant	Shape of claret jug with stopper beneath the lid
2659	29 February		Henry Gething Richardson, Stourbridge. Glass Maker	New design for glass globe to be used with comet fitting
3613/4	14 March		Burtles, Tate & Co., Manchester. Glass Makers	Ornamental design applicable for patterns
3658	15 March		Reuben Jackson, Sheffield, York. Cut Glass Manufacturer	Shape of a circular glass cruet
4242	27 March		Alfred & James Davies, Stourbridge. Glass Makers	Pattern and shape
4406	29 March		T. L. Willis, Winder & Co., London. Wine Merchant	Shape of bottle
4489	2 April		John Walsh Walsh (see prior)	Shape of the acorn
4546			James Dixon & Sons, Sheffield. Merchant	Shape
4589			Edward Webb, Wordsley, Stourbridge. Glass Maker	Pattern and shape
4833	7 April		Sowerby's Ellison Glass Works Ltd., Gateshead. Glass Maker.	Pattern
5418	18 April		Henry Johnson, Holborn. Glass Maker Agent	Pressed glass flower stand; pattern and shape
5442	19 April		Edward Webb (see prior)	Shape — crimping and decoration of flower stand
5849	29 April		Sowerby's Ellison Glass Works Ltd. (see prior)	Pattern and shape
6481	8 May		Sowerby's Ellison Glass Works Ltd. (see prior)	Pattern and shape of flower vase
6658	10 May		Percival, Vickers & Co. Ltd., (see prior)	Design for round platter in moulded glass
7978/9	5 June		Sowerby's Ellison Glass Works Ltd. (see prior)	Butter dish and cover; shape and pattern
8013	7 June		John Walsh Walsh (see prior)	Shape
8824	24 June		G. Murray Wilson, Hawick, Scotland. Manufacturer	Conical or pear-shaped ink bottle
9213	3 July		John Fuller Spong, Clapham, Surrey. Gentleman	Design for neck and stopper of glass bottle
9805-8	15 July		Alfred and James Davies (see prior)	Pattern and shape
10038	19 July		A. J. Smith, Birmingham. Manufacturing Jeweller	Ornamental glass case for scarf pins
10277	25 July		Thomas Webb & Sons, Stourbridge. Glass Maker	Shape of valence edge glass
10422	29 July		Thomas Rule, Leeds. Commercial Traveller	Shape of stopper

Registration No.	Date	Year	Registered Party	Design
10594	2 August	1884	Philip Schuyler Malcolm, London. Gentleman	Design for glass bottle
10595			Max Sugar, London. Manufacturer	Shape
10966	11 August		Sowerby's Ellison Glass Works Ltd., Gateshead. Glass Maker	Pattern and shape
10967			Sowerby's Ellison Glass Works Ltd. (see prior)	Sugar basin, shape and ornamentation
11109	12 August		Thomas Webb & Sons, Stourbridge. Glass Maker	Scent bottle
11344	15 August		Max Sugar & Co. (see prior)	Shape of boat flower vase
12723	10 September		Silber and Fleming, London. Foreign & Fancy goods dealers	Pattern and shape
12758/9	11 September		Thomas Webb & Sons (see prior)	Shape of bottle
12839/40	12 September		Thomas Webb & Sons (see prior)	Shape and decoration
13563	19 September		Sowerby's Ellison Glass Works Ltd. (see prior)	Handle of jug made at the side instead of at back opposite the lip.
13792	24 September		Sowerby's Ellison Glass Works Ltd. (see prior)	Shape of glass post pillar money box manufactured in one piece
13870	25 September		Groves and Company, London. Wine Merchant	Shape of Greek amphora-shaped bottle with foot added
14057	27 September		W. W. Harrison & Co., Montgomery Works, Sheffield. Electro Plate Manufacturer	Shape for biscuit or sugar basket
14390	3 October		Henry Greener, Wear Flint Glass Works, Sunderland and London. Glass Maker	Ornamental design for glasses for pavement lights, floor lights, etc.
15256	16 October		Henry Gething Richardson, Wordsley Flint Glass Works, Stourbridge. Glass Maker	Ornamental design for glass decoration
15332	18 October		Percival, Vickers & Co. Ltd., Manchester. Glass Makers	Shape and pattern in pressed glass
15352			Johnson, Sons & Edmonds, Bedford Row. Silversmiths	Pattern and shape of bottle
15353			Stevens & Williams, Brierley Hill Glass Works, Stafford. Glass Makers	Design for glass ornament to be used for decorating bowls, vases, etc.
16235	3 November		Selinger & Emanuel, London. Merchants	Design for an ornamental tray representing the Nile expedition
16475	7 November		Boulton & Mills, Audnam Glass Works, Stourbridge. Glass Maker	Shape of glass candlestick & flower-holder combined
16828/9	13 November		Thomas Webb & Sons (see prior)	Shape of scent bottle
16835			William Henry Wood, Jr., Birmingham. Manufacturer Iron, Tin & Zinc Goods	Glass cover for floral and artificial decoration; novel-shaped glass cover
17102/3	17 November		George Cole, London. Merchant	Pattern and shape of moulded and blown glass
17721	27 November		George Cole (see prior)	Pattern and shape of cruet set
18069	3 December		Joseph Lucas & Son, Birmingham. Lamp Manufacturer	Shape
18108/9	3 December		Sampson Mordan & Co., London. Manufacturer	Shape of perfume bottle
18749	10 December		Percival, Vickers & Co. Ltd. (see prior)	Railway and other lamps — pressed scolloped band on glass.

Registration No.	Date	Year	Registered Party	Design
18806	12 December	1884	Sampson Mordan & Co., London. Manufacturer	Shape of a perfume or salts bottle
18827	13 December		Francis Dixon Nuttal, Ravenhead Glass Bottle Works, St. Helens, Lancashire. Glass Bottle Manufacturer	Glass jars of novel shape, with straight sides internally and a projecting external flange or rim at the top.
19238	18 December		Edmond Rocher, Clichy, France. Glass Maker	Protection for bottle having internal lozenges, facets or prisms
19704	20 December		George Cole, London. Merchant	Shape for glass or china vase
19733	21 December		Lampereur & Bernard, Liege, Belgium. Manufacturer	Chimney for mineral oil and gas lamps
19740	23 December		Mills, Walker & Co., Glass Works, Stourbridge. Table Glass Manufacturer	Acorn and leaf running round article made in glass
19741			Mills, Walker & Co. (see prior)	Acorn and oak leaf supporting article made in glass
19742			Mills, Walker & Co. (see prior)	Acorn and oak leaf
19744	31 December		J. Dunlop Mitchell & Co., Glasgow. Merchant	Shape of combination bottle and top
19937	6 January	1885	Sowerby's Ellison Glass Works Ltd., Gateshead. Glass Maker	Pattern of sugar basin
20079	8 January		George Cole (see prior)	Shape and pattern of blown or moulded vase
20085			Burtles, Tate & Co., Poland Street Glass Works, Manchester. Glass Makers	Design for glass flower holder or bracket
20086			Burtles, Tate & Co. (see prior)	Design for glass flower holder
20355	14 January		Percival, Vickers & Co. Ltd., Manchester. Glass Maker	Pattern for pressed butter trencher
20634	19 January		Selinger & Emanuel, London. Merchants	Design for a bottle
20775	21 January		Sowerby's Ellison Glass Works Ltd. (see prior)	Pattern of water jug
20860			Jane Webb & Henry Fitzroy Webb, Coalbourn Hill Glass Works, Stourbridge. Glass Makers.	Embossed pine decoration for cutting and moulding in glass
20861			Jane Webb & Henry Fitzroy Webb (see prior)	Glass perfume bottle formed as a shell
20862			Jane Webb & Henry Fitzroy Webb (see prior)	Glass perfume bottle formed as a horn
20930	22 January		Edward Edwards, The Novelty Glass Works, Stourbridge. Glass Maker.	Shape for relief ornament for vases
20936			Percival, Vickers & Co. Ltd. (see prior)	Design for pressed glass marmalade
20972	24 January		Burtles, Tate & Co. (see prior)	Shape and pattern of flower stand
21108-10	28 January		Burtles, Tate & Co. (see prior)	Pattern and shape of flower stand
21284	31 January		Sowerby's Ellison Glass Works Ltd. (see prior)	Pattern of glass dish
21326/7	2 February		Burtles, Tate & Co. (see prior)	Shape and pattern of flower stand
21328/9			Burtles, Tate & Co. (see prior)	Shape and pattern of flower stand
21616	5 February		Boulton & Mills, Audnam Glass Works, Stourbridge. Glass Maker	Pattern of glass decoration
21620	6 February		James Hateley, Birmingham. Flint Glass Manufacturer	Pattern and shape
22179	17 February		Boulton & Mills (see prior)	Maiden Hair fern decoration on glass
22506	24 February		Thomas Edward Bladon, Birmingham. Tin & Iron Plate Worker	Pattern and shape of the glass

Registration No.	Date	Year	Registered Party	Design
22614	25 February	1885	C. George, Islington. Chemist	Pattern and shape of tumbler
22928	3 March		Heine Bros. & Co., London. Importers	Shape of glass globe, ornamental design
23040/1	5 March		Molineaux, Webb & Co., Manchester. Glass Maker	Pattern and shape
23184			Yeatman & Co., London. Manufacturer	Shape of the bottle
23333-8	10 March		Molineaux, Webb & Co. (see prior)	Pattern and shape
23378	11 March		Molineaux, Webb & Co. (see prior)	Pattern and shape
24100	20 March		Burtles, Tate & Co., Poland Street Glass Works, Manchester. Glass Makers	Shape and pattern of flower stand
24139	21 March		Joseph Braham, Soho. Silversmith	Shape of bottle for toilet or scent bottle representing a grenade
24953	13 April		Sowerby's Ellison Glass Works Ltd., Gateshead. Glass Maker	Shape of butter dish
25435	20 April		Thomas Webb & Sons, Stourbridge. Glass Maker	Pattern of decoration
25863-5	27 April		Thomas Webb & Sons (see prior)	Shape of bottle
26170	2 May		George Watts, Jr. Middlesex. Jeweller's Pattern Maker	Perfume bottle in the shape of a "walnut shell"
26173	4 May		Max Sugar & Co., London. Manufacturer	Pattern and shape
26480	7 May		Burtles, Tate & Co. (see prior)	Shape of glass shell
27072	16 May		Lotz, Abbot & Co., Middlesex. Merchant	Shape
27553	28 May		Percival, Vickers & Co. Ltd., Manchester. Glass Makers	Pattern for moulded marmalade
27624	1 June		Hardcastle & Co., London. East India Merchant	Shape
27642			Lotz, Abbot & Co. (see prior)	Shape
27985-90	5 June		William Oppenheim, London. Importer	Shape of lamp ornament or stick top
28338	12 June		J. Dunlop Mitchell & Co., Glasgow. Merchant	Shape and pattern of gas shade
28709	20 June		Sampson Mordan & Co. London. Manufacturer	Design for a scent bottle
28770	22 June		Miles Williams, Liverpool. Varnish Manufacturer	Glass bottle, three sides plain and one plain having a wide neck
29106	29 June		Burtles, Tate & Co. (see prior)	Pattern of flower boat
29145	1 July		Percival, Vickers & Co. Ltd. (see prior)	Design for pressed glass butter
29260	2 July		Sampson Mordan & Co. (see prior)	Design for scent bottle
29677	10 July		J. Shaw & Sons, Sheffield. Cut Glass Manufacturer	Pattern shown on the paper not the shape of bottle
29780/1	14 July		Molineaux, Webb & Co. (see prior)	Pattern and shape
30244	22 July		Sowerby's Ellison Glass Works Ltd. (see prior)	Pattern of a sugar
30345	24 July		Henry Johnson, Holborn. Glass Maker	Moulded glass horseshoe photograph frame
30704	1 August		Henry Johnson (see prior)	Moulded glass bowl attached to moulded glass stand
31844	21 August		Molineaux, Webb & Co. (see prior)	Shape and pattern

Registration No.	Date	Year	Registered Party	Design
32125/6	25 August	1885	George Seibdrat, Finsbury. Agent	Shape and pattern of cruet
32253	27 August		Sowerby's Ellison Glass Works Ltd., Gateshead. Glass Maker	Pattern of dish
33714/5	19 September		John Walsh Walsh, The Soho & Vesta Glass Works, Birmingham. Glass Maker.	Shape
34196	26 September		Burtles, Tate & Co., Poland Street Glass Works, Manchester. Glass Makers	Pattern and shape of glass flower vase
35063	7 October		Prince & Symmons, Lion Lamp Works, Shoreditch. Lamp Manufacturer	Pattern of a parrot to be used as a lamp
35064			Prince & Symmons (see prior)	Pattern of bulldog to be used as a lamp
35293	10 October		Percival, Vickers & Co. Ltd., Manchester. Glass Maker	Design for pressed glass cruets
35660	15 October		Thomas Seage, Heeley. Glass Mixer.	New form of glass jelly dish for mounting in silver electro plate metal
35709	18 October		Alfred Arculus, Birmingham. Glass Maker	Ornamentation on the shade
36184	22 October		John Walsh Walsh (see prior)	Honeysuckle made in glass and used as a decoration on glass
36477/8	26 October		M. Davis & Co., London. Lamp & Glass Manufacturer	Pattern on globes to be applied to lamps
36536	27 October		Guiseppe Vincenzo De Luca, London. Agent	Pattern
36846	30 October		Guiseppe Vincenzo De Luca (see prior)	Pattern of bottle
37026	2 November		Prince & Symmons (see prior)	Pattern and design of a bear to be used as a lamp
37027			Prince & Symmons (see prior)	Pattern and design of a dog to be used as a lamp
37110	4 November		Sowerby's Ellison Glass Works Ltd. (see prior)	Shape of sugar
37111			Sowerby's Ellison Glass Works Ltd. (see prior)	Pattern of sugar
37300	6 November		Julius Faulkner, Birmingham. General Brassfounder	Finger plate
37487	7 November		Saunders & Shepherd, London. Manufacturing Goldsmiths & Jewellers	Human hand holding egg adapted to scent bottles
38431	19 November		William James Green, Sudbury. Suffolk. Builder	Shape of round glass honey bell or jar
38486	21 November		Walter Edwards, London. Commercial Traveller	Pattern and shape of lamp representing tiger lily
38487			Walter Edwards (see prior)	Pattern and shape of lamp representing heartsease
38488			Walter Edwards (see prior)	Pattern and shape of lamp representing dog rose
38582	23 November		Greener & Co., Wear Flint Glass Works Sunderland & London. Glass Maker	Shape for glass mould
38983	1 December		Stevens & Williams, Brierley Hill Glass Works, Stafford. Glass Makers	Pattern for the ornamentation of flint glass table ware
39062-4	3 December		Sowerby's Ellison Glass Works Ltd. (see prior)	Pattern of sugar
39086	30 November		Sidney Wittmann, Wittmann & Roth, London. Glass & China Manufacturer	Raised pattern on glass surface to imitate hammered metal
39328	10 December		Robinson, Son & Skinner, Mersey Glass Works	Ornamental design for glass frame
39414	11 December		Edward Bolton, Orford Lane Glass Works, Warrington. Glass Maker	Pattern of glass boat

Registration No.	Date	Year	Registered Party	Design
39415	11 December	1885	Edward Bolton, Orford Lane Glass Works, Warrington. Glass Maker	Pattern of a flower trough
39626	15 December		Miles Bros. & W. Claridge, Hackney Road. Manufacturer of Coloured Glass	Scent bottle in the shape of a lemon
39648	16 December		Joseph Benson, Sheffield. Cut Glass Manufacturer	Glass marmalade dish
39807	18 December		Burtles, Tate & Co., Poland Street Glass Works, Manchester. Glass Maker	Pattern and shape of flower bracket
39984	21 December		Saunders & Shepherd, London. Manufacturing Goldsmiths & Jewellers	Pattern and shape of ornamental vessel
40484	1 January	1886	Percival, Vickers & Co. Ltd., Manchester. Glass Maker	Pressed glass cruet
40927	7 January		Batty & Company, London. Wholesale Italian Warehousemen	Pattern of bottle
41919	25 January		Saunders & Shepherd (see prior)	Elephant head as scent bottles
41925	26 January		Wittmann & Roth, London. Glass & China Manufacturer	Pattern worked on body of the glass to represent fish scales
42041	28 January		A. & R. Cochran, St. Rollox Flint Glass Works, Glasgow. Flint Glass Manufacturer	Pattern to be applied to gas and lamp globes
42538	3 February		Arthur Abraham, London. Glass Cutter	Pattern of mirror frame
42716	29 January		John Walsh Walsh, The Soho & Vesta Glass Works, Birmingham. Glass Maker	Shape of biscuit jar pushed in at four sides
42726	6 February		Meigh, Forester & Co., Longton.	Pattern
42947	10 February		Sowerby's Ellison Glass Works Ltd., Gateshead. Glass Maker	Pattern of dish
43069	11 February		Saunders & Shepherd (see prior)	Lighthouse as a design for scents, etc.
43165	10 February		Martin, Hall & Co. Ltd., Shrewsbury Works, Sheffield. Manufacturer of Silver and Electro Plated Goods	Pattern and shape
43197/8	15 February		W. H. Dixon & Co., Hull. Lamp Manufacturer	Shape of lamp chimneys
43501	19 February		Elkington & Co., London. Silversmiths	Ornamental group
43502			Blumberg & Co., London. Fancy Goods Merchant	Pattern and shape of flower bowl
43536	20 February		Gebhardt Rottmann & Co., Cheapside. Fancy Goods Warehouseman	Shape of combined inkstand, calendar and memorandum tablet
43650	22 February		James Testro & John Richard, Chandos Glass Works, London. Glass Maker	Shape of a bottle having a likeness to the Right Honorable W. E. Gladstone, M.P.
43749	24 February		James Aston, Birmingham. Designer on glass	Glass show card
43867	25 February		Henry Sarsons & Son, Chester Street Glass Works, Birmingham. Glass Maker	Shape of the glass vessel forming the inner part of the glass mustard pot
43869			James Testro & John Richard (see prior)	Shape of a bottle having a likeness to the late Right Honorable, the Earl of Beaconsfield.
44219	4 March		W. H. Dixon & Co. (see prior)	Fluted shape pine lamp glass

Registration No.	Date	Year	Registered Party	Design
44220	4 March	1886	W. H. Dixon & Co., Hull. Lamp Manufacturer	Serrated top fluted shape pine lamp glass
44408			J. H. Roger, Glasgow. Wine Merchant	Shape and pattern of jug
44445	8 March		Burtles, Tate & Company, Poland Street Glass Works, Manchester. Glass Maker	Pattern and shape of flower boat
44546	9 March		Blumberg & Co. Ltd., London. Fancy Goods Merchant	Pattern and shape of flower bowl
44659	11 March		Sowerby's Ellison Glass Works Ltd., Gateshead. Glass Maker	Shape of dish
45759	25 March		Sowerby's Ellison Glass Works Ltd. (see prior)	Pattern of sugar
45768			Henry Gething Richardson, Wordsley Flint Glass Works, Stourbridge. Glass Maker	Shape of improved "Ice Drainer"
45942	26 March		Percival, Vickers & Co. Ltd., Manchester. Glass Maker	Moulded glass marmalade or biscuit jar
46252	24 March		Edward Webb, Stourbridge. Glass Maker	Shape of bowl
46253	30 March		Jonas & Jules Lang, London. Glass & China Merchants	Shape of jug
46294/5	24 March		Hempton & Son (Kempton & Son), Lambeth. Glass Maker	Pattern of table lamp
46498	1 April		Henry G. Richardson, Stourbridge. Glass Maker	Combination of threads of glass of different shades of colour, arranged as to form a plaid, to be used for glass decoration
46897/8	9 April		Hempton & Son (see prior)	Shape of whole as a lampshade
47381-6	16 April		Alfred Arculus, Birmingham. Glass Maker	Shape
47514	21 April		Sowerby's Ellison Glass Works Ltd. (see prior)	Pattern and shape of pressed glass fan picture frame
47696	22 April		Moses Davis & Co., London. Lamp & Glass Manufacturer	Shape of a bottle having a likeness to H.R.H. The Prince of Wales
47698			Moses Davis & Co. (see prior)	Shape of bottle having a likeness to her Gracious Majesty Queen Victoria
47900	20 April		Mills, Walker & Co., Stourbridge. Table Glass Manufacturer	Design of flower dish
48008	28 April		Stead, Simpson & Nephews, Leicester. Boot & Shoe Manufacturer	Shape of an ash tray representing various kinds of boots and shoes in relief
48212			Mills, Walker & Co. (see prior)	Shape of glass fairy light
48228	4 May		Sowerby's Ellison Glass Works Ltd. (see prior)	Pattern and shape of butter
48352	5 May		Greener & Co., Wear Flint Glass Works, Sunderland & London. Glass Maker	Shape of glass dish
48909	11 May		Sowerby's Ellison Glass Works Ltd. (see prior)	Shape of celery
48910			Sowerby's Ellison Glass Works Ltd. (see prior)	Shape of sweetmeat
50071	1 June		Sowerby's Ellison Glass Works Ltd. (see prior)	Pattern of butter
50165	2 June		Alfred Arculus (see prior)	Shape
50422	3 June		Francis Paine Hill, Surrey. Glass Embosser	Pattern and shape
50425	5 June		Ward & Holloway, Birmingham. Glass Tablets Manufacturer	Spill box with glass front

Registration No.	Date	Year	Registered Party	Design
50594	8 June	1886	Mappin & Webb, London. Silversmiths	Pattern and shape of salad bowl
50725/6	10 June		Boulton & Mills, Audnam Glass Works, Stourbridge. Glass Maker	Pattern
50859	12 June		Alfred Arculus, Birmingham. Glass Maker	Shape
51026	16 June		Sampson Mordan & Co., London. Manufacturer	Design for a toilet bottle
51047	15 June		Thomas Webb & Sons, Stourbridge. Glass Maker	Pattern — hexagonal configuration with raised and sunk surfaces
51423	25 June		Max Emanuel, London. Foreign Agent	Shape of a card tray
51812	3 July		Baxendale & Co., Manchester. Manufacturer	Pattern
52218	9 July		Baxendale & Co. (see prior)	Pattern
52434	13 July		Sowerby's Ellison Glass Works Ltd., Gateshead. Glass Maker	Pattern and shape of boat stand
53013	23 July		William Cutler, Birmingham. Glass Maker	Shape and configuration of a show glass
53466	3 August		Percival Jones, Dublin. Glass & China Merchant	Shape of a handle for glass jugs
53468			Percival, Vickers & Co. Ltd., Manchester. Glass Maker	Moulded glass tumbler
53483	30 July		H. G. Richardson, Wordsley Flint Glass Works, Stourbridge. Glass Maker	Design for a Hyacinth glass made with two projections on the upper or cup part and having an indentation on the upper part of the body to carry and keep in position a stick or other support to the plant
53732	3 August		Stuart & Sons, Stourbridge, Glass Maker.	Pattern of a flower bowl for use with fairy lamps
53733	7 August		Stuart & Sons (see prior)	Pattern of a fairy lamp shade
53734			Stuart & Sons (see prior)	Pattern of a flower stand with fairy light on top
54040	13 August		A. & R. Cochran, St. Rollox Flint Glass Works, Glasgow. Flint Glass Manufacturer	Design for ornamenting glass globes, etc.
54098	14 August		Kempton & Sons (Hempton & Sons), Lambeth. Glass Maker	Pattern and shape
54314	18 August		Sowerby's Ellison Glass Works Ltd. (see prior)	Shape and design of moulded glass sugar basin
54315/6			Sowerby's Ellison Glass Works Ltd. (see prior)	Shape of moulded glass jelly dish
54702	19 August		Hauptman Albert & Co., Edinburgh. Glass Maker	Design of vase
55113	27 August		Stone, Fawdry & Stone, Birmingham. Glass Maker	Pattern of glass jelly dish
55162	28 August		Baxendale & Co. (see prior)	Pattern
55235	26 August		John Shaw & Sons, Latimer Glass Works, Sheffield. Cut Glass Manufacturer.	Shape of glass bottle
55272	30 August		Guiseppe Vincenzo De Luca, London. Agent	Shape
55275	27 August		Josiah Lane, Birmingham. Glass Maker	Pattern
55693	6 September		Stevens & Williams, Brierley Hill Glass Works, Stafford. Glass Maker	Pattern for the ornamentation of glassware
55773	7 September		Edward Webb, Stourbridge. Glass Maker	Design for configuration

Registration No.	Date	Year	Registered Party	Design
55865	8 September	1886	Atkin Brothers, London & Truro Works, Sheffield. Silversmiths	Shape of glass body to represent boar's tusk
55866			Atkin Brothers (see prior)	Shape of glass body to represent elephant's tusk
56047	11 September		Percival, Vickers & Co. Ltd., Manchester. Glass Maker	Pattern for pressed glass dish
56942/3	22 September		Sampson Mordan & Co., London. Manufacturer	Design and shape of scent bottle
56961-6	23 September		Sowerby's Ellison Glass Works Ltd., Gateshead. Glass Maker	Shape and pattern of sugar
57070	27 September		Henry Titterton Brockwell, London. Manufacturer	Design and shape of pear for scent bottle
57071			Henry Titterton Brockwell (see prior)	Design and shape of a lobster claw for scent bottle
57072			Henry Titterton Brockwell (see prior)	Design and shape of a shell for scent bottle
57073			Henry Titterton Brockwell (see prior)	Design and shape of a stone for scent bottle
58092	6 October		Saunders & Shepherd, London. Manufacturing Goldsmiths & Jewellers	Shape and pattern of a canoe for personal use or ornament
58103			Sampson Mordan & Company, London. Manufacturer	Shape and pattern of a scent bottle
58275	7 October		Edward Moore, Tyne Flint Glass Works, South Shields. Glass Maker	Pattern
58374	8 October		Thomas Webb & Sons, Stourbridge. Glass Maker	Diaper of semi-circular lines forming a decorative pattern
58375			Thomas Webb & Sons (see prior)	Diaper of irregular lines forming a watery or wavy pattern on the surface of glass
59136	19 October		Boulton and Mills, Audnam Glass Works, Stourbridge. Glass Maker	Pattern
59777	26 October		Henry Holcroft, London. Agent	Shape of lamp vase or fountain with legs
59794			Hayward Bros. & Eckstein, London. Manufacturing Ironmongers	Shape of glass tile
60108	29 October		Percival, Vickers & Co. Ltd., (see prior)	Design for a pressed glass pillar or lamp stand
60270			Carl Quitmann, London. Merchant	Pattern of a glass globe with the National Emblem
60351	1 November		Edward Webb, Stourbridge. Glass Maker	Pattern of chamber lamp
60872	8 November		Edward Webb (see prior)	Shape of plate
61091/2	11 November		Powell, Bishop & Stonier, Hanley, Staffordshire. Manufacturer	Design for a shape
61211	12 November		Sampson Mordan & Co. (see prior)	Shape of a scent bottle
61357	15 November		Stevens & Williams, Brierley Hill Glass Works, Stafford. Glass Maker	Pattern for the ornamentation of glass
61922	22 November		Johnstone Sadler & Co., London. Wine Merchant	A pentagonal bottle
61923			Johnstone Sadler & Co. (see prior)	A hexagonal bottle

Registration No.	Date	Year	Registered Party	Design
61924	22 November	1886	Johnstone Sadler & Co. London. Wine Merchant	A heptagonal bottle
62029	23 November		Thomas Webb & Sons, Stourbridge. Glass Maker	For the form cylindrical, tapering, having six rows of arched corrugations
62325	19 November		Charles Kempton & Sons (Charles Hempton & Sons), Lambeth. Glass Maker	Shape of a combined flower stand and lamp
62584	1 December		Frederick Augustus Heepe & Co., London. Importer and Agent	Pattern and shape of cruet stand
62925	6 December		Hayward Brothers & Eckstein, London. Manufacturing Ironmongers	Shape of glass tile
63008			B. Cars, Lion Lamp Works, London.	Combination of flower stand mounted on plush base with fixed or loose lamps
63267	10 December		F. & C. Osler, Birmingham. Flint Glass Manufacturer	Shade for electric light
63473	14 December		John Mortlock & Co., London.	Magpies with landscape as applied to decoration of china and glass services
63474			Stevens & Williams, Brierley Hill Glass Works, Stafford. Glass Maker	Design for cameo glass lamp
63533-5	15 December		W. P. Phillips & G. Phillips, London. China and Glass Merchants	Shades for fairy lamps made in the shape of a cactus flower, of a dahlia and of a carnation
63543	15 December		Edward Moore, Tyne Flint Glass Works, South Shields. Glass Makers	Shape and pattern of a gas moon or shade
63665	17 December		Guiseppe Vincenzo De Luca, London. Agent	Pattern
63937	21 December		Guiseppe Vincenzo De Luca (see prior)	Pattern of glass bottle
64086	22 December		Sowerby's Ellison Glass Works Ltd., Gateshead. Glass Maker	Pattern of sugar
64087/8			Scotney & Earnshaw, London. Merchant	Pattern for the decoration of glass ware
64106	23 December		Sowerby's Ellison Glass Works Ltd. (see prior)	Pattern of butter
64234	28 December		Burtles, Tate & Co., Poland Street Glass Works, Manchester. Glass Maker	Pattern and shape of flower holder
64517			Powell, Bishop & Stonier, Hanley, Staffordshire. Manufacturer	Shape
64590	1 January	1887	C. Kempton & Sons (see prior)	Shape of glass stand or mount for lamp, etc.
64641	4 January		Mills, Walker & Co., Glass Works, Stourbridge. Table Glass Manufacturer	Shape of lamp
64766	6 January		Prince & Symmons, Lion Lamp Works, Shoreditch. Lamp Manufacturer	Pattern and shape of lamp shade
64920/1	7 January		Powell, Bishop & Stonier (see prior)	Pattern
64967-9	11 January		S. Falk, London. Merchant	Shape of globe
65229			Stevens & Williams (see prior)	Decoration of ornamental glass in colours and relief
65339	14 January		Edward Moore & Co. (see prior)	Shape and pattern of pressed gas shade
65455	17 January		Burtles, Tate & Co. (see prior)	Pattern and shape of new flower holder
65468	8 January		James Carpenter, Clapham Common, Surrey. Merchant	Design for the commemoration of the Jubilee of Queen Victoria

Registration No.	Date	Year	Registered Party	Design
65495	17 January	1887	Charles Kempton & Sons (Charles Hempton & Sons), Lambeth. Glass Maker	Shape of stand for holding lamp, etc.
65543	15 January		John Walsh Walsh, The Soho & Vesta Glass Works, Birmingham. Glass Maker	Shape
66273	25 January		C. Kempton & Sons (see prior)	Shape of stand for a lamp or flower vase
66450	27 January		C. Kempton & Sons (see prior)	Shape of a flower stand
66813	26 January		Alfred Arculus, Birmingham. Glass Maker	Ornamental design for use on gas, paraffin or other globes consisting of rose, shamrock and thistle wreath
67040	2 February		Wittmann & Roth, London. China & Glass Manufacturer	Pattern of lampshade
67113	3 February		James Buchanan & Co., London. Spirit Merchant	Shape and pattern of spirit jar
67124	4 February		C. Kempton & Sons (see prior)	Shape of a stand for flowers
67262	5 February		C. Kempton & Sons (see prior)	Shape of a dish or stand for flowers
67263			Stevens & Williams, Brierley Hill Glass Works, Stafford. Glass Maker	Design in glass lamp
67425	7 February		Edward Moore, Tyne Flint Glass Works, South Shields. Glass Maker	Shape and pattern of pressed glass gas shade
67646	9 February		John Grinsell & Sons, Birmingham. Silver & Art Metal Smiths	Water bottle
67941	10 February		Sampson Mordan & Co., London. Manufacturer	Pattern of decoration for a scent bottle
68066	16 February		William Leuchars, London. Silversmith	Pattern and shape of a tray with metal rim and glass bottom
68249	18 February		Edward Moore (see prior)	Shape and pattern of a pressed glass lampshade
68327	21 February		H. G. Richardson, Wordsley Flint Glass Works, Stourbridge. Glass Maker	Shape of a flower or lamp bowl with sides turned down or lapped over, shewing (sic) from side view a crescent shape
68633/4	24 February		William Leuchars (see prior)	Pattern and shape
68746	26 February		C. Kempton & Sons (see prior)	Shape of a bucket or lamp suitable for illumination
68806	28 February		Stevens & Williams (see prior)	Shape in glass for table ornament
68846	1 March		Sowerby's Ellison Glass Works Ltd., Gateshead. Glass Maker	Pattern of dish
68984			Fisher Brown & Co., Lion Works, Birmingham. Manufacturer of brass and iron bedsteads	Glass rose for ornamentation of bed
69362	8 March		William Oppenheim, London. Importer	Shape for lamp
69699	15 March		Wittman (sic) & Roth (see prior)	Pattern of lamp shade
69969	17 March		C. Kempton & Sons (see prior)	Shape of lamp
70422	23 March		Molineaux, Webb & Co., Manchester. Glass Maker	Shape
70868	29 March		Sampson Mordan & Co. (see prior)	Design to be applied for the decoration of circular smelling bottles, etc.
70872			J. Hayes	Pattern and shape
71216	1 April		J. Hayes	Pattern and shape of ornamental pincushion
71528	6 April		Molineaux, Webb & Co. (see prior)	Pattern
71534/5			J. Hayes	Shape of ornamental pincushion
71736	9 April		Greener & Co., Wear Flint Glass Works, Sunderland & London. Glass Maker	Design for the ornamentation of glass

Registration No.	Date	Year	Registered Party	Design
71753	12 April	1887	Edward Moore, Tyne Flint Glass Works, South Shields. Glass Maker	Shape and pattern of an oval covered dish
71816	13 April		Edward Moore (see prior)	Shape and pattern of a gas shade
71869	14 April		Percival, Vickers & Co. Ltd., Manchester. Flint Glass Manufacturers	Pattern of a moulded cruet
72071	16 April		J. Hayes	Pattern and shape of pincushion
72169	15 April		Saunders & Shepherd, London. Manufacturing Goldsmiths & Jewellers	Group of nuts as ornamental cruet stand
72345	25 April		Victoria Hansom Cab Co., Ltd., London. Cab Proprietors	Pattern, shape and ornament
72453	5 April		Daniel Judson & Son Ltd., Surrey. Manufacturer	Shape and pattern of scent bottles and vinaigrettes
72790	28 April		Philip M. Beck, London. Glass Maker	Design for glass tumbler
72815			Edward Moore (see prior)	Pattern for a pressed glass shade
72884	29 April		Edward Moore (see prior)	Pattern for pressed glass shade
73319	6 May		Guiseppe V. De Luca, London. Agent	Shape of bottle
73351	7 May		Sir Robert Burnett & Co., Vauxhall. Distillers	Shape and pattern of bottle
73836	17 May		Scotney & Earnshaw, London. Merchant	Pattern for decoration of table glass ware
74164	21 May		C. Kempton & Sons, Lambeth. Glass Maker	Shape of an illumination lamp can also be used as a flower vase
74556	26 May		John Walsh Walsh, The Soho & Vesta Glass Works, Birmingham. Glass Maker	Flower holder in the form of a tree trunk
74878	4 June		J. Hayes	Shape and pattern of pincushion
74879			J. Hayes	Shape and pattern of thimble case
75015/6	8 June		Edward Moore (see prior)	Pattern
75091/2	9 June		Edward Moore (see prior)	Pattern
75175			W. P. & G. Philips (sic), London. Glass Maker	Shape of a jug in glass or china
75843	25 June		Wittmann & Roth, London. China & Glass Manufacturer	Pattern
75942	29 June		Percival, Vickers & Co. Ltd., Manchester. Glass Maker	Pattern for moulded glass marmalade
76057	1 July		Wittmann & Roth (see prior)	Pattern
76682	11 July		Alfred & James Davies, Stourbridge. Glass Maker	Pattern and shape of flower stand
76759	9 July		J. H. & A. Hawkesford, Birmingham. Fancy tin plate workers	Shape and ornament of a money box
76762-5	12 July		Alfred & James Davies (see prior)	Pattern and shape of flower stand
76878-80	13 July		Edward Moore (see prior)	Shape
76935	14 July		Edward Moore (see prior)	Pattern
77116	20 July		J. H. & A. Hawkesford (see prior)	Shape and ornament of spill box
77341	25 July		Edward Moore (see prior)	Pattern
77881	2 August		Sowerby's Ellison Glass Works Ltd., Gateshead. Glass Maker	Pattern and shape of butter
77967	3 August		Sowerby's Ellison Glass Works Ltd. (see prior)	Pattern and shape of biscuit

Registration No.	Date	Year	Registered Party	Design
78084	3 August	1887	Sowerby's Ellison Glass Works Ltd., Gateshead. Glass Maker	Pattern and shape of sugar and cover
78233	5 August		Guiseppe V. De Luca London. Agent	Shape and pattern
78551	11 August		Sowerby's Ellison Glass Works Ltd. (see prior)	Pattern of sugar
78688	12 August		Mills, Walker & Co., Stourbridge. Table Glass Manufacturer	Shape of lamp
78704	13 August		Sowerby's Ellison Glass Works Ltd. (see prior)	Pattern of sugar
78754			Woodall & Son, Birmingham. Glass Maker	Squat shaped globe with crimped and threaded top
78795/6	15 August		Mills, Walker & Co. (see prior)	Shape of lamp
80012	1 September		Edward Moore, Tyne Flint Glass Works, South Shields. Glass Maker	Shape and pattern
80013			Edward Moore (see prior)	Shape and pattern
80153	3 September		Guiseppe V. De Luca (see prior)	Shape of menthol stand
80167	5 September		Thomas Webb & Sons, Stourbridge. Glass Maker	Shape for particular form of edge
80260	6 September		Saunders & Shepherd, London. Manufacturing Goldsmiths & Jewellers	Shape of scent bottle
80530	10 September		Sowerby's Ellison Glass Works Ltd. (see prior)	Pattern of sugar basin in glass
80632	12 September		Percival, Vickers & Co. Ltd., Manchester. Glass Maker	Pattern of pressed glass celery vase
80687			Guiseppe V. De Luca (see prior)	Shape and pattern of menthol stand
81051	15 September		Stevens & Williams, Brierley Hill Glass Works, Stafford. Glass Maker	Pattern of ornamental glass
81158			S. Mordan & Co., London. Manufacturer	Design for scent bottle
81159			S. Mordan & Co. (see prior)	Pattern and shape of pencil case
81160			Greener & Co., Wear Flint Glass Works, Sunderland & London. Glass Maker	Pattern of table glass
81959	24 September		Edward Moore (see prior)	Shape and pattern
82606	30 September		Edward Moore (see prior)	Shape and pattern
82776/7	3 October		William Blenko, Clapton Park. Glass Maker	Pattern of stained glass window pane
83773	12 October		Edward Moore (see prior)	Shape
83777	7 October		Sowerby's Ellison Glass Works Ltd. (see prior)	Pattern and shape of a advertising plate in pressed glass
84001	15 October		Sowerby's Ellison Glass Works Ltd. (see prior)	Pattern of sugar
84218	18 October		Sowerby's Ellison Glass Works Ltd. (see prior)	Pattern of dish
84495	17 October		W. P. & G. Phillips, London. Glass Maker	Shape of drinking glass
84747	21 October		Sowerby's Ellison Glass Works Ltd. (see prior)	Pattern of butter
85870	1 November		Sowerby's Ellison Glass Works Ltd. (see prior)	Shape of comportier and dish
85913	1 November		Samuel Clarke, London. Night Light Manufacturer.	Shape and ornament of fairy lamps

Registration No.	Date	Year	Registered Party	Design
86044	3 November	1887	T. Stapleton & Son, London. Silversmiths	Pattern and shape of glass bottle — the novelty being the concave depression in one side of the bottle for the hand
86246	5 November		Thomas Webb & Sons Ltd., Stourbridge. Glass Maker	Shape — a particular form of edging
87058	15 November		Sowerby's Ellison Glass Works Ltd., Gateshead. Glass Maker	Pattern and shape of shoe
87082			J. Hayes	Pattern and shape of boot pincushion
87083			J. Hayes	Pattern and shape of shoe pincushion
87259	18 November		Johnson & Company	Pattern and shape of a lemon squeezer
87776	24 November		Sowerby's Ellison Glass Works Ltd. (see prior)	Pattern of sugar
87777			Sowerby's Ellison Glass Works Ltd. (see prior)	Pattern of salt
88120	26 November		Greener & Co., Wear Flint Glass Works, Sunderland & London. Glass Maker	Pattern or shape of a dish
88124	29 November		Edward Moore, Tyne Flint Glass Works, South Shields. Glass Maker	Shape
88125			Edward Moore (see prior)	Pattern
88254	30 November		S. Mordan & Co., London. Manufacturer	Shape of scent bottle
88730	5 December		Edward Moore (see prior)	Shape
88940	7 December		Richard Morgan, Masbro. Glass Blower	Shape of bottle
89209	9 December		Wilson Salamon & Co., London. Agent	Shape of bottle
89920	20 December		Saunders & Shepherd, London. Manufacturing Goldsmiths & Jewellers	Filbert for a scent bottle with neck for stopper
90268	28 December		Samuel Clarke, London. Night Light Manufacturer	Pattern of a fairy lamp
91241	11 January	1888	Samuel Clarke (see prior)	Shape of a cup for food warmers
91359	13 January		Henry John Manton, Birmingham. Glass Maker	Shape
91431	14 January		Sowerby's Ellison Glass Works Ltd. (see prior)	Pattern of dish
91432			Sowerby's Ellison Glass Works Ltd. (see prior)	Pattern of sugar
91449	11 January		Greener & Company (see prior)	Pattern of a plate
91857	20 January		J. Hayes	Pattern and shape of a ladies companion
92045	23 January		Edward Moore (see prior)	Shape
92226	26 January		W. P. & G. Phillips, London. Glass Maker	Fairy or any other lamp shade in the form of a plum
92229			W. P. & G. Phillips (see prior)	Lamp shade in the form of a fir cone
92230			W. P. & G. Phillips (see prior)	Lamp shade in the shape of an orange
92231			W. P. & G. Phillips (see prior)	Lamp shade in the form of an apple
92571	30 January		J. Stembridge & Co., Holborn. Importers	Pattern table decoration — lamp
92631-3	31 January		W. P. & G. Phillips (see prior)	Lamp shades in the forms of a raspberry, a cabbage and a strawberry
93225	9 February		Charles Edward Hill, Brighton. Importer	Shape
93320	11 February		Samuel Clarke (see prior)	Shape of a fairy lamp
93450			Guiseppe Vincenzo De Luca, London. Agent	Shape of bottle

Registration No.	Date	Year	Registered Party
93905	18 February	1888	Percival, Vickers & Co. Ltd., Manchester. Glass Makers
94025	17 February		Stevens & Williams, Brierley Hill Glass Works, Stafford. Glass Maker
94100/1	18 February		Mills, Walker & Co., Stourbridge. Table Glass Manufacturer
94181	22 February		Frederick Watson Bach, London. Manufacturer
94543	25 February		Greener & Company, Wear Flint Glass Works, Sunderland & London. Glass Maker
94775	1 March		W. P. & G. Phillips, London. Glass Maker
94820			Edward Moore, Tyne Flint Glass Works, South Shields. Glass Maker
95106	2 March		W. P. & G. Phillips (see prior)
95114	5 March		Samuel Clarke, London. Night Light Manufacturer
95300	7 March		Sowerby's Ellison Glass Works Ltd., Gateshead. Glass Maker
95382/3	8 March		The Glasgow Plate Glass Co., Glasgow. Glass Maker
95461	9 March		Guiseppe Vincenzo De Luca, London. Agent
95482			Samuel Clarke (see prior)
95625	12 March		Edward Moore (see prior)
95676	13 March		Falk, Stadlemann & Co.
95775	14 March		Edward Moore (see prior)
95894	16 March		Sowerby's Ellison Glass Works Ltd. (see prior)
95935			Greener & Company (see prior)
96679	27 March		Powell, Bishop & Stonier, Hanley, Staffordshire. Manufacturer
96775/6			Greener & Co. (see prior)
96813	29 March		Charles E. Hill, Brighton. Importer
96945	31 March		Thomas Davidson, Teams Glass Works, Gateshead on Tyne. Glass Maker
97198	5 April		George Watts & Co.
97380	29 March		James A. Cox, London. China & Glass Manufacturer
97697	12 April		W. P. & G. Phillips (see prior)
98215/6	18 April		Sowerby's Ellison Glass Works Ltd. (see prior)
98242			Frederick Leslie Jeyes, The Chandos Glass Works, Bermondsey. Glass Maker
98551	21 April		Greener & Co. (see prior)
98578	23 April		Burtles, Tate & Co., Poland Street Glass Works, Manchester. Glass Maker
98658	24 April		W. P. & G. Phillips (see prior)

Registration No.	Date	Year	Registered Party
98744	25 April	1888	A. & R. Cochran, Glasgow. Flint Glass Manufacturer
99487	7 May		W. P. & G. Phillips (see prior)
99489			W. P. & G. Phillips (see prior)
99490			J. Stembridge & Co., Holborn. Importers
99715	9 May		Sowerby's Ellison Glass Works Ltd. (see prior)
99911	10 May		H. G. Richardson, Wordsley Flint Glass Works, Stourbridge. Glass Maker
99928-39	9 May		Samuel Clarke (see prior)
100004	12 May		John Walsh Walsh, Birmingham. Glass Maker
100207/8	14 May		J. Stembridge & Co. (see prior)
100404	18 May		Guiseppe V. De Luca (see prior)
100456	19 May		Thomas Webb & Sons, Stourbridge. Glass Maker
100724	25 May		Warrick Bros, London. Wholesale Perfumers
101007	31 May		Wittman (sic) & Roth, London. Glass & China Manufacturer
101008			Hinrichs & Co., New York, U.S.A. Glass & China Merchant
101809	13 June		George Watts & Company
101901	12 June		Wade & Co., Burslem, Staffordshire. Jet & Rockingham Manufacturer
101985	15 June		The Glasgow Plate Glass Co., Glasgow. Glass Maker
102405	22 June		Powell, Bishop & Stonier (see prior)
102902	28 June		Boulton & Mills, Audnam Glass Works, Stourbridge. Glass Makers
102939	2 July		W. P. & G. Phillips (see prior)
102977	3 July		John Tams, Longton. Manufacturer
103434	11 July		Greener & Co. (see prior)
103532	12 July		Wittmann & Roth (see prior)
103703/4	16 July		Charles E. Hill, Brighton. Importer
103949	18 July		John Walsh Walsh (see prior)
103954			Charles E. Hill (see prior)
103975	17 July		Greener & Co. (see prior)
104051	19 July		W. P. & G. Phillips (see prior)
104241/2	23 July		Charles E. Hill (see prior)
104759	31 July		Duncan Webb, Manchester. Glass Maker
104890	2 August		Boulton & Mills (see prior)
105233	9 August		W. P. & G. Phillips (see prior)
105464	11 August		Edward Bolton & Sons, Orford Lane Glass Works, Warrington. Glass Maker
105558	13 August		Samuel Clarke (see prior)

Registration No.	Date	Year	Registered Party
105713/4	13 August	1888	Charles E. Hill, Brighton. Importer
105830	14 August		Thomas Webb & Sons, Stourbridge. Glass Maker
106892	30 August		Sowerby's Ellison Glass Works Ltd., Gateshead. Glass Maker
106938	31 August		Sowerby's Ellison Glass Works Ltd. (see prior)
106954/5			Charles E. Hill (see prior)
107316	5 September		Edward Moore, Tyne Flint Glass Works, South Shields. Glass Maker
107409	6 September		Duncan Webb, Manchester. Glass Maker
107697	10 September		Wittmann & Roth, London. Glass & China Manufacturer
107808/9	12 September		John Walsh Walsh, The Soho & Vesta Glass Works, Birmingham. Glass Maker
108018/9	14 September		Greener & Co., Wear Flint Glass Works Sunderland & London. Glass Makers
108129	15 September		Mills, Walker & Co., Stourbridge. Table Glass Manufacturer
108271	18 September		W. P. & G. Phillips, London. China & Glass Merchants
108469			Wittmann & Roth (see prior)
108470	19 September		Caspar & Co., London. Manufacturer of Crystallized Glass
109330/1	28 September		Wittmann & Roth (see prior)
109338	26 September		Wittmann & Roth (see prior
109461/2	29 September		Greener & Co. (see prior)
109531	1 October		Burtles, Tate & Co., Poland Street Glass Works, Manchester. Glass Makers
109568	2 October		The Glasgow Plate Glass Co., Glasgow
109612			Edward Moore (see prior)
109926	5 October		Guiseppe V. De Luca, London. Agent
110458/9	11 October		Robert E. Finley, Birmingham. Cut Glass Manufacturer
110914	12 October		Wittmann & Roth (see prior)
110916	10 October		Cartier & Amez Droz, Geneve, Suisse. Watchmakers
111269/70	17 October		Sowerby's Ellison Glass Works Ltd. (see prior)
111289/90			Duncan Webb (see prior)
111295	16 October		Max Emanuel, London. Foreign Agent
111661	19 October		Matthew Turnbull, Cornhill Glass Works, Sunderland. Flint Glass Manufacturer

Registration No.	Date	Year	Registered Party
112468	1 November	1888	John T. Creasy & James Dingwall, Blackfriars. Glass Maker
112730/1	1 November		Robert Emmett Finley (see prior)
113389	10 November		Wittmann & Roth (see prior)
113560	13 November		Sowerby's Ellison Glass Works Ltd. (see prior)
113746	15 November		Wade & Co., Burslem, Staffordshire. Jet & Rockingham Manufacturer
113896			Greener & Co. (see prior)
113915-7			Samuel Clarke, London. Night Light Manufacturer
113989	16 November		Thomas Goode & Co.
114006	14 November		Boulton & Mills, Audnam Glass Works, Stourbridge. Glass Maker
114044	17 November		Sowerby's Ellison Glass Works Ltd. (see prior)
114297	21 November		E. Ackroyd & J. Ridgway, Bedford Works, Stoke-on-Trent. Manufacturer
114667	27 November		Charles E. Hill (see prior)
115000	1 December		Thomas Goode & Co.
115077	28 November		Percival, Vickers & Co. Ltd., Manchester. Glass Makers
115156	5 December		The Army & Navy Cooperative Society Ltd., London. Manufacturer
115743	14 December		Greener & Co. (see prior)
115748	12 December		Stone, Fawdry & Stone Union Glass Works, Birmingham. Glass Maker
115910	17 December		John Shaw & Sons, Latimer Glass Works, Sheffield, Cut Glass Manufacturer
116148-50	20 December		Thomas Goode & Co.
116158-61	19 December		Georges Dreyfus, Paris. Merchant
116254			Charles Horner, Halifax. Jeweller
116983	8 January	1889	The Army & Navy Cooperative Society Ltd. (see prior)
117086	9 January		John Walsh Walsh (see prior)
117556/7	14 January		Burtles, Tate & Co (see prior)
117569	17 January		Sowerby's Ellison Glass Works Ltd. (see prior)
117815	21 January		Matthew Turnbull (see prior)
118152	24 January		J. Stembridge & Co., London. Importer
118285	26 January		A. & R. Cochran, St. Rollox Flint Glass Works, Glasgow. Flint Glass Manufacturer
118358/9	26 January		Chance Bros. & Co. Ltd., West Smethwick. Glass Maker

Registration No.	Date	Year	Registered Party
118485	28 January	1889	Max Emanuel, London. Foreign Agent
118864	2 February		Boulton & Mills, Audnam Glass Works, Stourbridge. Glass Maker
119318	9 February		Matthew Turnbull, Cornhill Glass Works, Sunderland. Flint Glass Manufacturer
119981	18 February		John Mortlock & Co., London. Glass & China Dealer
120229	23 February		Sowerby's Ellison Glass Works Ltd., Gateshead. Glass Maker
120374	26 February		Falk, Stadelmann & Co. Ltd.
120437			Edward Moore, Tyne Flint Glass Works, South Shields. Glass Maker
120451	27 February		Henry G. Richardson, Wordsley Flint Glass Works, Stourbridge. Glass Maker
120547	25 February		Frederick S. Balls, Cambridge. Glass & China Merchant
120760	2 March		Monot & Stump, Pantin, France. Glass Maker
120808	4 March		Burtles, Tate & Co., Poland Street Glass Works, Manchester. Glass Makers
121729-31	19 March		James Couper & Sons, City Glass Works, Glasgow. Glass Maker
121760	20 March		Russell, Jones & Price, London. Wholesale Glass & China Merchant
121841	22 March		Charles E. Hill, Brighton. Importer
121891/2	21 March		George (sic) Dreyfus, Paris. Merchant
121894	22 March		William Brown, London. China & Glass Warehouseman
121927	23 March		Arthur W. Pennington, Birmingham. Silversmith
121984			C. & G. E. Asprey, London. Dressing Case Makers
121985			Greener & Co., Wear Flint Glass Works, Sunderland & London. Glass Makers
122046	20 March		Russell, Jones & Price (see prior)
122047	25 March		Russell, Jones & Price (see prior)
122093/4	26 March		Guiseppe V. De Luca, London. Agent
122096			Boulton & Mills (see prior)
122274	28 March		F. & C. Osler, Birmingham. Flint Glass Manufacturer
122393	30 March		Sowerby's Ellison Glass Works Ltd. (see prior)
122519	2 April		Sowerby's Ellison Glass Works Ltd. (see prior)

Registration No.	Date	Year	Registered Party
122521	2 April	1889	J. Hulls & A. Griffiths, Birmingham. Glass Beveller
122581			Pilkington Bros., Lancaster. Glass Maker.
122583			T. Stapleton & Son, London. Silversmiths
122790	5 April		John Henry Downing, Birmingham. Glass Merchant
123030	8 April		Charles H. Reynolds, Stoke-on-Trent. Engraver
123198	10 April		G. Davidson & Co., Teams Flint Glass Works, Gateshead-on-Tyne. Glass Maker
123702/3	20 April		W. P. & G. Phillips, London. China & Glass Merchants
124116	25 April		Pilkington Bros (see prior)
124771	8 May		The Glasgow Plate Glass Co., Glasgow. Glass Maker
124835			Richard Vann, Birmingham. Glass Toy Manufacturer
125024	10 May		C. Stolzles Sohne, Vienna, Manufacturer
125028	11 May		W. P. & G. Phillips (see prior)
125490	16 May		W. P. & G. Phillips (see prior)
125847	22 May		Charles Kempton & Sons, Lambeth. Glass Maker
126244	30 May		Charles E. Hill (see prior)
126315	31 May		F. & C. Osler (see prior)
126688	1 June		Boulton & Mills (see prior)
126694	5 June		G. Davidson & Co. (see prior)
126869	8 June		Percival, Vickers & Co. Ltd., Manchester. Glass Makers
126940	11 June		Sowerby's Ellison Glass Works Ltd. (see prior)
126941			Wittmann & Roth, London. Glass & China Manufacturer
127512	21 June		W. P. & G. Phillips (see prior)
127515/6	22 June		Matthew Turnbull (see prior)
127704-6	26 June		Charles E. Hill (see prior)
128472	10 July		Charles Kempton & Sons (see prior)
128665	13 July		C. Stolzles Sohne (see prior)
128763	16 July		Wittmann & Roth (see prior)
128882-4	17 July		Greener & Co., (see prior)
129295/6	29 July		Alfred Arculus, Birmingham. Glass Maker
129933	31 July		Edward Moore (see prior)
130641	13 August		G. Davidson & Co. (see prior)
130643			G. Davidson & Co. (see prior)
130648	14 August		Horton & Allday, Birmingham. Manufacturing Jeweller
131653	23 August		Stuart & Sons, Red House Glass Works, Stourbridge. Glass Maker
132189	31 August		Edward Moore (see prior)

Registration No.	Date	Year	Registered Party
132777	7 September	1889	Charles E. Hill, Brighton. Importer
132789/90	9 September		James Abraham Cox, London. Glass & China Manufacturer
133053	11 September		Sowerby's Ellison Glass Works Ltd., Gateshead. Glass Makers
133560	18 September		Edward Moore, Tyne Flint Glass Works, South Shields. Glass Maker
133643/4	20 September		Charles E. Hill (see prior)
133909	24 September		Sowerby's Ellison Glass Works Ltd. (see prior)
134350	1 October		William J. Blenko, London. Glass Maker
134907	5 October		Percival, Vickers & Co. Ltd., Manchester. Glass Makers
134908			Molineaux, Webb & Co., Manchester. Glass Makers
135780	16 October		Henry Dreydel, London. China & Glass Manufacturer
135946	18 October		Elkington & Co. Ltd., London. Silversmiths
136053	21 October		Saunders & Shepherd, London. Manufacturing Goldsmiths & Jewellers
136495	25 October		Johnson, Sons & Edmonds, London. Silversmiths
136980	28 October		Stevens & Williams, Brierley Hill Glass Works, Stafford. Glass Makers
137288	4 November		Stevens & Williams (see prior)
138051	14 November		Greener & Co., Wear Flint Glass Works, Sunderland & London. Glass Makers
138055			W. Thornhill & Co., London. Silversmiths
138523	19 November		Henry Dreydel (see prior)
139101	26 November		Pilkington Brothers, Lancaster. Glass Maker
139589	4 December		Edward Moore (see prior)
139808	6 December		Sowerby's Ellison Glass Works Ltd. (see prior)
140021	10 December		Falk, Stadelmann & Co.
140225	12 December		Haynes & Fisher, London. Glass Merchant
141068	24 December		Edward Moore (see prior)
141080	27 December		Sowerby's Ellison Glass Works Ltd. (see prior)
141128	27 December		F. & C. Osler, Birmingham. Flint Glass Manufacturer
141892/3	6 January	1890	Edward J. Shaw & Co., Astral Works, Walsall. Lamp Manufacturer
141980	11 January		Haynes & Fisher (see prior)
142179	15 January		Phillips (sic), London. China & Glass Merchants
142433	18 January	1890	Boulton & Mills, Audnam Glass Works, Stourbridge. Glass Makers
142675	22 January		Sowerby's Ellison Glass Works Ltd. (see prior)
142755/6	23 January		Siebdrat & Schmidt, London. Manufacturer
142985	28 January		Burtles, Tate & Co., Poland Street Glass Works, Manchester. Glass Makers
143135	30 January		Guiseppe V. De Luca, London. Agent
143153	28 January		Molineaux, Webb & Co. Ltd. (see prior)
143884	11 February		Matthew Turnbull, Cornhill Glass Works, Sunderland. Flint Glass Manufacturer
144725	24 February		James Dixon & Sons, Sheffield. Silver Plate Manufacturer
144779	25 February		Molineaux, Webb & Co. Ltd. (see prior)
144848	26 February		George Jackson & Sons, London. Interior Decorator
145000	28 February		Phillips (sic) (see prior)
145008			Matthew Turnbull (see prior)
145580	11 March		Greener & Co. (see prior)
145668	12 March		Samuel Clarke, London. Night Light Manufacturer
145813	14 March		A. & R. Cochran, St. Rollox Flint Glass Works, Glasgow. Flint Glass Manufacturer
145999			Frederick S. Balls, Cambridge. Glass & China Manufacturer
146042	18 March		Mappin & Webb, London. Silversmiths
146125	19 March		Wittmann & Roth, London. Glass & China Manufacturer
146736	28 March		Samuel Clarke (see prior)
147123	3 April		Samuel Clarke (see prior)
147194/5	5 April		Charles E. Hill (see prior)
147747	16 April		Samuel Clarke (see prior)
147915	15 April		The General Electric Co. Ltd., London. Manufacturing Electricians
148640	30 April		Phillips (sic) (see prior)
148661			Burtles, Tate & Co. (see prior)
148740			C. & G. E. Asprey, London. Silversmiths
149002	5 May		Charles Kempton & Sons, Lambeth. Glass Maker
149468	14 May		John Walsh Walsh, The Soho & Vesta Glass Works, Birmingham. Glass Maker
149470			Schindler & Co., London. Glass Maker
149959	22 May		James Bridger, Upper Edmonton. Glass Merchant
150045/6	24 May		Charles Kempton & Sons (see prior)

Registration No.	Date	Year	Registered Party
150063	27 May	1890	Charles E. Hill, Brighton. Importer
150087	28 May		Henry Mayer & Co., London. Glass & China Exporters
150166/7	31 May		Wittmann & Roth, London. Glass & China Manufacturer
150277	3 June		Greener & Co., Wear Flint Glass Works, Sunderland & London. Glass Makers
150401	5 June		Greener & Co. (see prior)
150532	7 June		Chance Bros. & Co. Ltd., Birmingham. Glass Maker
150552	4 June		Rowland Ward & Co., London. Naturalist
150597	10 June		Chance Bros. & Co. Ltd. (see prior)
150662	11 June		Charles E. Hill (see prior)
151046	18 June		Siebdrat & Schmidt, London. Manufacturers
151548	27 June		Phillips (sic), London. Glass & China Manufacturer
151657	1 July		Stevens & Williams, Brierley Hill Glass Works, Stafford. Glass Makers
151745	2 July		Falk, Stadelmann & Co.
152059	8 July		M. J. Reynolds, Stoke-on-Trent. Engraver
152135	10 July		Charles E. Hill (see prior)
152257			Samuel Clarke, London. Night Light Manufacturer
152546	9 July		M. J. Reynolds (see prior)
152906-8	21 July		Franz Aut Mehlem, Bonn, Germany. China & Glass Manufacturer
153858	2 August		George Davidson & Co., Teams Flint Glass Works, Gateshead-on-Tyne. Glass Makers
153901/2	5 August		Phillips (sic) (see prior)
154104	7 August		Louis Hats-chek & Co., Vienna & London. Importers
154350	1 August		John Tams, Longton, Staffordshire. Manufacturer
154486	15 August		William S. Thomson, London. Perfumer
154679	19 August		Edward John Shaw, Astral Works, Walsall. Lamp Manufacturer
154744/5	20 August		F. H. Davy & Co., Upper Edmonton. Glass Merchants
154849	19 August		The Pendleton Flint Glass Co. Ltd., Lancaster. Flint Glass Manufacturer
155744	2 September		John Walsh Walsh, The Soho & Vesta Glass Works, Birmingham. Glass Maker
155890	4 September		William Walker
156218-20	8 September		Louis Sepulchre, Herstal les Liege, Belgium. Manufacturer
156417	10 September	1890	F. H. Davy & Co. (see prior)
156626			Saunders & Shepherd, London. Manufacturing Goldsmiths & Jewellers
157103	19 September		William Walker
157164	20 September		Samuel Clarke (see prior)
157979	30 September		Siebdrat & Schmidt (see prior)
158283	4 October		Saunders & Shepherd (see prior)
158327/8	6 October		L. Straus & Sons, New York. Merchants
158336			Samuel Clarke (see prior)
158804	9 October		Schindler & Co., London. Glass Maker
158841			Schindler & Co. (see prior)
158948	15 October		Molineaux, Webb & Co. Ltd., The Manchester Flint Glass Works, Manchester. Glass Maker
158967			Schindler & Co. (see prior)
159189	18 October		Percival, Vickers & Co. Ltd., Manchester. Flint Glass Manufacturer
160244	3 November		Greener & Company (see prior)
162057	29 November		M. J. Reynolds (see prior)
163075	16 December		Greener & Co. (see prior)
163179	17 December		James Marshall, Novelty Glass Works, Stourbridge. Glass Manufacturer
163914	1 January	1891	Martin Gray, London. China & Glass Merchant
164521	12 January		Molineaux, Webb & Co. Ltd. (see prior)
164606/7	13 January		Stone, Fawdry & Stone, The Union Glass Works, Birmingham. Flint Glass Manufacturers
164670	14 January		John Walsh Walsh (see prior)
165012	20 January		John Walsh Walsh (see prior)
165559	30 January		Sowerby's Ellison Glass Works Ltd., Gateshead-on-Tyne. Glass Maker
166178	10 February		Burtles, Tate & Co., Poland Street Glass Works, Manchester. Glass Makers
166347	12 February		A. & R. Cochran, St. Rollox Flint Glass Works, Glasgow. Flint Glass Manufacturer
166359/60			Max Emanuel, London. Merchant
166650/1	18 February		The Glass & Metal Engraving Co. Ltd., Glasgow. Engravers
166677			Mappin & Brothers, Queens Cutlery Works, Sheffield. Silversmiths & Cutlers
166680			James Deakin & Sons, London. Silversmiths

Registration No.	Date	Year	Registered Party
166960	24 February	1891	John Grinsell & Sons, Birmingham. Silversmiths
167269	2 March		Francis A. Coles, Birmingham. Silversmiths
167516	5 March		Thomas Webb & Sons, Stourbridge. Glass Maker
168065	12 March		Edward J. Shaw, Astral Works, Walsall. Lamp Manufacturer
168130	13 March		Percival, Vickers & Co. Ltd., Manchester. Glass Makers
168132			Samuel Clarke, London. Night Light Manufacturer
168237	14 March		Henry C. Stephens, London. Ink Manufacturer
168686	24 March		James Hateley & Co., Aston Glass Works, Birmingham. Glass Maker
169054	2 April		Alfred Arculus, Birmingham. Glass Maker
169069			Wittmann & Roth, London. Glass & China Manufacturer
169292	8 April		Wittmann & Roth (see prior)
169406-9	9 April		Wittmann & Roth (see prior)
169410			Matthew Turnbull, Sunderland. Flint Glass Manufactuer
170269/70	24 April		Wittmann & Roth (see prior)
170363	25 April		A. & R. Cochran, St. Rollox Flint Glass Works, Glasgow. Flint Glass Manufacturer
170658	30 April		Stevens & Williams, Brierley Hill Glass Works, Stafford. Glass Makers
170909	6 May		Wittmann & Roth (see prior)
171058	7 May		Saunders & Shepherd, London. Manufacturing Goldsmith & Jeweller
171377	13 May		Guiseppe V. De Luca, London. Agent
171770-2	20 May		Charles E. Hill, Brighton. Importer
171774			Charles E. Hill (see prior)
171819/20	22 May		Charles E. Hill (see prior)
172125	29 May		John Walsh Walsh, The Soho & Vesta Glass Works, Birmingham. Glass Maker
172810	11 June		John Walsh Walsh (see prior)
173044	18 June		Percival, Vickers & Co. Ltd. (see prior)
173059			Sowerby & Co., Lemington Glass Works, Newcastle-on-Tyne. Glass Maker
173528	26 June		S. Mordan & Co., London. Manufacturer
173566	27 June		M. J. Reynolds, Stoke-on-Trent. Engraver
173968	3 July		Charles E. Hill (see prior)
173976			Guiseppe V. De Luca (see prior)
174527	14 July		Guiseppe V. De Luca (see prior)

Registration No.	Date	Year	Registered Party
174850/1	18 July	1891	Edward J. Shaw & Co. (see prior)
174913	20 July		John Line & Sons, Reading & London. Paperhanging & Glass Merchant
175031	23 July		Boulton & Mills, Stourbridge. Glass Makers
175420	29 July		Wittmann & Roth (see prior)
175802	4 August		Thomas Webb & Sons (see prior)
175894	6 August		Schindler & Co., London. Importers
176239	10 August		Greener & Co., Wear Flint Glass Works, Sunderland. Glass Makers
176566	15 August		George Davidson & Co., Teams Flint Glass Works, Gateshead-on-Tyne. Glass Maker
176642	17 August		Hukin & Heath, Imperial Works, Birmingham. Silversmiths
176677			Edward Coppin, London. China, Glass & Bottle Contractors
176723	18 August		Hukin & Heath (see prior)
176764	19 August		The Glasgow Plate Glass Co., Glasgow. Glass Maker
177399	28 August		Boulton & Mills (see prior)
177733	2 September		John Walsh Walsh (see prior)
178065/6	7 September		Thomas Goode & Co., London. Glass & China Merchant
178133	8 September		Hukin & Heath (see prior)
178135/6			Weiss & Biheller, London. Importers
178174	9 September		Thomas Webb & Sons Ltd. (see prior)
178653	16 September		Thomas Webb & Sons Ltd. (see prior)
179709	29 September		J. & W. B. Smith, London. Glass Maker
179726			Henry J. Latham, New York City. Manufacturer
181040	16 October		Hukin & Heath (see prior)
181041-3			Army and Navy Cooperative Society Ltd., London. Manufacturer
181057			G. Heath & Co., London. Silversmith
181326-9	22 October		Richard Schmidt, Finsbury. Agent
181572	27 October		Stevens & Williams (see prior)
181922	29 October		John Walsh Walsh (see prior)
182002	30 October		Greener & Co. (see prior)
182180/1	3 November		Webb Shaw & Co. Ltd., Stourbridge, Glass Maker
183187	17 November		Hukin & Heath (see prior)
183264	18 November		S. Mordan & Co. (see prior)

Registration No.	Date	Year	Registered Party
183415-7	20 November	1891	John Walsh Walsh, The Soho & Vesta Glass Works, Birmingham. Glass Maker
183637	23 November		Richard Schmidt, Finsbury. Agent
183799	26 November		Joseph Holdcroft, Longton, Staffordshire. Manufacturer
184359	4 December		Stone, Fawdry & Stone, Birmingham. Glass Maker
184501	7 December		John Walsh Walsh (see prior)
184548	8 December		John Walsh Walsh (see prior)
184582	9 December		Falk, Stadelmann & Co. Ltd.
184619			Richard Thomas Grocott, Whitehall Works, Longport, Staffordshire. Manufacturer
185045	17 December		Hukin & Heath, Imperial Works, Birmingham. Silversmiths
185803	4 January	1892	Stuart & Sons, Red House Glass Works, Stourbridge, Glass Maker
185823/4	5 January		Falk, Stadelmann & Co.
185847			Henry J. Latham, New York City. Manufacturer
185911	7 January		Thomas Webb & Sons Ltd. Stourbridge, Glass Maker
186137	12 January		John Walsh Walsh (see prior)
186286	14 January		Richard Wilkes, Cross Glass Works, Dudley. Glass Maker
186335			John Henry Downing, Birmingham. Glass Merchant
186382	15 January		Boulton & Mills, Audnam Glass Works, Stourbridge, Glass Maker.
186546	21 January		John Walsh Walsh (see prior)
186567			John Walsh Walsh (see prior)
186770	25 January		Thomas Webb & Sons Ltd. (see prior)
187037	29 January		Saunders & Shepherd, London. Manufacturing Goldsmiths & Jewellers
187105	30 January		Francis Fether, London. Glass Blower
187145	1 February		Hukin & Heath (see prior)
187169	2 February		Schindler & Co., London. Glass Maker
187222	3 February		Price's Patent Candle Co., Battersea. Manufacturer
187759	15 February		Hukin & Heath (see prior)
187891	17 February		Edward John Shaw, Astral Works, Walsall. Lamp Manufacturer
188148	22 February		Hukin & Heath (see prior)
188440	27 February		Charles E. Hill, Brighton. Importer
188489	29 February		Edward John Shaw (see prior)
188944/5	10 March		Alfred Arculus & Co., Birmingham. Glass Maker

Registration No.	Date	Year	Registered Party
189247	15 March	1892	Percival, Vickers & Co. Ltd., Manchester. Glass Makers
189324	16 March		Sowerby's Ellison Glass Works Ltd., Gateshead-on-Tyne. Glass Maker
189344	16 March		Percival, Vickers & Co. Ltd. (see prior)
190428	2 April		Boulton & Mills (see prior)
190543	5 April		J. & J. Price, Birmingham. Glass Maker
190696	7 April		Saunders & Shepherd (see prior)
191042	14 April		Frederick Hewitt, North Shields. Glass and China Merchant
191191	20 April		Mrs. Marcus Stone, London. Gentlewoman
191254	21 April		Pilkington Bros., Lancaster. Glass Maker
191384	22 April		Guiseppe V. De Luca, London. Agent
191886	3 May		Webb, Shaw & Co. Ltd., Stourbridge. Glass Maker
191932	4 May		Boulton & Mills (see prior)
192298	10 May		Robinson, Skinner & Co., Warrington. Glass Maker
192350	11 May		The Lamp Manufacturing Co. Ltd.
192553	14 May		Saunders & Shepherd (see prior)
192595	16 May		Thomas Webb & Sons Ltd. (see prior)
192602-4			Charles E. Hill (see prior)
192807	20 May		Thomas Webb & Sons Ltd. (see prior)
192876	21 May		Percival, Vickers & Co. Ltd. (see prior)
193196	28 May		Zeno & Company, London. Perfumers
193365	1 June		George Davidson & Co., Teams Flint Glass Works, Gateshead-on-Tyne. Glass Maker
193492/3	3 June		M. J. Reynolds, Stoke-on-Trent. Engraver
193624	4 June		Schindler & Co. (see prior)
193626			Schindler & Co. (see prior)
193691	8 June		Soane & Smith, London. China & Glass Merchant
193694/5	9 June		Percival, Vickers & Co. Ltd. (see prior)
193821	14 June		Percival, Vickers & Co. Ltd. (see prior)
193826/7			Krausse & Auerbach, London. Foreign Agents
193917	15 June		Saunders & Shepherd (see prior)
194040/1	17 June		Schindler & Co. (see prior)

Registration No.	Date	Year	Registered Party
194188	21 June	1892	George Betjemann & Sons, London. Dressing Case Manufacturer
194189	21 June		Charles E. Hill, Brighton. Importer
194562	24 June		John Grinsell & Sons, Birmingham. Art Metal Smiths
194616	25 June		Chance Brothers & Co. Ltd., West Smethwick. Glass Manufacturers
194638	27 June		Percival, Vickers & Co. Ltd., Manchester. Glass Makers
194696	28 June		Mappin & Webb, London. Silversmiths
194813	30 June		Soane & Smith, London. China & Glass Merchant
195324	12 July		William Ault, Swadlincote. Manufacturer
195482	15 July		I. & W. B. Smith, London. Glass Makers and Importers
195689	21 July		M. J. Reynolds, Stoke-on-Trent. Engraver
196009	26 July		S. Reich & Co., London. Glass Maker
196342	3 August		Mappin & Webb (see prior)
196639	10 August		Percival, Vickers & Co. Ltd. (see prior)
196641			Greener & Co., Wear Flint Glass Works, Sunderland. Glass Makers
196748/9	12 August		Pilkington Brothers, St. Helens. Glass Maker
196953/4	17 August		Herbert Price & Co., London. Wholesale China and Glass Merchant
197221	20 August		Charles E. Hill (see prior)
198233	8 September		Guiseppe V. De Luca, London. Agent
198248			William Ault (see prior)
198959	17 September		Wittmann & Roth, London. Glass & China Manufacturer
199109	20 September		Henry G. Richardson, Wordsley Flint Glass Works, Stourbridge. Glass Maker
199110			Woodall & Son, London. Glass Maker
199284	23 September		Woodall & Son (see prior)
199590	28 September		Francis A. Coles, Birmingham. Silversmith
200502	11 October		Stone, Fawdry & Stone, Birmingham. Glass Maker
200505			Boulton & Mills, Audnam Glass Works, Stourbridge. Glass Makers
201102	19 October		Richard Schmidt, Finsbury. Agent
201139	20 October		Herbert Price & Co. (see prior)

Registration No.	Date	Year	Registered Party
201225	21 October	1892	Molineaux, Webb & Co. Ltd., The Manchester Flint Glass Works. Manchester. Glass Makers
201392	25 October		John Shaw & Sons, Latimer Glass Works, Sheffield. Cut Glass Manufacturer
201648	31 October		Walter Thornhill & Co., London. Silversmiths
201902	3 November		Wittmann & Roth (see prior)
202200/1	8 November		John Stewart, Glasgow. Glass Stainer and Embosser
202625-9	15 November		Walter Thornhill & Co. (see prior)
202675	16 November		Saunders & Shepherd, London. Manufacturing Goldsmiths & Jewellers
203135	25 November		John Walsh Walsh, The Soho & Vesta Glass Works, Birmingham. Glass Maker
203159			Weiss & Biheller, London. Importers
203235-7	28 November		Hukin & Heath, Imperial Works, Birmingham. Silversmiths
203327	30 November		Max Emanuel & Co., London. Merchant
204089-91	12 December		William Ault (see prior)
204189	14 December		Josiah Lane, Birmingham. Glass Maker
204438	17 December		Henry Mayer & Co., London. China & Glass Merchants
204629	21 December		Phillips's, London. Glass & China Manufacturer
205238	31 December		Schindler & Co., London. Glass Maker
205280/1	3 January	1893	Zimmermann & Co., London. Lamp Manufacturer
205884	14 January		Schindler & Co. (see prior)
205994	17 January		Boulton & Mills (see prior)
206025/6	18 January		Webb Brothers Ltd., Manchester. Flint Glass Manufacturer
206204	2 February		Phillips's (see prior)
206612	27 January		Thomas Webb & Sons Ltd., Stourbridge. Glass Maker
206623/4			Guiseppe V. De Luca (see prior)
207004	3 February		Edward John Shaw, Astral Works, Walsall. Lamp Manufacturer
207065	4 February		Webb, Shaw & Co. Ltd., Stourbridge. Glass Maker
207120	7 February		Wood Brothers & Co., Borough Flint Glass Works, Barnsley. Glass Maker
207243	9 February		Guiseppe V. De Luca (see prior)

150

Registration No.	Date	Year	Registered Party
207909	20 February	1893	G. Davidson & Co., Teams Flint Glass Works, Gateshead-on-Tyne. Glass Maker
208112	24 February		Schindler & Co., London. Glass Maker
208367	1 March		Matthew Turnbull, Cornhill Glass Works, Sunderland. Flint Glass Manufacturer
208600	6 March		Saunders & Shepherd, London. Manufacturing Goldsmiths & Jewellers
208658	7 March		Saunders & Shepherd (see prior)
209222	15 March		William Ault, Derby. Manufacturer
209414	17 March		Molineaux, Webb & Co. Ltd., The Manchester Flint Glass Works, Manchester. Glass Maker
209465	18 March		Herbert Price & Co., London. Wholesale China and Glass Merchant
209493	20 March		Stevens & Williams, Brierley Hill Glass Works, Stafford. Glass Makers
210371	10 April		Greener & Company, Wear Flint Glass Works, Sunderland. Glass Makers
210373			M. J. Reynolds, Stoke-on-Trent. Engraver
210704	15 April		Stone, Fawdry & Stone, Birmingham. Glass Maker
210719			Stone, Fawdry & Stone (see prior)
210755	17 April		Thomas Webb & Sons Ltd., Stourbridge. Glass Maker
211129	24 April		Guiseppe V. De Luca, London. Agent
211352	28 April		Max Emanuel & Co., London. Merchant
211616	3 May		M. J. Reynolds (see prior)
211617			Percival, Vickers & Co. Ltd., Manchester. Glass Makers
211778	6 May		John Walsh Walsh, The Soho & Vesta Glass Works, Birmingham. Glass Maker
211800	8 May		M. J. Reynolds (see prior)
212166	15 May		Max Emanuel & Co. (see prior)
212315	17 May		Pilkington Brothers, Lancaster. Glass Maker
212319			John Mortlock & Co., London. China and Glass Dealer
212459	19 May		Thomas Goode & Co., London. China & Glass Merchant
212679	25 May		De Grelle, Houdret & Co., London. Manufacturer

Registration No.	Date	Year	Registered Party
212684	25 May	1893	George Davidson & Co. (see prior)
212730	29 May		Thomas Webb & Sons Ltd. (see prior)
212735			Guiseppe V. De Luca (see prior)
212950	1 June		Richard Schmidt, Finsbury. Agent
212983	2 June		Francis A. Coles, Birmingham. Silversmith
213282	8 June		The Army & Navy Cooperative Soc. Ltd., London. Manufacturer
213324	9 June		Pilkington Brothers (see prior)
213374	10 June		Matthew Turnbull (see prior)
213381			Percival, Vickers & Co. Ltd. (see prior)
213455	13 June		Oppenheimer Son & Co. Ltd., London. Merchant
213768	21 June		Stone, Fawdry & Stone (see prior)
214578	5 July		William Ault (see prior)
215082	15 July		Sowerby's Ellison Glass Works Ltd., Gateshead-on-Tyne. Glass Maker
215154	18 July		Greener & Co. (see prior)
215774/5	28 July		Max Emanuel & Co. (see prior)
216088	3 August		Burtles, Tate & Co., Poland Street Glass Works, Manchester. Glass Makers
216157			Henry G. Richardson & Sons, Wordsley Flint Glass Works, Stourbridge. Glass Maker
216255/6	4 August		T. Wilkinson & Sons, Pelican Works, Birmingham. Electro Plate Manufacturer
216578	10 August		G. V. De Luca, Hill & Co. (see prior)
216626	11 August		Schindler & Co., London. Glass Maker
216627			Wittmann & Roth, London. Glass & China Manufacturer
216711	15 August		Arthur Mortimer, London. Glass Merchant
216779/80	16 August		Henry G. Richardson & Sons (see prior)
217198	25 August		M. J. Reynolds (see prior)
217199			Sowerby's Ellison Glass Works Ltd. (see prior)
217202			Henry G. Richardson & Sons (see prior)
217204			Saunders & Shepherd, London. Manufacturing Goldsmiths & Jewellers
217327	28 August		George Jackson & Sons, London. Manufacturer
217405	29 August		Saunders & Shepherd (see prior)

Registration No.	Date	Year	Registered Party
217448	30 August	1893	Phillips's, London. Glass & China Manufacturer
217651	4 September		Molineaux, Webb & Co. Ltd., The Manchester Flint Glass Works, Manchester. Glass Maker
217660			Saunders & Shepherd, London. Manufacturing Goldsmiths & Jewellers
217749	6 September		Greener & Co., Wear Flint Glass Works, Sunderland. Glass Makers
217752			G. Davidson & Co., Teams Flint Glass Works, Gateshead-on-Tyne. Glass Maker
217831/2	7 September		J. Defries & Son
217900	9 September		Henry G. Richardson & Sons, Wordsley Flint Glass Works, Stourbridge. Glass Maker
218085	11 September		Thomas Webb & Sons Ltd., Stourbridge. Glass Maker
218103	12 September		Stevens & Williams, Brierley Hill Glass Works, Stafford. Glass Makers
218417/8	18 September		De Grelle, Houdret & Co., London. Manufacturer
218710	20 September		Greener & Co. (see prior)
219465	2 October		M. J. Reynolds, Stoke-on-Trent. Engraver
219565	3 October		John Ford & Co., Holyrood Glass Works, Edinburgh. Manufacturer
219638	4 October		Matthew Turnbull, Cornhill Glass Works, Sunderland, Durham. Flint Glass Manufacturer
220471-3	14 October		Molineaux, Webb & Co. Ltd. (see prior)
220863	19 October		Stevens & Williams (see prior)
221006	21 October		James A. Cox, London. Glass & China Merchant
221175	25 October		Hukin & Heath, Imperial Works, Birmingham. Silversmiths
221354	27 October		Boulton & Mills, Audnam Glass Works, Stourbridge. Flint Glass Makers
221480	30 October		M. J. Reynolds, Stoke-on-Trent. Engraver
221684	2 November		M. J. Reynolds (see prior)
221728	3 November		Harold Faraday, London. Electric Light Fitting Manufacturer
222032/3	8 November		J. & J. Price, Birmingham. Glass Maker
222389	15 November		William Ault, Derby. Manufacturer
222451	16 November		Guiseppe V. De Luca, Hill & Co., London. Merchant
223294	4 December	1893	Saunders & Shepherd (see prior)
223362	5 December		John Ford & Co., (see prior)
223645	8 December		William Ault (see prior)
223742	11 December		Greener & Co. (see prior)
223873/4	13 December		G. V. De Luca, Hill & Co. (see prior)
224171	19 December		G. Davidson & Co. (see prior)
224229	20 December		J. Defries & Sons Ltd.
224362	22 December		Andrew Murray Malloch, Glasgow. Glass Maker
224603	28 December		Stevens & Williams (see prior)
224713	30 December		Saunders & Shepherd (see prior)
224765	1 January	1894	G. V. De Luca, Hill & Co. (see prior)
225794	20 January		Schindler & Co., London. Glass Maker
226750	3 February		Stevens & Williams (see prior)
226959	7 February		William Hutton & Sons Ltd., London. Manufacturing Silversmiths
226976	8 February		Schindler & Co. (see prior)
227177	10 February		Hukin & Heath (see prior)
227396	14 February		Wittmann and Roth, London. Glass & China Manufacturer
227564	15 February		Hukin & Heath (see prior)
227966	23 February		Hukin & Heath (see prior)
228608	6 March		Hukin & Heath (see prior)
228636	7 March		William Hutton & Sons Ltd. (see prior)
229738	24 March		William Hutton & Sons Ltd. (see prior)
230031	3 April		Jules Lang & Co., London. Glass and China Merchant
230286	7 April		John Ford & Co. (see prior)
230336	9 April		Falk, Stadelmann & Co. Ltd.
230704	14 April		Henry Briggs & Co., Hood Street Glass Works, Manchester. Glass Workers
230817	17 April		Falk, Stadelmann & Co. Ltd.
230818			Saunders & Shepherd (see prior)
231039	20 April		G. V. De Luca, Hill & Co. (see prior)
231387	26 April		Thomas Webb & Sons Ltd. (see prior)
231490	28 April		Henry Salsbury, London. Lamp Manufacturer
232529	22 May		Jules Lang & Co. (see prior)
232959-61	28 May		J. Defries & Sons Ltd.
233062	30 May		Matthew Turnbull (see prior)
233135	31 May		Hukin & Heath (see prior)
233181	1 June		Max Emanuel & Co., London. Merchant

Registration No.	Date	Year	Registered Party
233256-60	2 June	1894	Max Emanuel & Co., London. Merchant
233564	8 June		Leuchars & Son, London. Dressing Case Makers
233571			M. J. Reynolds, Stoke-on-Trent. Engraver
233766	11 June		Percival, Vickers & Co. Ltd., Manchester. Glass Makers
233768			Molineaux, Webb & Co. Ltd., The Manchester Flint Glass Works, Manchester. Glass Maker
233777			Henry Turner, London. Glass and China Manufacturer
233948	13 June		Richard Schmidt, Finsbury. Agent
234231	14 June		Greener & Co., Wear Flint Glass Works. Sunderland. Glass Makers
234288	15 June		Max Emanuel & Co (see prior)
234561/2	20 June		M. J. Reynolds (see prior)
235217	28 June		Phillips's, London. Glass & China Manufacturer
235230			Max Emanuel & Co. (see prior)
235824	12 July		Boulton & Mills, Audnam Glass Works, Stourbridge. Flint Glass Makers
237038	1 August		G. Davidson & Co., Teams Flint Glass Works, Gateshead-on-Tyne. Glass Maker
237567	10 August		J. Defries & Sons Ltd.
237641	13 August		M. J. Reynolds (see prior)
237720	14 August		A. Ruch & Co., London. Glass Bottle Manufacturer
238352	23 August		Sowerby's Ellison Glass Works Ltd., Gateshead-on-Tyne. Glass Maker
238623	27 August		Hukin & Heath, Imperial Works, Birmingham. Silversmiths
238687-90	28 August		Jules Lang & Co., London. Glass & China Merchant
238856	30 August		Jules Lang & Co. (see prior)
239188	4 September		Charles Parsons, Lancaster. Glass Merchant
239655	11 September		A. Ruch & Co. (see prior)
239938	15 September		Max Emanuel & Co (see prior)
240048	18 September		William Brown, London. Glass & China Warehouseman
240049			Hukin & Heath (see prior)
240703	25 September		C. H. Moody, London. Glass Bottle Manufacturer
240865	27 September		A. & R. Cochran, St. Rollox Flint Glass Works, Glasgow. Flint Glass Manufacturer
241122	28 September		Max Emanuel & Co (see prior)
241304/5	2 October		William Ault, Derby. Manufacturer
241570	4 October		Max Emanuel & Co (see prior)
241788	9 October	1894	Max Emanuel & Co (see prior)
241930	10 October		Greener & Co. (see prior)
242610	19 October		Hukin & Heath (see prior)
242706	22 October		M. J. Reynolds (see prior)
243177	27 October		Edward J. Shaw & Co., Astral Works, Walsall. Lamp Manufacturer
243452	1 November		Chance Brothers & Co. Ltd., Birmingham. Glass Maker
243946	9 November		M. J. Reynolds (see prior)
244076	12 November		Max Emanuel & Co (see prior)
244118/9	13 November		A. Ruch & Co. (see prior)
244245	14 November		C. Depinoix, Paris. Bottle Manufacturer
245039	27 November		M. J. Reynolds (see prior)
245044			Jules Lang & Co. (see prior)
245141	28 November		John Walsh Walsh, The Soho & Vesta Glass Works, Birmingham. Glass Maker
245520	5 December		Falk, Stadelmann & Co. Ltd.
245720	10 December		Matthew Turnbull, Cornhill Glass Works, Sunderland. Flint Glass Manufacturer
246383	18 December		A. Ruch & Co. (see prior)
246507	20 December		Zeno & Co., London. Perfumers
247064	2 January	1895	Alfred Arculus & Co., Birmingham. Glass Maker
247225	4 January		Alfred Arculus & Co (see prior)
247617	12 January		Alfred Arculus & Co (see prior)
247777	15 January		G. V. De Luca, Hill & Co., London. Merchant
247921	17 January		De Grelle, Houdret & Co., London. Manufacturer
248011	18 January		Roberts & Belk, Furnival Works, Sheffield. Silversmiths
248169-72	22 January		Max Emanuel & Co (see prior)
248507	26 January		Roberts & Belk (see prior)
248671	30 January		Thomas Webb & Sons Ltd., Stourbridge. Glass Maker
249009	5 February		G. V. De Luca, Hill & Co. (see prior)
249104	7 February		John Shaw, Latimer Glass Works, Sheffield. Cut Glass Manufacturer
249121/2			Max Emanuel & Co (see prior)
249450/1	14 February		Boulton & Mills (see prior)
249824	20 February		Schindler & Co., London. Glass Maker
249976	22 February		M. J. Reynolds (see prior)
250254	27 February		Webb, Shaw & Co., Stourbridge. Glass Maker
250515	2 March		Matthew Turnbull (see prior)
250842	7 March		Henry Turner, The Crown Pottery, London. Glass & China Manufacturer
251098-101	11 March		Gustav Doring, London. Glass Bottle Manufacturer

Registration No.	Date	Year	Registered Party
251168	12 March	1895	Alfred Arculus, Birmingham. Glass Maker
251393	15 March		Molineaux, Webb & Co. Ltd., The Manchester Flint Glass Works, Manchester. Glass Maker
251816	23 March		John Walsh Walsh. The Soho & Vesta Glass Works, Birmingham. Glass Maker
251997	27 March		A. Ruch & Co., London. Glass Bottle Manufacturer
252416	4 April		Oppenheimer Brothers & Co., London. Merchant
252587	5 April		Hukin & Heath, Imperial Works, Birmingham. Silversmiths
252957	10 April		Saunders & Shepherd, London. Manufacturing Goldsmiths & Jewellers
252968			Mills, Walker & Co. Ltd., London. Glass and China Manufacturer
253219	16 April		The Acme Patents China, Glass & Earthenware Co., London. Dealers
253348	18 April		Hukin & Heath (see prior)
253531	22 April		James Keiller & Sons Ltd., Dundee & London. Confectioners
253737	25 April		John Grinsell & Sons, Victoria Works, Birmingham. Silvermsith
253744			John Grinsell & Sons (see prior)
253880-3	27 April		Max Emanuel & Co., London. Merchant
253934/5	29 April		John Walsh Walsh (see prior)
254027	1 May		G. Davidson & Co., Teams Flint Glass Works, Gateshead-on-Tyne, Glass Maker
254070/1	2 May		M. J. Reynolds, Stoke-on-Trent. Engraver
254406	7 May		Percival, Vickers & Co. Ltd., Manchester. Glass Makers
254496/7	8 May		G. V. De Luca, Hill & Co., The French Flint Glass Bottle Co., London. Manufacturer
255279	23 May		William Hutton & Sons Ltd., London. Silversmiths
255999	8 June		Saunders & Shepherd (see prior)
256117	11 June		De Grelle, Houdret & Co., London. Manufacturer
256561	20 June		B. Peacock & Sons, Venetian & Industry Glass Works, Castleford. Glass Bottle Manufacturer
256562-5			Jules Lang & Co., London. Glass & China Merchant
256710	21 June		J. Dunlop Mitchell & Co., Glasgow. Bottle & Glassware Manufacturer
257024	27 June	1895	G. V. De Luca, Hill & Co. (see prior)
257357	2 July		Gustav Doring, London. Glass Bottle Manufacturer
257632	6 July		Joseph Hawkes, Birmingham. Silversmith
258032-4	12 July		Gustav Doring (see prior)
258147	15 July		John Walsh Walsh (see prior)
258156			Greener & Co., Wear Flint Glass Works, Sunderland. Glass Makers
259153	3 August		Herbert Price & Co., London. Wholesale China & Glass Merchant
259467	12 August		The Albion Lamp Co., Birmingham. Lamp Manufacturer
260128	20 August		Saunders & Shepherd (see prior)
260279	22 August		Max Emanuel & Co (see prior)
260538	26 August		Max Emanuel & Co (see prior)
260968	3 September		G. V. De Luca, Hill & Co. (see prior)
261065/6	4 September		Henry G. Richardson & Sons, Wordsley Flint Glass Works, Stourbridge. Glass Maker
261274	6 September		Allen & Hanbury's Ltd., London. Chemists
261292	7 September		Schindler & Co., London. Glass Maker
262018	16 September		Greener & Co. (see prior)
262255	19 September		G. V. De Luca, Hill & Co. (see prior)
263133/4	4 October		Max Emanuel & Co (see prior)
263426	10 October		Herbert Price & Co (see prior)
263675	12 October		A. Ruch & Co., London. Glass Bottle Manufacturer
264396/7	23 October		Herbert Price & Co (see prior)
264444	24 October		Max Emanuel & Co (see prior)
264500	25 October		Jules Lang & Co. (see prior)
264751	29 October		John Walsh Walsh (see prior)
264997	1 November		John Walsh Walsh (see prior)
265003			Jules Lang & Co. (see prior)
265102	4 November		Henry Salsbury, London. Lamp Manufacturer
265305	7 November		G. V. De Luca, Hill & Co. (see prior)
265365	8 November		A. Ruch & Co. (see prior)
265549	12 November		I. & E. Atkinson, London. Perfumers
265716	14 November		George C. Fowler & Morris B. Fowler, Brockley, Kent. Night Light Manufacturer
265925	19 November		Henry Salsbury (see prior)
266768	2 December		Eunson & Scurr, Sunderland. Glass Maker
266897	4 December		Pilkington Brothers Ltd., St. Helens. Glass Maker

Registration No.	Date	Year	Registered Party
267079	6 December	1895	Max Emanuel & Co. London. Merchant
267156	7 December		Saunders & Shepherd, London. Manufacturing Goldsmiths & Jewellers
267857	19 December		Max Emanuel & Co (see prior)
267930	20 December		Hukin & Heath, Imperial Works, Birmingham. Silversmiths
267931/2			Eunson & Scurr, Sunderland. Glass Maker
268126	27 December		Jules Lang & Co., London. Glass & China Merchant
268576-8	3 January	1896	Jules Lang & Co. (see prior)
268869	10 January		G. V. De Luca, Hill & Co. The French Flint Glass Bottle Co., London. Manufacturer
268968	13 January		Percival, Vickers & Co. Ltd., Manchester. Glass Makers
269113	15 January		Molineaux, Webb & Co. Ltd., The Manchester Flint Glass Works, Manchester. Glass Makers
269118			Tomlinson & Co. Ltd., Manor Flint Glass Works, Barnsley. Glass Blower
269203	16 January		Jules Lang & Co. (see prior)
269927-9	27 January		Thomas Webb & Sons Ltd., Stourbridge. Glass Maker
270110	30 January		E. H. Cutler & Co., Boston, U.S.A. Perfume Manufacturer
270546	7 February		Jules Lang & Co. (see prior)
270756	10 February		A. Ruch & Co., London. Glass Bottle Manufacturer
270831	12 February		Jules Lang & Co. (see prior)
270832			Max Emanuel & Co (see prior)
271344	20 February		Weiss & Biheller, London. Importers
271422	21 February		John Walsh Walsh, The Soho & Vesta Glass Works, Birmingham. Glass Maker
271500	22 February		John Grinsell & Sons, Victoria Works, Birmingham. Silversmiths
271534/5	24 February		McDougall & Sons, Glasgow. Glass & China Merchant
271700	26 February		Molineaux, Webb & Co. Ltd. (see prior)
271766	27 February		Wittmann & Co., London. Glass & China Merchant
272192	5 March		M. J. Reynolds, Stoke-on-Trent. Engraver
272238	6 March		Mappin & Webb, London. Silversmiths
272672	13 March		E. Coaney & Co., Birmingham. Glass Maker
273414	25 March		John Walsh Walsh (see prior)
273503	26 March		Hukin & Heath (see prior)
273702	30 March	1896	A. Ruch & Co (see prior)
273840	1 April		Davies & Stewart, Tower Glass Works, Birmingham. Manufacturer
274253	11 April		Edward J. Shaw, Astral Works, Walsall. Lamp Manufacturer
274427	15 April		C. H. Moody & Co., London. Glass Bottle Merchant
274732	21 April		Jules Lang & Co. (see prior)
274885	24 April		McDougall & Sons (see prior)
274887-9			John Walsh Walsh (see prior)
274897/8			William Ault, Derby. Manufacturer
275000-3	27 April		Edward J. Shaw (see prior)
275639	5 May		James Lewis, London. Wholesale & Export Perfumers
275802	7 May		Percival, Vickers & Co. Ltd. (see prior)
275897	8 May		G. V. De Luca, Hill & Co. (see prior)
275954	9 May		James L. Shepherd, Birmingham. Glass Merchant
276415-8	18 May		Edward J. Shaw (see prior)
276909	29 May		John Grinsell & Sons, Victoria Works, Birmingham. Silversmiths
276977	1 June		Greener & Co., Wear Flint Glass Works, Sunderland. Glass Makers
277168	4 June		Jules Lang & Co. (see prior)
277412	8 June		James Buchanan & Co., London. Whiskey Merchant
277775/6	15 June		A. Ruch & Co. (see prior)
277837-9	16 June		William Whiston, Birmingham. Lamp Manufacturer
278033/4	18 June		Phillips's, London. Glass & China Manufacturer
278141	20 June		Gustav G. Doring, London. Glass Bottle Manufacturer
278273	23 June		Arthur T. Woodhall, London. Glass Maker
278699	29 June		McDougall & Sons (see prior)
278782	30 June		M. J. Reynolds (see prior)
279511	13 July		James Buchanan & Co. (see prior)
279782	16 July		Falk, Stadelmann & Co. Ltd.
280388	28 July		Henry Mayer & Co., London, Glass & China Merchant
280525	30 July		Eunson & Scurr Ltd., Sunderland. Glass Maker
282113/4	25 August		Schindler & Co., London. Glass Maker
282607/8	31 August		John Walsh Walsh (see prior)
282614			John L. Grossmith, London. Manufacturer of Perfumery

Registration No.	Date	Year	Registered Party
282775	2 September	1896	Richter & Kuttner, London. Glass Bottle Manufacturer
283227	5 September		Henry Defries
283577	10 September		Thomas Webb & Sons Ltd., Stourbridge, Glass Maker
284403	19 September		Charles Melin, London. Glass Merchant
284639	23 September		Greener & Co., Wear Flint Glass Works, Sunderland. Glass Makers
284640			The Baccarat Glass Co., London. Glass Manufacturer
284895	26 September		Wittmann & Co., London. Glass & China Manufacturer
285342	2 October		G. Davidson & Co., Teams Flint Glass Works, Gateshead-on-Tyne. Glass Maker
286107	13 October		Hukin & Heath, Imperial Works, Birmingham. Silversmiths
286391	15 October		Soane & Smith, London. China & Glass Merchant
287135	27 October		Lea & Perrins, Midlands Works, Birmingham. Chandelier Manufacturer
287267	29 October		Hukin & Heath (see prior)
287472	2 November		Henry G. Richardson & Sons, Wordsley Flint Glass Works, Stourbridge. Glass Maker
287653	4 November		Percival, Vickers & Co. Ltd., Manchester. Glass Makers
287927	9 November		Wittmann & Co. (see prior)
288044	11 November		Mappin & Webb, London. Silversmiths
288049			Frederick W. Neuburger & Co., London. China & Glass Merchant
288442	17 November		James Cox, London. Glass Merchant
288785/6	20 November		A. Ruch & Co., London. Glass Bottle Manufacturer
288969	24 November		Phillips's, London. Glass & China Manufacturer
289233	27 November		G. V. De Luca, Hill & Co., The French Flint Glass Bottle Co., London. Manufacturer
290039	11 December		Jules Lang & Co., London. Glass & China Merchant
290299	15 December		William Ramsey, London. Glass Maker
290483	18 December		James Cox (see prior)
291659	8 January	1897	Henry G. Richardson & Sons (see prior)
291662			Eunson & Scurr, Sunderland. Glass Maker
291928/9	14 January		John Grinsell & Sons, Victoria Works, Birmingham. Silversmiths
291933	14 January	1897	Henry G. Aldridge, Marylebone. China & Glass Dealer
292005	15 January		Schindler & Co., London. Glass Maker
292506	23 January		Percival, Vickers & Co. Ltd. (see prior)
292744	27 January		John Grinsell & Sons (see prior)
292752			E. Coaney & Co., Birmingham. Glass & Earthenware Merchant
292875	28 January		Gustav Doring, London. Glass Bottle Manufacturer
292934	29 January		G. V. De Luca, Hill & Co. (see prior)
293046	1 February		M. J. Reynolds, Stoke-on-Trent. Engraver
293052			A. Ruch & Co. (see prior)
293210-3	3 February		John Walsh Walsh, The Soho & Vesta Glass Works, Birmingham. Glass Maker
293416	5 February		Briedenbach & Co., London. Perfumer
293484	6 February		John Grinsell & Sons (see prior)
293696/7	9 February		M. J. Reynolds (see prior)
295198	5 March		James Green & Nephew, London. China & Glass Merchant
295260	6 March		Wood Brothers & Co., Borough Flint Glass Works, Barnsley. Glass Maker
295653	15 March		John Walsh Walsh (see prior)
296025	22 March		John L. Grossmith, London. Manufacturer of Perfumery
296071	23 March		F. & C. Osler, Birmingham. Flint Glass Manufacturer
296134	24 March		James Green & Nephew (see prior)
296418-20	27 March		Alfred Arculus & Co., Birmingham. Glass Maker
297352	14 April		John Ford & Co., Holyrood Glass Works, Edinburgh. Manufacturer
297500	15 April		G. V. De Luca, Hill & Co. (see prior)
297595	17 April		Chance Brothers & Co. Ltd., Birmingham. Glass Maker
297675	21 April		Chance Brothers & Co. Ltd. (see prior)
297791	23 April		A. Ruch & Co. (see prior)
298560-3	8 May		William E. Barras, Middlesex. Glass Blower
299123/4	19 May		Charles Kempton, Sen., Lambeth. Glass Maker
299383	22 May		Schindler & Co. (see prior)

Registration No.	Date	Year	Registered Party
299464	22 May	1897	Alfred W. Levee, Manchester. Glass & China Merchant
299712	28 May		John Walsh Walsh, The Soho & Vesta Glass Works, Birmingham. Glass Maker
299974	3 June		A. Ruch & Co., London. Glass Bottle Manufacturer
300319	14 June		M. J. Reynolds, Stoke-on-Trent. Engraver
300657	23 June		Holophane Ltd., London. Manufacturer of Glass Globes & Shades
300950	1 July		H. Labern & Son, Stoke Newington. Wholesale Perfumers
301224	8 July		Schindler & Co., London. Glass Maker
301324	10 July		Charles Kempton, Sen., Lambeth. Glass Maker
301443	13 July		Jules Lang & Co., London. Glass & China Merchant
302034	23 July		Jules Lang & Co. (see prior)
302035			Richard Wittmann, London. Glass & China Manufacturer
302085	24 July		Richard Wittmann (see prior)
302165-9	27 July		The Glasgow Plate Glass Co., Glasgow. Glass Maker
302340	30 July		William Ault, Derby. Manufacturer
303344/5	16 August		Richard Wittmann (see prior)
303519	18 August		G. Davidson & Co., Teams Flint Glass Works, Gateshead-on-Tyne. Glass Maker
304097	30 August		Jules Lang & Co. (see prior)
304505	3 September		Greener & Co., Wear Flint Glass Works, Sunderland. Glass Makers
305840	20 September		Percival, Vickers & Co. Ltd., Manchester. Glass Makers
306459	4 October		M. J. Reynolds (see prior)
307899	23 October		Max & Jacques Guggenheim, London. Glass & China Importers
307946-8	25 October		G. V. De Luca, Hill & Co., The French Flint Glass Bottle Co., London. Manufacturer
308830	9 November		A. Ruch & Co. (see prior)
310593	10 December		Gustav G. Doring, London. Glass Bottle Manufacturer
310924/5	16 December		Scotney & Earnshaw, London. Glass Maker
311070-2	18 December		Herbert Price & Co., London. Wholesale China & Glass Merchant
311867	5 January	1898	Edward J. Shaw, Astral Works, Walsall. Lamp Manufacturer

Registration No.	Date	Year	Registered Party
312304	13 January	1898	G. V. De Luca, Hill & Co. (see prior)
314494	18 February		Percival, Vickers & Co. Ltd. (see prior)
314569	19 February		G. V. De Luca, Hill & Co. (see prior)
314989	26 February		James A. Cox, London. Glass & China Merchant
315340	4 March		John Walsh Walsh (see prior)
315841/2	15 March		Haswell J. Twiner, London. Glass & China Merchant
316068	18 March		Pilkington Brothers Ltd., Lancaster. Glass Maker
316351	23 March		The Lamp Manufacturing Co. Ltd., London. Lamp Manufacturer
316413	24 March		Burtles, Tate & Co., Poland Street Glass Works, Manchester. Glass Makers
316997	5 April		Hukin & Heath, Imperial Works, Birmingham. Silversmiths
317331	15 April		Jules Lang & Co. (see prior)
317448	18 April		Henry G. Richardson & Sons, Wordsley Flint Glass Works, Stourbridge. Glass Maker
317720	23 April		Antony Rueckl, Bienenthal, Bohemia, Austria. Glass Maker
317767	25 April		William Breffit, York. Glass Maker
318345	6 May		Henry G. Richardson & Sons (see prior)
319082	18 May		Jules Lang & Co. (see prior)
319151	19 May		Percival, Vickers & Co. Ltd. (see prior)
319400	24 May		Alfred Arculus & Co., Birmingham. Glass Maker
319604/5	27 May		James Stevens & Son
320124	10 June		G. Davidson & Co. (see prior)
320494/5	18 June		Schindler & Co. (see prior)
321093	29 June		The British & Foreign Bottle Co., London. Glass Maker
321637	7 July		G. V. De Luca, Hill & Co. (see prior)
321667	8 July		Alfred Arculus & Co. (see prior)
322001	15 July		Alfred Arculus & Co. (see prior)
322177	20 July		John Walsh Walsh (see prior)
323035	4 August		The Improved Electric Glow Lamp Co. Ltd., London. Lamp Manufacturer
323220	8 August		M. J. Reynolds (see prior)
323288/9	9 August		John Walsh Walsh (see prior)

Registration No.	Date	Year	Registered Party
323997	20 August	1898	Percival, Vickers & Co. Ltd., Manchester. Glass Makers
324169	23 August		Alfred Arculus & Co., Birmingham. Glass Maker
324870	2 September		James Green & Nephew, London. China & Glass Merchant
325071	7 September		Jules Lang & Co., London. Glass & China Merchant
325194	9 September		Greener & Co., Wear Flint Glass Works, Sunderland. Glass Maker
325497	14 September		The Improved Electric Glow Lamp Co. Ltd., London. Lamp Manufacturer
325539	15 September		Greener & Co. (see prior)
325615	16 September		Alfred Arculus & Co. (see prior)
327603	18 October		Schindler & Co., London. Glass Maker
328530/1	3 November		James Stevens & Son
328630-2	4 November		Webb, Shaw & Co. Ltd., The Dial Glass Works, Stourbridge. Glass Maker
328770-4	7 November		Laurie & Lazarus, London. Art Ware Merchant
330042	30 November		Josef R. Sohne, Dux, Bohemia. Glass Maker
330700	12 December		M. J. Reynolds, Stoke-on-Trent. Engraver
331189	19 December		Henry G. Richardson & Sons, Wordsley Flint Glass Works, Stourbridge. Glass Maker
332356-9	16 January	1899	M. J. Reynolds (see prior)
332563	21 January		Alfred Arculus & Co. (see prior)
332564/5			John Walsh Walsh, The Soho & Vesta Glass Works, Birmingham. Glass Maker
332798	25 January		Hukin & Heath, Imperial Works, Birmingham. Silversmiths
333004	28 January		Johnsen & Jorgensen, London. Commission Merchant
333324	4 February		Thomas Webb & Sons Ltd., Stourbridge. Glass Maker
333367	6 February		Johnsen & Jorgensen (see prior)
333665	13 February		G. V. De Luca, Hill & Co., The French Flint Glass Bottle Co., London. Manufacturer
333753	14 February		J. & R. Craw, London. Glass Merchant
333851/2	16 February		John Walsh Walsh (see prior)
333944	18 February		John Walsh Walsh (see prior)
334085	21 February		Weiss & Biheller, London. Importers

Registration No.	Date	Year	Registered Party
334241	23 February	1899	Johnsen & Jorgensen (see prior)
334242			Weiss & Biheller (see prior)
334596	1 March		Johnsen & Jorgensen (see prior)
334659	2 March		The York Glass Co., Ltd., York. Glass Maker
334962	9 March		Jules Lang & Co. (see prior)
334976			Weiss & Biheller (see prior)
335468	18 March		G. V. De Luca, Hill & Co. (see prior)
335478	20 March		M. J. Reynolds (see prior)
335479			Johnsen & Jorgensen (see prior)
335692	23 March		A. Ruch & Co., London. Glass Bottle Manufacturer
335854	27 March		La Societe Anonyme des Glaces de Charleroi, Roux, Belgium. Glass Makers
336112	1 April		Schindler & Co. (see prior)
336261	6 April		Burtles, Tate & Co., Poland Street Glass Works, Manchester. Glass Makers
336510	12 April		Percival, Vickers & Co. Ltd. (see prior)
336752	18 April		John Walsh Walsh (see prior)
336967/8	22 April		Jules Lang & Co. (see prior)
337349-53	28 April		Johnsen & Jorgensen (see prior)
337607/8	2 May		Jules Lang & Co. (see prior)
337930	9 May		Johnsen & Jorgensen (see prior)
338590	20 May		Molineaux, Webb & Co. Ltd., The Manchester Flint Glass Works, Manchester. Glass Makers
339015	2 June		Laurie & Lazarus (see prior)
339343	8 June		Burtles, Tate & Co. (see prior)
339350			S. Reich & Co., London. Austrian Glass Manufacturer
339402/3	9 June		Webb, Shaw & Co. Ltd., The Dial Glass Works, Stourbridge. Glass Maker
340647/8	3 July		Johnsen & Jorgensen (see prior)
340825	5 July		G. Davidson & Co., Teams Flint Glass Works, Gateshead-on-Tyne. Glass Maker
341077	10 July		The British & Foreign Bottle Co., London. Glass Maker
341684	17 July		The Crown Perfumery Co., London. Manufacturing Perfumery
342692	4 August		Laurie & Lazarus (see prior)
342852	8 August		James A. Cox, London. Glass & China Merchant
343063	11 August		Greener & Co. (see prior)

Registration No.	Date	Year	Registered Party
344484	4 September 1899		Federick (sic) E. Payton, Birmingham. Glass Merchant
345228	15 September		Thomas Shorter & Sons, London. Glass, China & Earthenware Merchant
345789	23 September		Laurie & Lazarus, London. Art Ware Merchant
346764	9 October		The Lamp Manufacturing Co. Ltd., London. Lamp Manufacturer
346841	10 October		Mappin & Webb Ltd., London. Silversmiths
347446	19 October		Henry Salsbury, London. Lamp Manufacturer
349043	11 November		G. V. De Luca, Hill & Co., The French Flint Glass Bottle Co. Ltd., London. Manufacturer
349881	27 November		M. & J. Guggenheim, London. Glass & China Importers
350115	4 December		Thomas Webb & Corbett Ltd., The White House Glass Works, Stourbridge. Glass Maker
350676	14 December		Scotney & Earnshaw, London. Merchants & Glass Manufacturers
351372	5 January	1900	Burtles, Tate & Co., Poland Street Glass Works, Manchester. Glass Makers
352198	20 January		Molineaux, Webb & Co. Ltd., The Manchester Flint Glass Works, Manchester. Glass Makers
352530	27 January		Johnsen & Jorgensen, London. Commission Merchant
353374	16 February		John Walsh Walsh, The Soho & Vesta Glass Works, Birmingham. Glass Maker
355149	24 March		F. & C. Osler, Birmingham. Glass Maker
355232	26 March		John Ford & Co., Holyrood Glass Works, Edinburgh. Manufacturer
355424	29 March		Harry Salsbury (see prior)
356046	12 April		James Green & Nephew, London. China & Glass Merchant
358727	13 June		George Sowerby Ltd., Lemington Glass Works, Newcastle in (sic) Tyne. Glass Maker
359416	27 June		Charles E. Hill, Brighton. Importer
360167	13 July		G. Davidson & Co., Teams Flint Glass Works, Gateshead-on-tyne. Glass Maker

Registration No.	Date	Year	Registered Party
360332	14 July	1900	Greener & Co., Wear Flint Glass Works, Sunderland. Glass Maker
361366	3 August		Percival, Vickers & Co. Ltd., Manchester. Glass Makers
361580	8 August		Jules Lang & Co., London. Glass & China Merchant
362212	22 August		Schindler & Co., London. Glass Maker
362643	31 August		Jules Lang & Co. (see prior)
363130	8 September		George Sowerby Ltd. (see prior)
363606-8	18 September		Jules Lang & Co. (see prior)
364576/7	10 October		The Glasgow Plate Glass Co., Glasgow. Glass Maker
366190	13 November		Schindler & Co. (see prior)
366297	14 November		Henry Salsbury (see prior)
366502	20 November		Stevens & Williams, Brierley Hill Glass Works, Stafford. Glass Makers
367054	3 December		Thomas Webb & Sons Ltd., Stourbridge. Glass Maker
367883	20 December		Weiss & Biheller, London. Importers
368149	31 December		Jules Lang & Co. (see prior)
368272/3	3 January	1901	A. Ruch & Co., London. Glass Bottle Manufacturer
368460/1	9 January		J. Grossmith Son & Co., London. Wholesale Perfumer
369254-6	28 January		Hateleys Ltd., Aston. Glass & Chandelier Manufacturer
369858	9 February		Weiss & Biheller (see prior)
370017	13 February		Alfred Arculus & Co., Birmingham. Glass Maker
370273	19 February		Alfred Arculus & Co. (see prior)
370320	20 February		Jules Lang & Co. (see prior)
370835	1 March		Weiss & Biheller (see prior)
371401	9 March		Johnsen & Jorgensen Ltd. (see prior)
371438/9	11 March		Edward J. Shaw, Astral Works, Walsall. Lamp Manufacturer
371480	12 March		The Improved Electric Glow Lamp Co. Ltd., London. Lamp Manufacturer
371553	14 March		Alfred Arculus & Co. (see prior)
371639	16 March		Alfred Arculus & Co. (see prior)
371733	19 March		Weiss & Biheller (see prior)
371885	22 March		A. Ruch & Co. (see prior)
372309	3 April		G. V. De Luca (see prior)
373032/3	20 April		Schott & Gen, Jena, Germany. Glass Maker
373598-600	3 May		S. Reich & Co., London. Glass Maker

Registration No.	Date	Year	Registered Party
373634	4 May	1901	Jules Lang & Co., London. Glass & China Merchant
374215	16 May		Weiss & Biheller, London. Importers
374792	1 June		George Sowerby Ltd., Lemington Glass Works, Newcastle-on-Tyne. Glass Maker
375464	17 June		Johnsen & Jorgensen Ltd., London. Commission Merchant
375533	18 June		Thomas Webb & Son Ltd., Stourbridge. Glass Maker
375896	25 June		John Walsh Walsh, The Soho & Vesta Glass Works, Birmingham. Glass Maker
375977	26 June		The Glasgow Plate Glass Co., Glasgow. Glass Maker
376659	9 July		Phillips's Ltd., London. Glass & China Dealers
376708	10 July		Johnsen & Jorgensen Ltd. (see prior)
377055/6	18 July		Robinson, King & Co.
377126	20 July		Wood Brothers & Co., Borough Flint Glass Works, Barnsley. Glass Maker
377322	25 July		Johnsen & Jorgensen Ltd. (see prior)
377323			Chance Brothers & Co. Ltd., Birmingham. Glass Maker
377726/7	1 August		Johnsen & Jorgensen Ltd. (see prior)
378198	14 August		Johnsen & Jorgensen Ltd. (see prior)
378648/9	23 August		John Walsh Walsh (see prior)
378765	27 August		Greener & Co., Wear Flint Glass Works, Sunderland. Glass Makers
378861	28 August		Jules Lang & Co. (see prior)
379455	9 September		Schindler & Co., London. Glass Maker
381210	8 October		Schindler & Co. (see prior)
381646/7	18 October		John Walsh Walsh (see prior)
381704/5	19 October		John Walsh Walsh (see prior)
381854-7	22 October		Weiss & Biheller (see prior)
382225	28 October		Messenger & Sons, Birmingham. Lamp & Chandelier Manufacturer
382298	29 October		Federick (sic) E. Payton, Staffordshire. Glass & China Merchant
383623	25 November		Johnsen & Jorgensen Ltd. (see prior)
384633	14 December		Schindler & Co. (see prior)
385754	15 January	1902	Johnsen & Jorgensen Ltd. (see prior)
385793	16 January		Johnsen & Jorgensen Ltd. (see prior)

Registration No.	Date	Year	Registered Party
385795-8	16 January	1902	Chance Brothers & Co. Ltd. (see prior)
386121/2	23 January		John Walsh Walsh (see prior)
386174	24 January		Phillips's Ltd. (see prior)
386488	30 January		John Walsh Walsh (see prior)
386616/7	3 February		Burtles, Tate & Co., Poland Street Glass Works, Manchester. Glass Makers
387680	24 February		James G. James, London. Glass Letter Manufacturer
387780	26 February		James Hateley & Co., Birmingham. Flint Glass Manufacturer
388142	5 March		Johnsen & Jorgensen Ltd. (see prior)
388143			Mortlocks Ltd., London. Glass & China Merchant
388197	6 March		Greener & Co. (see prior)
388595	15 March		Molineaux, Webb & Co. Ltd., The Manchester Flint Glass Works, Manchester. Glass Makers
388857	20 March		Burtles, Tate & Co. (see prior)
389019	24 March		Thomas Dukes, Stourbridge. Glass Maker
389876	17 April		G. V. De Luca, London. Merchant
390019	22 April		Percival, Vickers & Co. Ltd., Manchester. Glass Makers
390020/1			Thomas Dukes (see prior)
391285	21 May		Molineaux, Webb & Co. Ltd. (see prior)
391513	27 May		Johnsen & Jorgensen Ltd. (see prior)
391761	2 June		Schott & Gen., Jena, Germany. Glass Maker
391814	3 June		Burtles, Tate & Co. (see prior)
392571	17 June		G. V. De Luca (see prior)
393177/8	2 July		Falk, Stadelmann & Co. Ltd.
393328	4 July		Federick (sic) E. Payton (see prior)
394152	21 July		The Union Plate Glass Co. Ltd.
394747/8	1 August		Schott & Gen. (see prior)
394758	1 August		Jonas Lang & Co., London. Glass Merchant
396001/2	26 August		Falk, Stadelmann & Co. Ltd.
396074	27 August		T. (sic) Reich & Co. London. Glass Maker
397605	19 September		Johnsen & Jorgensen Ltd. (see prior)
398503	7 October		John Walsh Walsh (see prior)
399983	31 October		George Farmiloe & Sons Ltd., London. Lead & Glass Merchant

Registration No.	Date	Year	Registered Party
400075	3 November	1902	M. J. Reynolds, Stoke-on-Trent. Engraver
400564	11 November		M. & J. Guggenheim, London. Glass & China Importers
401196	25 November		Weiss & Biheller, London. Importers
401278-80	26 November		Oesterreichische Glaskutten-Geselkschaft, Austria. Glass Maker
402635/6	23 December		Johnsen & Jorgensen Ltd. London. Commission Merchant
402712/3	24 December		Falk, Stadelmann & Co. Ltd.
403012	3 January	1903	John Walsh Walsh, The Soho & Vesta Glass Works, Birmingham. Glass Maker
403015			Weiss & Biheller (see prior)
403028	5 January		Thomas Webb & Sons Ltd., Stourbridge. Glass Maker
403073	6 January		Weiss & Biheller (see prior)
403075			Weiss & Biheller (see prior)
403657	17 January		Burtles, Tate & Co., Poland Street Glass Works, Manchester. Glass Makers
404248	29 January		Jules Lang & Co., London. Glass & China Merchant
404514	4 February		Guiseppe V. De Luca, The French Flint Glass Bottle Co., London. Glass Maker
404676	6 February		Schindler & Co., London. Glass Maker
404678			Wood Brothers & Co., Borough Flint Glass Works, Barnsley. Glass Maker
404686			Johnsen & Jorgensen Ltd. (see prior)
405034-6	11 February		Liberty & Co. Ltd., London. Merchant
405100-3	12 February		The Societe Anonyme des Manufactures des Glaces et Produits Chimiques de St. Gobain, Paris. Manufacturer
405139	13 February		William Dow, Aberdeen. Glass Merchant
405727	25 February		Sir Hiram Maxim Electrical & Engineering Co. Ltd., London. Manufacturers of Electrical Lamps
406300	5 March		Burtles, Tate & Co. (see prior)
407269	23 March		Sir Hiram Maxim Electrical & Engineering Co. Ltd. (see prior)
407375	25 March		Jules Lang & Co. (see prior)
407480	27 March		Sir Hiram Maxim Electrical & Engineering Co. Ltd. (see prior)
408211	8 April		Richard F. Isherwood, Manchester. Glass Maker
408379	11 April	1903	Jules Lang & Co. (see prior)
408782-6	21 April		S. Reich & Co., London. Glass Maker
409057	27 April		A. Riess & Co., London. Importers of Foreign Glass & China
409145	28 April		S. Reich & Co. (see prior)
409508-13	5 May		S. Reich & Co. (see prior)
409768	9 May		Stevens & Williams, Brierley Hill Glass Works, Stafford. Glass Makers
409769			John Walsh Walsh (see prior)
409876	12 May		William Ritchie, Glasgow. Glass Merchant
410290-8	19 May		S. Reich & Co. (see prior)
410468	21 May		Federick (sic) E. Payton, Handsworth. Glass & China Merchant
410529	22 May		Stafford Hill, The Eclipse Glass Works, London. Glass Bottle Manufacturer
411103	3 June		The British & Foreign Bottle Co., London. Glass Maker
411733-41	16 June		William Ritchie (see prior)
413200	7 July		J. Harrison & Co., Stafford. Glass Merchant
413692	14 July		The Glasgow Plate Glass Co., Glasgow. Glass Maker
413701			G. Davidson & Co., Teams Flint Glass Works, Gateshead-on-Tyne. Glass Maker
414327	23 July		Weiss & Biheller (see prior)
414362-67	24 July		Schott & Gen, Jena, Germany. Glass Maker
414496	27 July		S. Reich & Co. (see prior)
415219	10 August		The British & Foreign Bottle Co. (see prior)
415221			Johnsen & Jorgensen Ltd. (see prior)
415661	18 August		John Southerst, Manchester. Glass Maker
415705-7	19 August		Johnsen & Jorgensen Ltd. (see prior)
415804	20 August		William A. Bailey, London. Potter & Glass Manufacturer
415969	24 August		William Ritchie (see prior)
416126/7	26 August		Johnsen & Jorgensen Ltd. (see prior)
416157-67	27 August		William Ritchie (see prior)
416239	28 August		Chance Brothers & Co. Ltd., Birmingham. Glass Maker
416507/8	3 September		Chance Brothers & Co. (see prior)
416512-9			S. Reich & Co. (see prior)
416529	4 September		Schindler & Co. (see prior)
417253	11 September		The Eclipse Glass Works Ltd. (see prior)

Registration No.	Date	Year	Registered Party
417598/9	19 September	1903	Johnsen & Jorgensen Ltd., London. Commission Merchant
417965	25 September		John Walsh Walsh, The Soho & Vesta Glass Works, Birmingham. Glass Maker
418052	28 September		John Southerst, Flint Glass Bottle Works, Manchester. Bottle Manufacturer
419077	8 October		Johnsen & Jorgensen Ltd. (see prior)
419358	13 October		James Green & Nephew, London. China & Glass Merchant
419488	15 October		The British & Foreign Bottle Co., London. Glass Maker
420155-60	27 October		Matthew Tytler & Sons, Greenock. Glass Makers
421474	14 November		The French Flint Glass Bottle Co. Ltd., London. Manufacturer
421546	17 November		The French Flint Glass Bottle Co. Ltd. (see prior)
422146/7	25 November		The British & Foreign Bottle Co. (see prior)
423257/8	14 December		Johnsen & Jorgensen Ltd. (see prior)
423313	15 December		Jules Lang & Co., London. Glass & China Merchant
423693-9	23 December		S. Reich & Co., London. Glass Maker
424157/8	4 January	1904	Weiss & Biheller, London. Importers
424198-201	5 January		S. Reich & Co. (see prior)
424247	6 January		Jules Lang & Co. (see prior)
424618	13 January		Jules Lang & Co. (see prior)
424756/7	15 January		Messenger & Sons, Birmingham. Lamp & Chandelier Manufacturer
425609	29 January		S. Reich & Co. (see prior)
426067	5 February		A. Ruch & Co., London. Glass Bottle Manufacturer
426322	9 February		Jules Lang & Co. (see prior)
426846-8	17 February		Jules Lang & Co. (see prior)
427017	19 February		Schindler & Co., London. Glass Maker
427029-33	19 February		Weiss & Biheller (see prior)
427524	25 February		Burtles, Tate & Co., Poland Street Glass Works, Manchester. Glass Makers
427847	1 March		M. J. Reynolds, Stoke-on-Trent. Engraver
427894	2 March		Schindler & Co. (see prior)
427905			Weiss & Biheller (see prior)
427995	3 March		William A. Bailey, London. Potter & Glass Manufacturer
428875	16 March		William A. Bailey (see prior)
429277/8	22 March		Schindler & Co. (see prior)
429743	29 March	1904	J. Grossmith, Son & Co., London. Perfumer
430325	12 April		Harry Peck & Co., London. Manufacturer
430630	16 April		Johnsen & Jorgensen Ltd. (see prior)
430944	21 April		Pilkington Brothers Ltd., Lancaster. Glass Maker
431162-4	25 April		Johnsen & Jorgensen Ltd. (see prior)
431293-6	27 April		Johnsen & Jorgensen Ltd. (see prior)
431365	28 April		The British & Foreign Bottle Co. (see prior)
431862	6 May		Jules Lang & Co. (see prior)
431924	7 May		John Southerst (see prior)
432256	12 May		Johnsen & Jorgensen Ltd. (see prior)
432431	14 May		Salsbury & Son Ltd., London. Lamp Manufacturer
432703	17 May		Chance Brothers & Co. Ltd., Birmingham. Glass Maker
432755	18 May		Jules Lang & Co. (see prior)
433624	31 May		Jules Lang & Son (see prior)
433625			William Ritchie, Glasgow. Glass Merchant
433867	2 June		Frederick Payton, Birmingham. Glass Dealer
434662-70	15 June		William Ritchie (see prior)
435141	22 June		Jules Lang & Son (see prior)
435651/2	28 June		John Walsh Walsh (see prior)
435959	1 July		John Walsh Walsh (see prior)
435962			Johnsen & Jorgensen Ltd. (see prior)
436260	5 July		Chance Brothers & Co. Ltd. (see prior)
436719	11 July		Salsbury & Son Ltd. (see prior)
436804	12 July		G. Davidson & Co., Teams Flint Glass Works, Gateshead-on-Tyne. Glass Maker
436862/3	13 July		John Walsh Walsh (see prior)
436876			The Improved Electric Glow Lamp Co. Ltd., London. Manufacturer
436943	14 July		Jules Lang & Son (see prior)
437164	18 July		Schott & Gen., Jena, Germany. Glass Maker
437349/50	21 July		Alfred Arculus & Co., Birmingham. Glass Maker
437570	23 July		Jules Lang & Son (see prior)
437601	25 July		Jules Lang & Son (see prior)
437654	26 July		Breidenbach & Co., London. Manufacturing Perfumer
438209	4 August		Harry Peck & Co., London. Manufacturer

Registration No.	Date	Year	Registered Party
438542	9 August	1904	R. Wittmann, London. China & Glass Manufacturer
438787	12 August		Johnsen & Jorgensen Ltd., London. Commission Merchant
439007	17 August		Glashutte Vormals Gebruder Siegwart and Cie Actien Gesellschaft, Rheinland, Germany. Glass Manufacturer
439199	19 August		Johnsen & Jorgensen Ltd. (see prior)
439537	24 August		Falk, Stadelmann & Co. Ltd.
439965	29 August		Jules Lang & Son, London. Glass Merchant & Bottle Manufacturer
440645-51	7 September		S. Reich & Co., London. Glass Maker
440767	9 September		John Walsh Walsh, The Soho & Vesta Glass Works, Birmingham. Glass Maker
441530	17 September		Schindler & Co., London. Glass Maker
441666	20 September		John Walsh Walsh (see prior)
441788-92	22 September		Jules Lang & Son (see prior)
441804/5			Johnsen & Jorgensen Ltd. (see prior)
442961	8 October		Jules Lang & Son (see prior)
443151	12 October		Thomas Webb & Corbett Ltd., White House Glass Works, Wordsley. Glass Maker
444212	29 October		S. Reich & Co. (see prior)
444370	1 November		The Eclipse Glass Works Ltd., London. Glass Bottle Manufacturer
444417	2 November		Jules Lang & Son (see prior)
444419/20			Alfred Arculus & Co., Birmingham. Glass Maker
444601-3	5 November		S. Reich & Co. (see prior)
444604			G. Davidson & Co., Teams Flint Glass Works, Gateshead-on-Tyne. Glass Maker
444605			Johnsen & Jorgensen Ltd. (see prior)
444681	7 November		William A. Bailey, London. Potter & Glass Manufacturer
444744	8 November		Alfred Arculus & Co. (see prior)
445181	16 November		Falk, Stadelmann & Co. Ltd.
445653	24 November		Jules Lang & Son (see prior)
446067	2 December		Jules Lang & Son (see prior)
446079-81			Falk, Stadelmann & Co. Ltd.
446594	12 December		M. & J. Guggenheim, London. Glass & China Importers
446747	14 December		The French Flint Glass Bottle Co. Ltd., London. Manufacturer

Registration No.	Date	Year	Registered Party
446924	17 December	1904	Weiss & Biheller, London. Importers
447006	20 December		John Walsh Walsh (see prior)
447316	27 December		Chance Brothers & Co. Ltd., Birmingham. Glass Makers
447543-5	31 December		S. Reich & Co. (see prior)
447615/6	3 January	1905	M. & J. Guggenheim (see prior)
448090	12 January		Alfred Arculus & Co. (see prior)
448364/5	16 January		Johnsen & Jorgensen Ltd. (see prior)
448986	26 January		Chance Brothers & Co. Ltd. (see prior)
449885	8 February		The French Flint Glass Bottle Co. Ltd. (see prior)
449988	9 February		The French Flint Glass Bottle Co. Ltd. (see prior)
450630/1	21 February		Schindler & Co. (see prior)
450823	23 February		John Walsh Walsh (see prior)
450838-42			Johnsen & Jorgensen Ltd. (see prior)
451273	1 March		William A. Bailey (see prior)
451544	4 March		Hukin & Heath, Imperial Works, Birmingham. Silversmiths
452043	11 March		Johnsen & Jorgensen Ltd. (see prior)
452189	14 March		Jules Lang & Son (see prior)
452425	16 March		Richard Wittmann (see prior)
452954	23 March		Weiss & Biheller (see prior)
453077/8	24 March		Falk, Stadelmann & Co. Ltd.
453483	31 March		Hukin & Heath (see prior)
454322/3	12 April		S. Reich & Co. (see prior)
454444/5	13 April		Messenger & Son, Birmingham. Lamp & Chandelier Manufacturer
454455/6			William A. Bailey (see prior)
455225	27 April		Schindler & Co. (see prior)
455497/8	2 May		S. Reich & Co. (see prior)
456270	13 May		Thomas G. Webb, Manchester. Glass Maker
456577	18 May		Hukin & Heath (see prior)
456828	22 May		Henry G. Richardson & Son, Wordsley Flint Glass Works. Stourbridge. Glass Maker
457361	26 May		Jules Lang & Son (see prior)
457832	1 June		Jules Lang & Son (see prior)
458014	3 June		The French Flint Glass Bottle Co. Ltd. (see prior)
458218	6 June		Weiss & Biheller (see prior)
458344	8 June		John Walsh Walsh (see prior)
458346			Herbert Price & Co., London. China & Glass Merchant
458785	17 June		William A. Bailey (see prior)
458983	21 June		S. Reich & Co. (see prior)

Registration No.	Date	Year	Registered Party
459027	22 June	1905	Samuel Keeling, Falcon Glass Works, Hanley. Glass Merchant
460510	14 July		Schindler & Co., London. Glass Maker
460944	19 July		The Eclipse Glass Works Ltd., London. Glass Bottle Manufacturer
460949/50			William A. Bailey, London. Potter & Glass Manufacturer
460989	20 July		Jules Lang & Son, London. Glass Merchant & Bottle Manufacturer
462109/10	4 August		S. Reich & Co., London. Glass Maker
462690	16 August		F. W. Neuburger & Co., London. China & Glass Merchant
464073	2 September		James Hateley, Birmingham. Flint Glass Manufacturer
464621	11 September		G. Davidson & Co., Teams Flint Glass Works, Gateshead-on-Tyne. Glass Maker
464696	12 September		John Walsh Walsh, The Soho & Vesta Glass Works, Birmingham. Glass Maker
465540	22 September		Johnsen & Jorgensen Ltd., London. Commission Merchant
465660	23 September		William A. Bailey (see prior)
465892	26 September		Greener & Co., Wear Flint Glass Works, Sunderland. Glass Makers
466431	4 October		Schindler & Co. (see prior)
466544	5 October		Johnsen & Jorgensen Ltd. (see prior)
468077	30 October		Fred Day, Barnsley. Glass Blower
468590-2	8 November		Johnsen & Jorgensen Ltd. (see prior)
468873	11 November		Jules Lang & Son (see prior)
469519/20	22 November		Johnsen & Jorgensen Ltd. (see prior)
470127	1 December		Jules Lang & Son (see prior)
470262	4 December		Pilkington Brothers Ltd., Lancaster. Glass Maker
471692	4 January	1906	Johnsen & Jorgensen Ltd. (see prior)
471761-70	5 January		S. Reich & Co. (see prior)
472064-76	11 January		S. Reich & Co. (see prior)
472207	13 January		Jules Lang & Son (see prior)
472301	16 January		Johnsen & Jorgensen Ltd. (see prior)
472480	19 January		Falk, Stadelmann & Co. Ltd.
472625	22 January		Reynolds & Sons, Stoke-on-Trent. Engravers
473273	31 January		William A. Bailey (see prior)

Registration No.	Date	Year	Registered Party
473435	2 February	1906	Hukin & Heath, Imperial Works, Birmingham. Silversmiths
473554	6 February		Johnsen & Jorgensen Ltd. (see prior)
474109/10	16 February		Jules Lang & Son (see prior)
474238	19 February		James Green & Nephew, London. China & Glass Merchant
474329	20 February		Burtles, Tate & Co., Poland Street Glass Works, Manchester. Glass Makers
474330			John Walsh Walsh (see prior)
474924	28 February		Falk, Stadelmann & Co. Ltd.
475286	7 March		Burtles, Tate & Co. (see prior)
475366	8 March		Johnsen & Jorgensen Ltd. (see prior)
475648	14 March		Frederick C. Payton, Birmingham. Glass Merchant
476078	21 March		John Walsh Walsh (see prior)
476270	24 March		Jules Lang & Son (see prior)
476366	27 March		Weiss & Biheller, London. Importers
476448	29 March		Henry Mayer & Co., London. Glass & China Importers
476516	30 March		Henry Richardson & Sons, Wordsley Flint Glass Works, Stourbridge. Glass Maker
476881	4 April		The French Flint Glass Bottle Co. Ltd., London. Manufacturer
476986	5 April		Clarke's Pyramid and Fairy Light Co. Ltd., London. Manufacturer
477092	6 April		William Ault, Derby. Manufacturer
478191/2	1 May		S. Reich & Co. (see prior)
478834	9 May		Thomas Goode & Co., London. Glass & China Merchant
478903	10 May		Jules Lang & Son (see prior)
479162	12 May		Jules Lang & Son (see prior)
479368	17 May		Jules Lang & Son (see prior)
479730	23 May		William Ault (see prior)
480105/6	30 May		Ingram & Kemp Ltd., London Works, Birmingham. Chandelier Manufacturer
480125			Clarke's Pyramid & Fairy Light Co. Ltd. (see prior)
480885	18 June		Samuel Eaton & Sons, Birmingham. Chandelier Manufacturer
481519-22	27 June		Liberty & Co. Ltd., London. Merchant
483573	23 July		Schindler & Co. (see prior)
483793	26 July		Johnsen & Jorgensen Ltd. (see prior)

Registration No.	Date	Year	Registered Party
484799	11 August	1906	John Walsh Walsh, The Soho & Vesta Glass Works, Birmingham. Glass Maker
484918	14 August		Jules Lang & Son, London. Glass Merchant & Bottle Manufacturer
486003	28 August		Jules Lang & Son (see prior)
486198	31 August		Schindler & Co., London. Glass Maker
486298	1 September		George Davidson & Co., Teams Flint Glass Works, Gateshead-on-Tyne. Glass Maker
486381	4 September		John Walsh Walsh (see prior)
486685	8 September		Stuart & Sons, Stourbridge. Glass Maker
486706	10 September		Schindler & Co. (see prior)
486969	13 September		John Walsh Walsh (see prior)
487200	15 September		Schindler & Co. (see prior)
487788	25 September		John Walsh Walsh (see prior)
487789			Schindler & Co. (see prior)
488023	27 September		Jules Lang & Son (see prior)
488368	2 October		Jules Lang & Son (see prior)
488888	8 October		C. & E. Bougard, Manage, Belgium. Glass Maker
489099/100	10 October		The London Sand Blast Decorative Glass Works Ltd., London. Manufacturer of Decorative Glass
489326	15 October		S. Reich & Co., London. Glass Maker
489719	22 October		Schott & Gen., Jena, Germany. Glass Maker
489850	23 October		The British & Foreign Bottle Co., London. Glass Maker
489854			Weiss & Biheller, London. Importers
489947	24 October		Schott & Gen. (see prior)
491329	15 November		Johnsen & Jorgensen Ltd., London. Commission Merchant
491837	23 November		United States Glass Co., London. Glass Maker
492244	30 November		John Walsh Walsh (see prior)
492468-70	6 December		Max Kray & Co., London. Manufacturer
492726-8	11 December		Weiss & Biheller (see prior)
493080	18 December		Thomas Webb & Corbett Ltd., The White House Glass Works, Stourbridge. Glass Maker
493237/8	21 December		F. W. Neuburger & Co., London. China & Glass Merchant
493373	28 December		Jules Lang & Son (see prior)
493475	31 December		Thomas Webb & Corbett Ltd. (see prior)
493485/6	31 December	1906	Falk, Stadelmann & Co. Ltd.
493532	2 January	1907	John Walsh Walsh (see prior)
493686	5 January		Max Kray & Co. (see prior)
493785	8 January		A. Ruch & Co., London. Glass Bottle Manufacturer
494747	24 January		M. & J. Guggenheim, London. Glass & China Importers
495273	1 February		Falk, Stadelmann & Co. Ltd.
495408/9	5 February		Schindler & Co. (see prior)
495682	8 February		Falk, Stadelmann & Co. Ltd.
496110	14 February		Schindler & Co. (see prior)
496449	19 February		Gustav Boehm, London. Perfumery Manufacturer
496583/4	21 February		Johnsen & Jorgensen Ltd. (see prior)
497306-11	4 March		S. Reich & Co. (see prior)
497354	5 March		Herbert Mew, Isle of Wight. China & Glass Merchant
497532	7 March		Johnsen & Jorgensen Ltd. (see prior)
497724	11 March		Jules Lang & Son (see prior)
497726			A. Ruch & Co. (see prior)
497872	13 March		Jules Lang & Son (see prior)
498162	15 March		Weiss & Biheller (see prior)
498958	26 March		Jules Lang & Son (see prior)
499022	27 March		Johnsen & Jorgensen Ltd. (see prior)
499334	4 April		Johnsen & Jorgensen Ltd. (see prior)
499445	5 April		Mabel Priem, London. Glass Merchant
499974	15 April		Schindler & Co. (see prior)
500502	20 April		John Walsh Walsh (see prior)
500650	23 April		Schindler & Co. (see prior)
501603	8 May		Schindler & Co. (see prior)
501821/2	11 May		Burtles, Tate & Co., Poland Street Glass Works, Manchester. Glass Makers
502044	15 May		Burtles, Tate & Co. (see prior)
502904/5	22 May		Weiss & Biheller (see prior)
504941/2	19 June		Weiss & Biheller (see prior)
505105-7	21 June		S. Reich & Co. (see prior)
505499	26 June		Johnsen & Jorgensen Ltd. (see prior)
505767	29 June		Johnsen & Jorgensen Ltd. (see prior)
506632/3	10 July		John Walsh Walsh (see prior)
506634			The Army & Navy Cooperative Society Ltd., London. Manufacturer
506873	12 July		Constantin Kopp, Settenz, Bohemia. Glass Maker
507206	15 July		The French Flint Glass Bottle Co. Ltd., London. Manufacturer
507457	19 July		S. Reich & Co. (see prior)

Registration No.	Date	Year	Registered Party
507678	22 July	1907	Schindler & Co., London. Glass Maker
508970	9 August		Schindler & Co. (see prior)
509943	23 August		Weiss & Biheller, London. Importers
510076/7	26 August		The French Flint Glass Bottle Co. Ltd., London. Manufacturer
510395	28 August		Schindler & Co. (see prior)
510403			Guiseppe V. De Luca, Bromley, Kent. Merchant
510504	29 August		Burtles, Tate & Co., Poland Street Glass Works, Manchester. Glass Makers
510978/9	6 September		Thomas Webb & Corbett Ltd., The White House Glass Works, Stourbridge. Glass Maker
511318	11 September		John Walsh Walsh, The Soho & Vesta Glass Works, Birmingham. Glass Maker
511401	12 September		Jules Lang & Son, London. Glass Merchant & Bottle Manufacturer
511845	17 September		John Walsh Walsh (see prior)
511929	18 September		George F. Webb, Manchester. Glass Maker
512195	21 September		Jules Lang & Son (see prior)
512560	25 September		George Davidson & Co., Teams Flint Glass Works, Gateshead-on-Tyne. Glass Maker
512874	1 October		S. Mordan & Co. Ltd., London. Manufacturer
513163	4 October		Thomas Webb & Corbett Ltd. (see prior)
513236	5 October		Pilkington Brothers Ltd., Lancaster. Glass Maker
513721	12 October		Henry G. Richardson & Sons, Wordsley Flint Glass Works, Stourbridge. Glass Maker

Registration No.	Date	Year	Registered Party
514062	18 October	1907	S. Reich & Co., London. Glass Maker
514133	19 October		James Green & Nephew, London. China & Glass Merchant
514597	28 October		Weiss & Biheller (see prior)
514650	29 October		Schindler & Co. (see prior)
514681			Georges Lemiere, London. Glass Blower
514796	31 October		Greener & Co., Wear Flint Glass Works, Sunderland. Glass Makers
514848	1 November		George Davidson & Co. (see prior)
516674	28 November		William A. Bailey, London. Glass Manufacturer
517385	10 December		Henry Hunt, Manchester. Glass Maker
517677	16 December		Jules Lang & Son (see prior)
517826	18 December		Falk, Stadelmann & Co. Ltd.
518541	3 January	1908	Weiss & Biheller (see prior)
518739	10 January		Falk, Stadelmann & Co. Ltd.
518867	15 January		Falk, Stadelmann & Co. Ltd.
518913	16 January		John Walsh Walsh (see prior)
519017	20 January		Schindler & Co. (see prior)
519087	21 January		Weiss & Biheller (see prior)
519330	28 January		Weiss & Biheller (see prior)
519389	30 January		Weiss & Biheller (see prior)
519900/1	7 February		Weiss & Biheller (see prior)
519902			The British & Foreign Bottle Co., London. Glass Makers
520168	13 February		The British & Foreign Bottle Co. (see prior)
520225	14 February		John Walsh Walsh (see prior)
520386/7	18 February		S. Reich & Co. (see prior)
520598	24 February		Jules Lang & Son (see prior)
520674	25 February		George Davidson & Co. (see prior)
520878	28 February		Weiss & Biheller (see prior)

Supplement

Foreword

For the past ten years and more, the interest in Pressed Glass has increased enormously and prices of the glass have gone up in conjunction with the interest.

The pioneer work of Dr Colin Lattimore in his book "English 19th Century Press Moulded Glass", published in 1979 by Barrie & Jenkins, was of immeasurable value and started us off on a treasure hunt of knowledge.

We owe the discovery that the Sowerby Nursery Rhyme pieces were taken from designs by Walter Crane to Mrs. Barbara Morris in a lecture to the Glass Circle, published in the Circle's Newsletter, and further discoveries since then have been written about in other books and journals.

There is still much more to be discovered on this fascinating subject and I am sure it will be in the future. Meantime, I hope this supplement will add a bit more interest for Collectors.

Jenny Thompson

Acknowledgements

I owe many thanks to the Ceramics Department under Dr. Oliver Watson of the Victoria and Albert museum for all their continued help and good will.

I acknowledge the custody of the Design Registers and the Representations by the Public Records Office and thank them most gratefully as before for permission to publish these lists.

Equally I would like to thank all those who have given their time and expertise to make my knowledge of English glass sounder and, I hope, better.

My references are mainly from the Design Registrations and Representations themselves for this supplement.

Reference Books:

1) *British Glass 1800-1914*. Charles R. Hajdamach

2) *English Pressed Glass*. Raymond Slack.

3) *Sowerby Gateshead Glass*. Simon Cottle.

4) *Victorian Table Glass & Ornaments*. Barbara Morris.

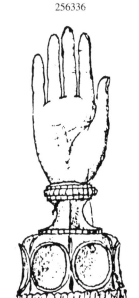

256336

3 October 1871

Class 3 Ornamental (Glass)
Design for a Chimney Piece Ornament
by Messrs. Burtles, Tate & Co.,
Poland Street, Manchester

120808

4 March 1889

Design for Flower Vase
by Burtles, Tate & Co.,
Poland Street, Manchester.

Introduction

This supplement contains additional drawings from the Design Registrations for the Glass Houses shown in *"The Identification of English Pressed Glass"* (ISBN 0 9515491 0 3).

There are several new names included such as Matthew Turnbull for the firm's long standing importance in the North East and the variety of the pressed glass items. Matthew Turnbull first registered a design in 1879 and although there were not many registrations the firm continued well into the twentieth century and survived longer than many of the other glass works.

Pressed glass is most often associated with the North East and Manchester areas; however, there were other firms making pressed glass in different parts of the country. The glass works of Joseph Webb were situated at Coalbourn Hill, Stourbridge. His early registrations, along with some of the drawings, are included along with a flower trough of December 19th 1872, registered by Jane Webb and Joseph Hammond trading as "The Executors of the late Joseph Webb". It is similar to an Edward Bolton flower trough of a much later date and it is included to show that pressed glass designs, regardless of area, followed certain trends. Thus many of the flower troughs and boats are similar and, without a registration, it would be hazardous to guess a maker. The Dolphin motif was popular in the 1870s and 1880s, as can be seen in the Dolphin series of J. J. and T. Derbyshire and W. H. Heppell. Even a stylish, distinctive sauce bottle registered as early as 1865 by Crosse & Blackwell, and probably for Anchovy Sauce, is a work of art, complete with scales and large fishy eye and a stance similar to the Heppell jug of 1882 in outline.

Pressed glass imitating cut class reached its heyday in the 1880s to 1890s, followed by the swirling curves of Art Nouveau by the beginning of the twentieth century. All the firms produced similar shapes and patterns, although some are so well known by now that they are instantly recognisable.

From the Collectors' point of view, the most original pressed glass must be that of Sowerby followed by Davidson's Pearline. Sowerby's glass is distinctive not only for the variety of design and colour but also for the shape of many of the handles and feet, some of which are set so angularly that they almost might have been influenced by the designs of Christopher Dresser.

There is still so much to learn and discover!

The charm of Sowerby lies in the many aesthetic pieces, the wonderful ivory Queen's Ware, together with the Nursery Rhyme additions from the designs of Walter Crane. Their versatility was an art in itself and now is deservedly recognised. The paperweights of John Derbyshire fall into this category too, as they are distinguished, handsome pieces and are of good quality in many different colours.

Most of the firms produced a variety of flower troughs and vases. As well as there being an immense number in pressed glass there were also a great many items registered by other firms in Fancy Glass. The registrations of John Walsh Walsh show such ingenuity of design that they have been included along with the registrations of the following, which must be of importance and interest to all collectors of Victorian Glass.

1)   Stuart & Sons.

2)   Boulton & Mills.

3)   W. H., B. and J. Richardson.
      Hodgetts, Richardson & Pargeter.
      H. G. Richardson.

4)   Thomas Webb & Sons.

G. Davidson & Co.
James Derbyshire & Brother

217752

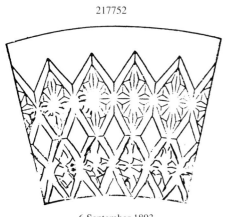

6 September 1893
G. Davidson & Co., Teams Flint Glass Works,
Gateshead-on-Tyne
(Imitation cut)

224171

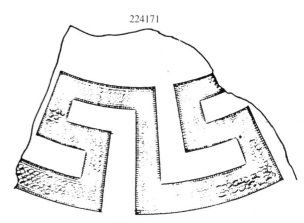

19 December 1893
G. Davidson & Co., Teams Flint Glass Works,
Gateshead-on-Tyne
(Pattern of dots with a form
similar to Greek key pattern)

180699

2 November 1864
James Derbyshire & Brother, Hulme, Manchester
Design for a Glass Butter Cooler

228612

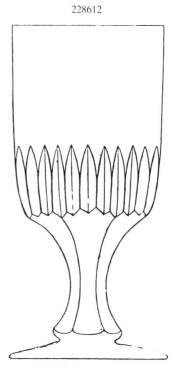

13 April 1869
James Derbyshire & Brother, Hulme, Manchester
Goblet

J. J. & T. Derbyshire

267727

268739

193264

6 November 1872
J. J. & T. Derbyshire, Hulme, Manchester
Roman Vase

11 December 1872
J. J. & T. Derbyshire,
Hulme, Manchester
Ornamental Design
for a Dolphin
Comport
(above side
elevation;
right stand;
below front view
of dish)

6 December 1865
Crosse & Blackwell, Soho Square
Sauce Bottle

J. J. & T. Derbyshire

268810

OVAL DISH

ROUND DISH

SUGAR

CREAM

BISCUIT BOX

BUTTER DISH & COVER

COMPORT

DRAWN HALF SIZE

FLOWER VASE & CELERY

FRONT VIEW OF BUTTER DISH

14 December 1872
J. J. & T. Derbyshire, Hulme, Manchester
Design for Breakfast Set

Greener & Co.

250723

2 March 1871
Henry Greener, The Wear Flint Glass Works, Sunderland
Glass Plate

150401

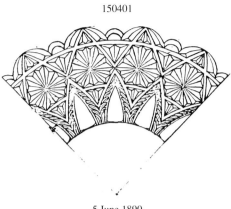

5 June 1890
Greener & Co., Sunderland
(Pattern imitation cut mostly)

258156

15 July 1895
Greener & Co., Sunderland
(Imitation cut with star pattern and lines
forming diamonds)

103434

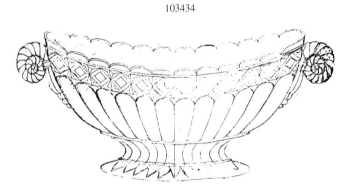

11 July 1888
Greener & Co., Sunderland
Dish

262018

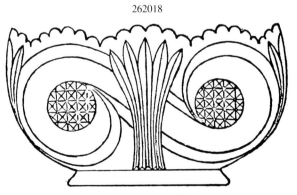

16 September 1895
Greener & Co., Sunderland
(Imitation difficult cut)

Molineaux, Webb & Co.

191555

31 October 1865
Molineaux, Webb & Co., Manchester
Glass Dish

215734

13 January 1868
Molineaux, Webb & Co., Manchester
Comport or elevated dish

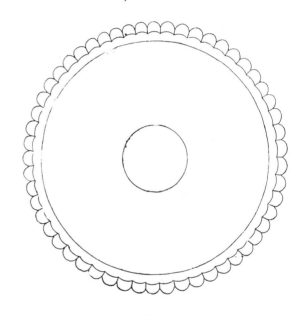

216348

31 January 1868
Molineaux, Webb & Co., Manchester
Comport or elevated dish

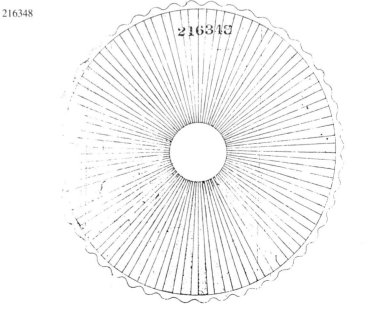

Molineaux, Webb & Co.

242968

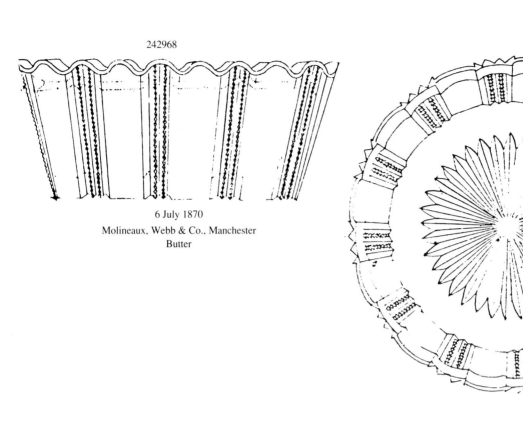

6 July 1870
Molineaux, Webb & Co., Manchester
Butter

247463

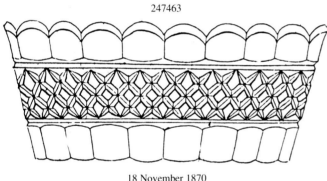

18 November 1870
Molineaux, Webb & Co., Manchester
Butter

249600

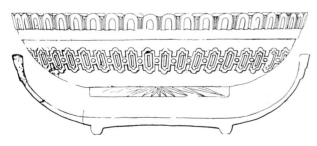

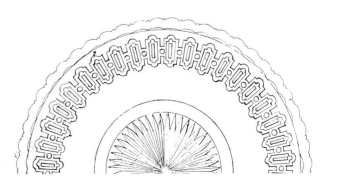

17 January 1871
Molineaux, Webb & Co., Manchester
Dish

Molineaux, Webb & Co.
Edward Moore & Co.
Sowerby & Co.

316862

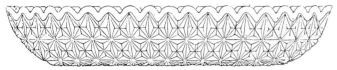

6 December 1877
Molineaux, Webb & Co., Manchester
Dish

92045

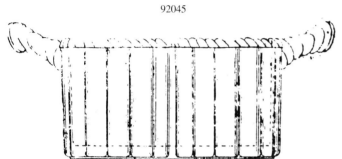

23 January 1888
Edward Moore & Co.,
Tyne Flint Glass Works, South Shields
Shape (imitation cut quatrefoil shape. Twisted handles)

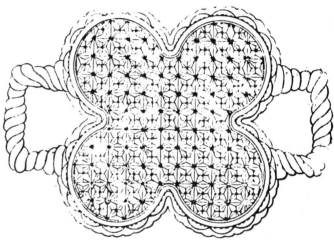

260184

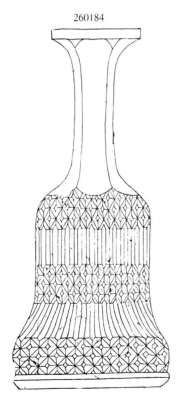

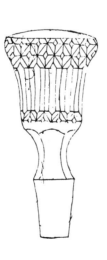

2 February 1872
Sowerby & Co.,
Ellison Glass Works,
Gateshead-on-Tyne
Decanter

2 February 1872
Sowerby & Co.,
Ellison Glass Works,
Gateshead-on-Tyne
Decanter

260185

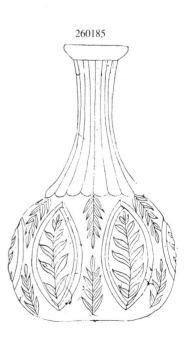

Sowerby & Co.

260405

12 February 1872
Sowerby & Co., Ellison Glass Works, Gateshead-on-Tyne
(Sugar)

260802

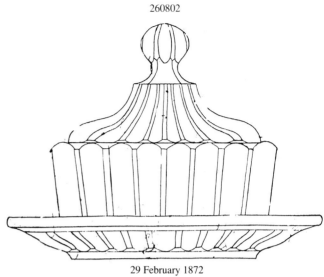

29 February 1872
Sowerby & Co., Ellison Glass Works, Gateshead-on-Tyne
(Covered Butter)

299051

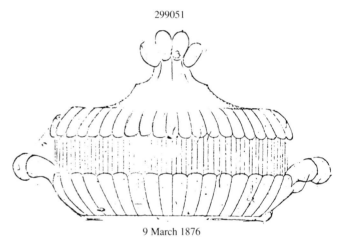

9 March 1876
Sowerby & Co., Ellison Glass Works, Gateshead-on-Tyne
Covered Dish

298872

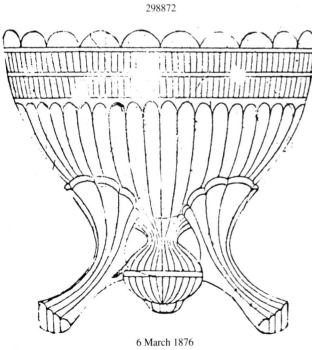

6 March 1876
Sowerby & Co., Ellison Glass Works,
Gateshead-on-Tyne (Sugar)

308714

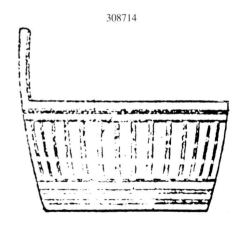

22 March 1877
Sowerby & Co., Ellison Glass Works,
Gateshead-on-Tyne (Trinket Dish)

Sowerby & Co.

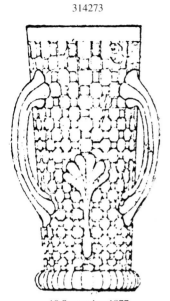

314273

18 September 1877
Sowerby & Co., Ellison Glass
Works, Gateshead-on-Tyne
Vase

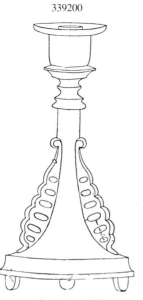

339200

4 September 1879
Sowerby & Co., Ellison Glass
Works, Gateshead-on-Tyne
New Candlestick with
Perforations

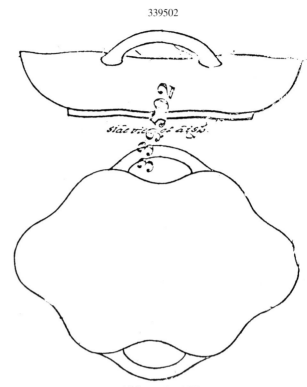

339502

12 September 1879
Sowerby & Co., Ellison Glass Works, Gateshead-on-Tyne
Jelly Dish

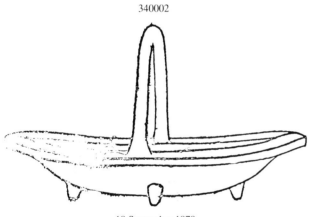

340002

18 September 1879
Sowerby & Co., Ellison Glass Works, Gateshead-on-Tyne
Basket

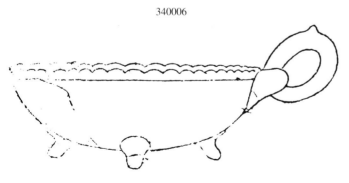

340006

18 September 1879
Sowerby & Co., Ellison Glass Works, Gateshead-on-Tyne
Handled Jelly

340005

18 September 1879
Sowerby & Co., Ellison Glass Works,
Gateshead-on-Tyne
Square Vase

Sowerby & Co.

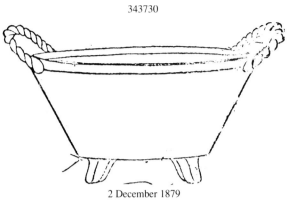

343730

2 December 1879
Sowerby & Co., Ellison Glass Works,
Gateshead-on-Tyne
Vase

106892

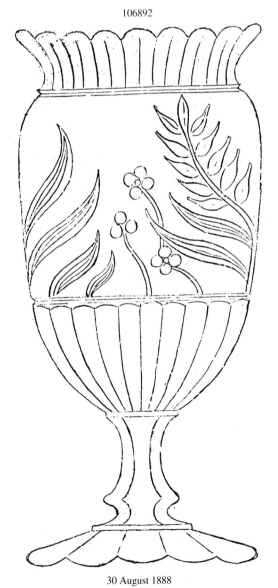

30 August 1888
Sowerby & Co., Ellison Glass Works, Gateshead-on-Tyne
Vase & Pattern

Sowerby & Co., Ellison Glass Works, Gateshead-on-Tyne
Top: Ales (glasses) Below: Baskets for Flowers from Sowerby's Pattern Book 1880s
Those marked with diamond lozenge were Design Registered.

Sowerby & Co.

Sowerby & Co., Ellison Glass Works, Gateshead-on-Tyne
Biscuit Boxes & Cheese Stand from Sowerby's Pattern Book 1880s
Those marked with diamond lozenge were Design Registered.

Sowerby & Co., Ellison Glass Works, Gateshead-on-Tyne
Moulded Sugars & Creams from Sowerby's Pattern Book about 1890.

Percival, Vickers & Co. Ltd.

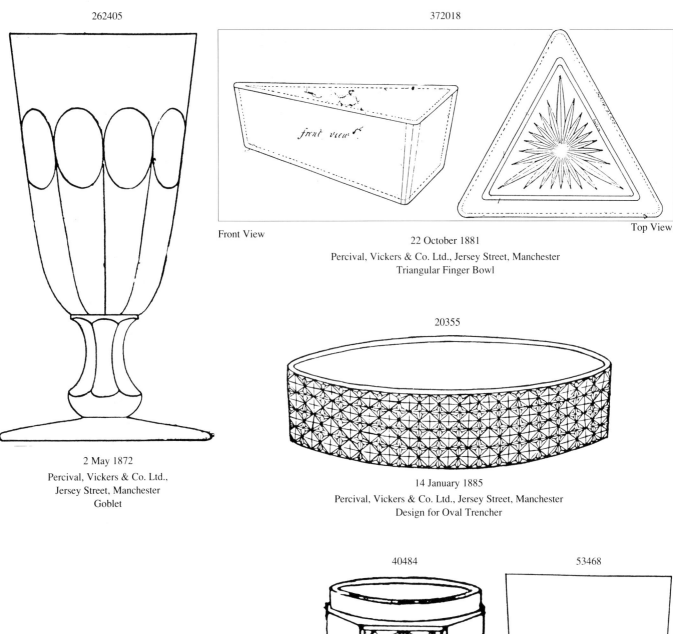

262405

372018

Front View

Top View

22 October 1881
Percival, Vickers & Co. Ltd., Jersey Street, Manchester
Triangular Finger Bowl

2 May 1872
Percival, Vickers & Co. Ltd.,
Jersey Street, Manchester
Goblet

20355

14 January 1885
Percival, Vickers & Co. Ltd., Jersey Street, Manchester
Design for Oval Trencher

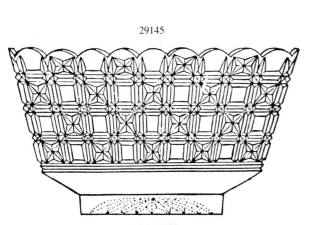

29145

1 July 1885
Percival, Vickers & Co. Ltd., Jersey Street, Manchester
Design for Pressed Glass Butter

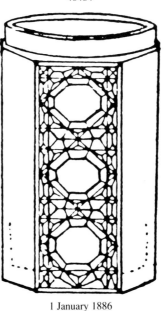

40484

1 January 1886
Percival, Vickers & Co. Ltd., Jersey
Street, Manchester. Glass Cruet

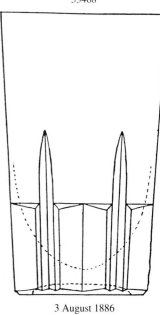

53468

3 August 1886
Percival, Vickers & Co. Ltd., Jersey
Street, Manchester. Glass Tumbler

Percival, Vickers & Co. Ltd.

60108

29 October 1886
Percival, Vickers & Co. Ltd., Jersey Street,
Manchester. Lamp Stand or
Pressed Glass Pillar (in form of lighthouse)

126869

8 June 1889
Percival, Vickers & Co. Ltd., Jersey Street,
Manchester. Vase

196639

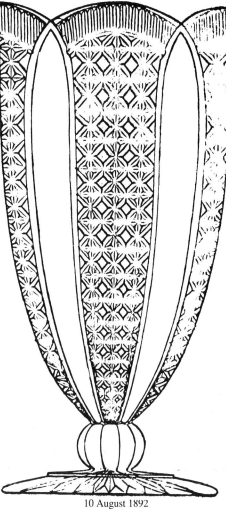

10 August 1892
Percival, Vickers & Co. Ltd., Jersey Street, Manchester.
Celery Glass

319151

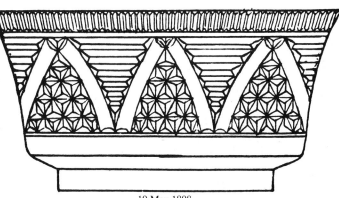

19 May 1898
Percival, Vickers & Co. Ltd., Jersey Street, Manchester. Butter Dish
It is interesting to see that the designs were registered so quickly after being
submitted.

Matthew Turnbull, Cornhill Glass Works, Southwick, Sunderland

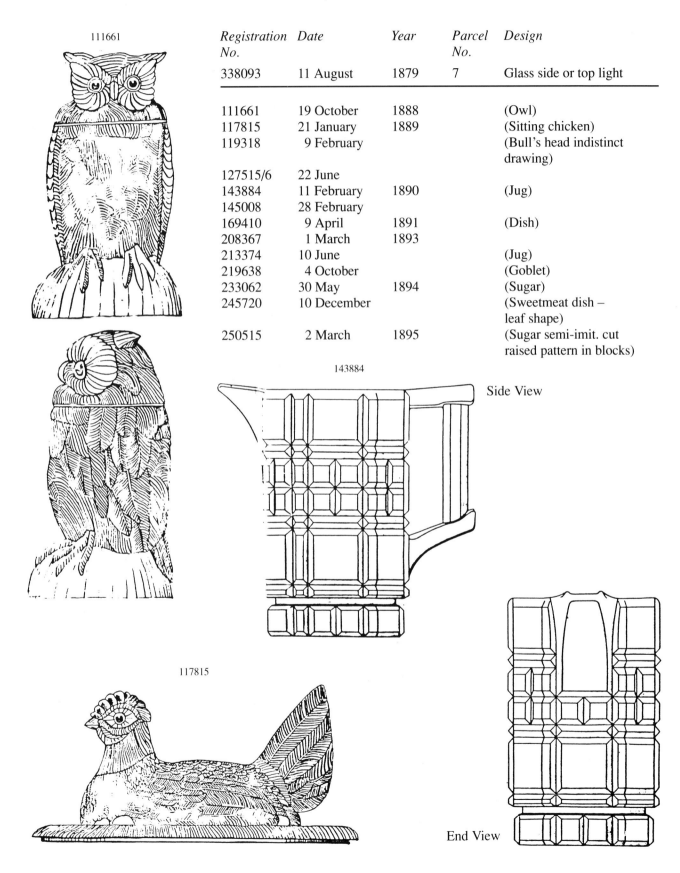

111661

Registration No.	Date	Year	Parcel No.	Design
338093	11 August	1879	7	Glass side or top light
111661	19 October	1888		(Owl)
117815	21 January	1889		(Sitting chicken)
119318	9 February			(Bull's head indistinct drawing)
127515/6	22 June			
143884	11 February	1890		(Jug)
145008	28 February			
169410	9 April	1891		(Dish)
208367	1 March	1893		
213374	10 June			(Jug)
219638	4 October			(Goblet)
233062	30 May	1894		(Sugar)
245720	10 December			(Sweetmeat dish – leaf shape)
250515	2 March	1895		(Sugar semi-imit. cut raised pattern in blocks)

143884

Side View

117815

End View

184

Joseph Webb, Coalbourn Hill, Stourbridge

Registration No.	Date	Year	Parcel No.	Design
80929	11 October	1851	3	Dish (star shape)
84300	18 March	1852	5	(Fluted vase shape)
84386	23 March		1	(Decanter shape – pattern of diamonds)
91476	23 June	1853	2	Sugar basin (oval pattern)
93626	17 December		1	Bowl with cover and stand (similar oval pattern)
96056	15 June	1854	2	(Similar)
96544	3 August		1	Pressed glass basin and cover to be used with or without cover
98201	18 November		4	Pressed glass dish (similar oval pattern)
109434	21 March	1857	3	Design for ornamenting glass dishes (petal pattern in centre, main body consists of oval pattern forming rows of bands)
114989	28 August	1858	2	Design for ornamenting pressed glass dishes (similar to above)

93626

Similar design in Edward Moore's Supplement to the Pottery Gazette, 1888.

96544

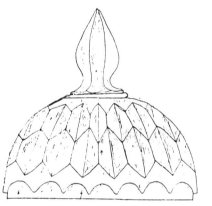

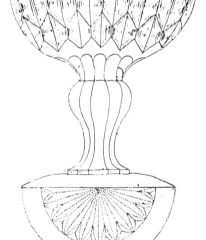

Registered 19th December 1872 by Jane Webb and Joseph Hammond trading as the Executors of the late Joseph Webb, Glass Manufacturers, Stourbridge. Design for Ornamental Pressed Glass Flower Boat for Table Decoration.

268883

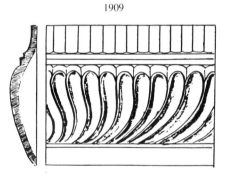

90767

1909

John Walsh Walsh, Soho & Vesta Glass Works, Birmingham

This firm registered several items in the 1850s but chiefly is remembered for a series of realistic flower holders in the 1880s and 1890s. Between 1880 and 1883, however, they registered two jelly dishes, two glass decanters, one sugar basin and one ornamental design for a socket block for a flower stand, which were unexciting in comparison with the registrations of the years which followed.

In 1884 they registered an arch-topped rolled over pillar known as the "Queen Anne" and applied to glass. This was an important registration in classical style which was followed by the gadrooned pieces of Edward Moore in 1887 and 1888, by Sowerby in 1887 and a set of pillared dishes by Edward Bolton in 1888. From 1885 on came the naturalistic shapes and flower holders.

In 1885 there was the registration of a honeysuckle to be made in glass and used as a decoration on glass. There was nothing in 1886 except for a biscuit jar shape pushed in at four sides, but in 1887 there was a flower holder in the form of a tree trunk and another tree vase in 1888, shaped like a palm tree. In that year there was a lovely water lily flower stand for holding flowers and candles and a double vase in the form of thistles. Other flower holders simulating plants were in the shape of a fern in 1889, some double crocus vases in 1891, a double vase in the form of two tulips and the top of a vase in the shape of a pansy in 1892. As well there was a rose lamp for burning Clarke's Fairy Light Candles in 1890 and a wine glass leg bent round to look like the stem of a flower in 1891. Continuing the flower theme, in 1891 there were four registrations for flower shaped light shades, and the naturalistic theme continued throughout the 1890s, whilst elaborate flower holders were registered in metal and glass during the beginning of the twentieth century. Apart from the flower shapes, there were "animal" holders for flowers; an owl in 1890, a wyvern in 1891 and a vase in the form of a snake in 1894.

During these years, the firm produced some lovely vases and centre pieces which were fashionable, decorative and graceful.

John Walsh Walsh

Registration No.	Date	Year	Parcel No.	Design
84598	6 April	1852	1	Claret decanter
90767	12 April	1853	7	Ink stand
91634	9 July		1	Soda water bottle
99882	18 April	1855	4	Glass ink and cover
356807	18 October	1880	14	Jelly dish
357608	3 November		1	Socket block for flower stand (ornamental design)
389157/8	31 October	1882	11	Glass clareteens
393243	25 January	1883	20	Sugar basin
393244			20	Jelly Dish (angular)
1909	14 February	1884		Arch-topped, rolled over pillar known as the "Queen Anne" and applied to glass
4489	2 April			Shape of the acorn
8013	7 June			Shape (Dragonfly)

39415

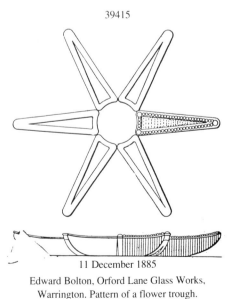

11 December 1885

Edward Bolton, Orford Lane Glass Works, Warrington. Pattern of a flower trough.

John Walsh Walsh (continued)

Registration No.	Date	Year	Design
33714/5	19 September	1885	Shape
36184	22 October		Honeysuckle made in glass and used as a decoration on glass
42716	29 January	1886	Shape of biscuit jar pushed in at four sides
65543	15 January	1887	Shape (Design for glass boat to hold flowers and a lamp in the centre)
74556	26 May		Flower holder in the form of a tree trunk
100004	12 May	1888	(Vase in form of a palm tree)
103949	18 July		(Water lily flower and bud for holding flowers and candles)
107808/9	12 September		(809 Double vase in form of thistles)
117086	9 January	1889	(Flower holder in shape of a fern)
149468	14 May	1890	(Flower vase in shape of an owl)
155744	2 September		(Rose lamp for burning Clarke's Fairy light candles)
164670	14 January	1891	(Flower holder in the shape of a wyvern)
165012	20 January		(Wine glass leg bent round to look like the stem of a flower)
172125	29 May		(Cylindrical glass vessel)
172810	11 June		(New shape top for wine glass)
177733	2 September		(Double crocus vases)
181922	29 October		(Cut glass vase)
183415 to 17	20 November		(Flower shaped electric shades)
184501	7 December		(Candle holder)
184548	8 December		(Flower shaped shade)
186137	12 January	1892	(Double vase in form of two tulips)
186546 186567	21 January		(Cornucopia vase)
203135	25 November		(Ice pail)
211778	6 May	1893	(Top of flower vase in shape of a pansy)
245141	28 November	1894	(Vase in form of snake)
251816	23 March	1895	(Flint glass for silver mounting in shape of horse's hoof)
253934 253935	29 April		(Horse shoe shape – probably ink well)
258147	15 July		(Design for cutting in glass)
264751	29 October		(Naturalistic flower holder)
264997	1 November		(Flower holder cornucopia supported on trellis of glass rods)
271422	21 February	1896	(Naturalistic flower centre arum lilies)
273414	25 March		(Ink wells and pen holder stand)
282607/8	31 August		(Very naturalistic)
293210/11	3 February	1897	(211 twig flower holders, harp shaped)

15353

18 October 1884
Stevens & Williams, Brierley Hill Glassworks.
Design for glass ornament to be used for
decorating bowls etc., compare with
36184, John Walsh Walsh
Used on "Matsu-no-kee" Pieces

36184

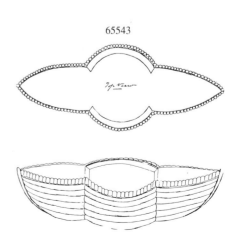

65543

74556

26 May 1887

100004

12 May 1888

103949

18 July 1888

John Walsh Walsh (continued)

Registration No.	Date	Year	Design
293212/13	3 February	1897	(212 twig flower holders, anchor shaped 213 bell shaped flowers on base)
295653	15 March		(Naturalistic flower holder, twig shapes)
299712	28 May		(Ice pail)
315340	4 March	1898	(Design for flint and opal glass shade)
322177	20 July		
323288/9	9 August		(288 Naturalistic with cutting on flower holders 289 candlestick and flower holder combined for table decoration. Similar vases to 288)
332564/5	21 January	1899	(Naturalistic set of flower holders for table decoration in cut or fancy glass)
333851/2	16 February		(Bottle with stopper and jar)
333944	18 February		(Ink bottle)
336752	18 April		(Naturalistic bowl on leaves for feet)
353374	16 February	1900	(Bowl representing an Imperial Yeomanry hat)
375896	25 June	1901	(Design for glass shade)
378648/9	23 August		(Naturalistic flower holders, vases in the shape of leaves)
381646/7	18 October		(Naturalistic glass and metal flower holders)
381704/5	19 October		(The same)
386121	23 January	1902	(Misc. individual naturalistic flower holders in coloured glass)
386122			(Naturalistic single glass and metal holder)
386488	30 January		(Naturalistic glass and metal flower holder but mainly glass)
398503	7 October		(Naturalistic glass and metal flower holder)
403012	3 January	1903	(Naturalistic glass and metal thistle shape vases)
409769	9 May		(Set of flower holders in metal and glass combined)
417965	25 September		(Naturalistic flower holder)
435651/2	28 June	1904	
435959	1 July		
436862/3	13 July		(Petal shaped shades)
440767	9 September		(Naturalistic flower holder convolvulus shape)
441666	20 September		(Naturalistic set of flower holders in glass and metal)
447006	20 December		(Misc. flower holders, wholly glass. Naturalistic wavy stems)
450823	23 February	1905	(Design for decorating light shades)
458344	8 June		(Design for ornamenting glass shades in moulding and etching combined)

John Walsh Walsh (continued)

Registration No.	Date	Year	Design
464696	12 September	1905	(Flower holders, free shapes quatrefoil tops but not naturalistic)
474330	20 February	1906	(Shade, decoration to be done by etching)
476078	21 March		(Pattern)
484799	11 August		(Multiple chain flower holders)
486381	4 September		(Set of symmetrical flower holders with metal fittings)
486969	13 September		
487788	25 September		
492244	30 November		(Rustic set of flower holders to be made in glass or porcelain with festoons of silk ribbons)
493532	2 January	1907	(Similar in shape to above but glass connected)
500502	20 April		(Light shade)
506632/3	10 July		(506633 pattern – palm leaf shapes)
511318	11 September		(Spiral in glass)
511845	17 September		(Handle of vase and flower support in glass and metal)
518913	16 January	1908	(Design for glass rustic support for vases)
520225	14 February		

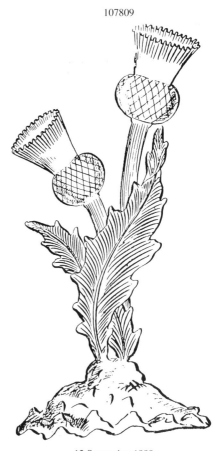

107809

12 September 1888

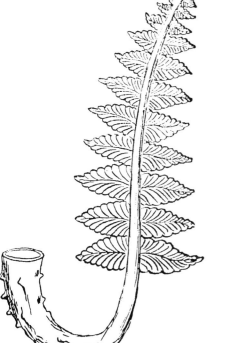

117086
9 January 1889

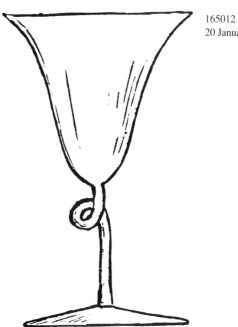

165012
20 January 1891

Stuart & Mills, Stourbridge

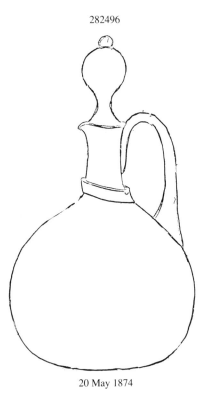

282496

Registration No.	Date	Year	Parcel No.	Design
251131 to 33	22 March	1871	3	Designs for lamps

20 May 1874

Philip Pargeter, Red House Glass Works, Stourbridge

Registration No.	Date	Year	Parcel No.	Design
254864	17 August	1871	4	(Centre piece)
272981	16 May	1873	4	
282496	20 May	1874	10	With Percival Jones of Westmoreland St., Dublin The drip cup claret jug

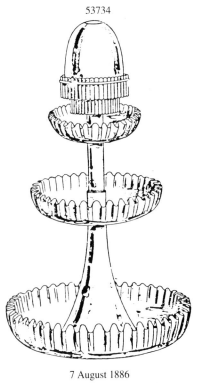

53734

Stuart and Sons, Red House Glass Works, Stourbridge

This firm did three registrations in 1886, namely: pattern of a flower bowl for use with fairy lamps, pattern of a fairy lamp shade and pattern of a flower stand with fairy light on top. In 1889 there was a design for the neck of a flower stand and in 1892 for a flower holder, connected by chains, which was reminiscent of the Webb's registration. The main registrations were for the pieces concerned with fairy lamps.

Registration No.	Date	Year	Design
53732	3 August	1886	Pattern of a flower bowl for use with fairy lamps
53733	7 August		Pattern of a fairy lamp shade
53734			Pattern of a flower stand with fairy light on top
131653	23 August	1889	(Design for neck of flower stand)
185803	4 January	1892	(Flower holders. Connected by chains)
486685	8 September	1906	(Bowl. Art nouveau design. Presumably hand made)

7 August 1886

Boulton & Mills, Audnam Glass Works, Stourbridge.
Design Registrations 1863-1893

Only two items were registered between 1864 and 1870, namely an epergne and a jug in 1868 with a distinctive handle. This was followed in 1870 with the registration for a design for handle, spout and feet. Hodgetts, Richardson & Pargeter equally registered in 1870 handle and ornaments for jug and goblet, ewer and bowl and both sets of these designs were similar to that of Thomas Webb's registration of 1867. In 1871 Boulton & Mills registered plateaux of silvered glass with plated or gilt rims but their more interesting designs were from 1884 to 1894, when they produced a series of imaginative, naturalistic flower holders.

A glass candle-stick and flower holder combined was registered in 1884 and in 1885 a maiden hair fern decoration. In 1888 there were three vases which were depicted as being shaped as a pineapple, a fern leaf and a tree trunk. Variations of the latter pattern were fairly common and were registered by John Walsh Walsh about the same time and, equally, were made by Thomas Webb and Sons Ltd., towards the end of the century onwards.

The next series came in 1891, starting with a flower holder with raised decoration of bell shaped flowers and a tree trunk vase with raised decoration of honeysuckle type flowers. In 1892 there were similar vases with applied decoration; one with lily of the valley, the top shaped like the petals of a flower, another with flower and leaf decoration, the base resembling leaves. In 1893 there were two designs, one a series of bamboo holders with connecting pieces and one a vase in the shape of a flower, the stem and leaves forming a base. Some of these were in coloured glass including straw opal.

221498

10 September 1868
Boulton & Mills
Please compare with 238052,
Hodgetts, Richardson & Pargeter

238593/4

3 February 1870
Boulton & Mills
Please compare with Thomas Webb and
Hodgetts, Richardson & Pargeter

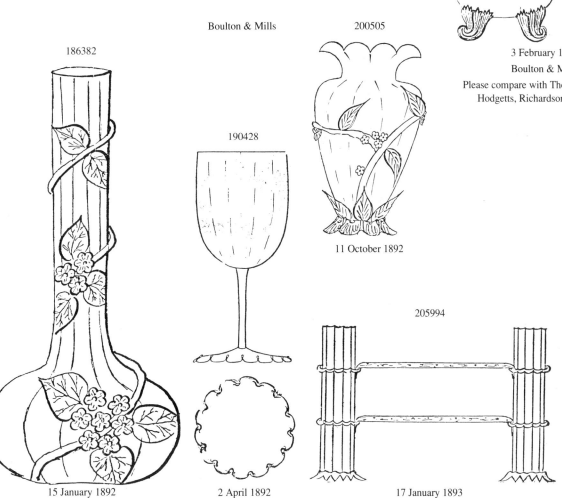

Boulton & Mills

186382

190428

200505

11 October 1892

205994

15 January 1892   2 April 1892   17 January 1893

191

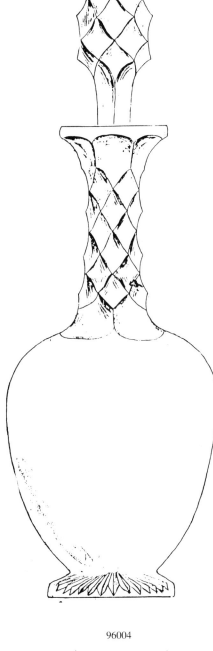

75675

W.H., B. and J. Richardson, Wordsley, near Stourbridge

Registration No.	Date	Year	Parcel No.	Design
42634/5	16 April	1847	2	Goblets
43924 to 27	6 July		2	Vase, ornaments
52158	30 May	1848	1	Jug
52159				Dish
52160				Candlestick
52179	1 June		6	Decanter
52328/9	13 June		4	Water jugs
59686	24 April	1849	3	Sugar basin
62923	13 October		2	Tumbler
75674	11 January	1851	3	Carafe and glass
75675				Decanter
81613	18 November		7	Glass vase

Benjamin Richardson, Wordsley Flint Glass Works, Nr. Stourbridge

Registration No.	Date	Year	Parcel No.	Design
95056	14 February	1854	3	
96004	3 June		3	Stems of wines
96703	26 August		2	Pattern upon all kinds of table glass (shown on jug)
97346	23 October		6	Mustard or for all kinds of table glass
98170	16 November		2	Pattern for all kinds of glasses, globes or shades, or pedestals etc (shown on vase)
103724	9 February	1856	3	(Diamond pattern shown on vase)
104212	25 March		6	(Elaborate cut decanter and stopper)
106216	8 September		3	(Pattern of ovals)
106366	20 September		3	(Globe – for lamps?)
110109	9 June	1857	2	For all kinds of flint table glass for the use of the table and ornaments
111878	6 November		3	Classes III and IV (spout of jug and handle)
114082	29 June	1858	2	For all kinds of table glass (Bark-like pattern)

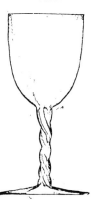

96004

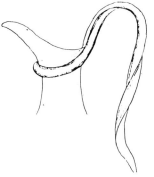

111878

Hodgetts, Richardson & Pargeter, Wordsley, Nr. Stourbridge

In 1865 and 1866 the firm registered a flower stand, one for each year. The registration of 1870 for the ornamental design for parts of a jug and goblet was followed by the important one of the handle and ornaments for ewer and bowl, which can be compared with that of Boulton & Mills in the same year and inevitably with that of Thomas Webb a few years earlier. By 1872 the registrations were in the name of Hodgetts, Richardson & Son. They did a swan shape in that year which became popular, but in the next 10 years the firm produced some curious registrations such as a design in the shape of a crucible and tripod, presumably for a flower holder in 1872, and in 1875 a design shaped like a pump and bucket equally for a flower holder. The last registration in 1882, before the firm became Henry Gething Richardson, was that of a jug in a bird shape.

One of the more important registrations this firm made in 1883 was for the "leaf motif for application" and consists of eight segments of leaf on either side of the stalk. The ornamental design in 1884 for glass decoration by acid etching, was a flower pattern with chrysanthemum and peony shapes and it is interesting because it was consistent both with the year and the fashionable Japanese influence of the day.

Again, in 1886 there was a most important registration of a "combination of threads of glass of different shades of colour arranged as to form a plaid, to be used for glass decoration". The next most important one was in 1887 for the "shape of a flower or lamp bowl with sides turned down or lapped over, showing from side view a crescent shape". These two registrations were of considerable interest and influence amongst the Stourbridge firms.

In 1889 there was a naturalistic flower holder and in 1892 and 1893 respectively two interesting patterns, one of birds in a fruit tree and one allegorical design of a fox and grapes.

These are for the design registrations, whereas the name of Richardson with the variety of glass made by this firm is synonymous with that of "Stourbridge".

Hodgetts, Richardson & Pargeter, Wordsley, Nr. Stourbridge

Registration No.	Date	Year	Parcel No.	Design
186478	3 May	1865	1	Flower stand in flint glass
205210	27 December	1866	3	Flower stand
238052	12 January	1870	8	Ornamental design for parts of a jug and goblet
239241/2	28 February		8	Handle and ornaments for ewer and bowl
246153	22 October		6	(Comport)

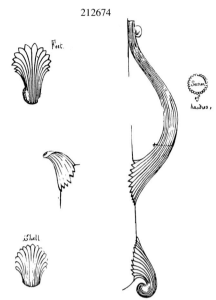

212674

19 October 1867
Thomas Webb
Please compare with 238052,
Hodgetts, Richardson & Pargeter

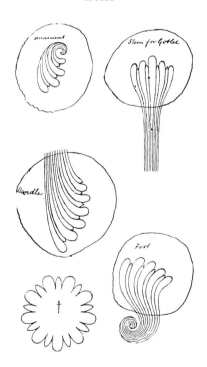

238052

12 January 1870
Hodgetts, Richardson & Pargeter
Ornamental design for parts of a jug and
goblet. The only parts registered are shown
within the circles.
† Base of all the parts

Hodgetts, Richardson & Son

Registration No.	Date	Year	Parcel No.	Design
260648 to 50	22 February	1872	6	(Basket) (649, swan shape 650, boat shape)
261125 to 27	14 March		2	
275856	6 September	1873	2	(Ornamental design)
286525	26 October	1874	5	
290890	23 April	1875	14	(Flower holder)
292040/1	12 June		9	Glass flower holder and fish holder
294575	18 September		4	
299158	11 March	1876	10	
299427	28 March		1	
333128/9	8 March	1879	8	
356111	5 October	1880	1	**Thomas Pargeter Richardson** (Mirror)
362453	4 March	1881	4	Part of a flower vase. (Shell ornamentation on rim)
376428	26 January	1882	8	A jug (bird shape)

362453

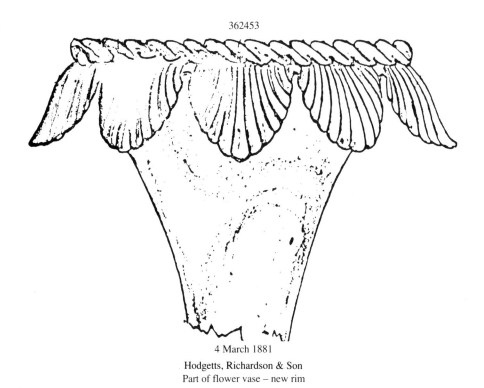

4 March 1881

Hodgetts, Richardson & Son
Part of flower vase – new rim

Henry Gething Richardson, Wordsley Flint Glass Works (Stourbridge)

Registration No.	Date	Year	Parcel No.	Design
379463	12 April	1882	7	Ornamental flower vase
395786	19 March	1883	6	(Leaf motif for application)
397828	8 May		5	Design for glass ornamentation

2659	29 February	1884		New design for glass globe to be used with comet fitting
15256	16 October			Ornamental design for glass decoration
45768	25 March	1886		Shape of improved 'Ice Drainer'
46498	1 April			Combination of threads of glass of different shades of colour, arranged as to form a plaid, to be used for glass decoration.
53483	30 July			Design for a Hyacinth glass made with two projections on the upper or cup part, and having an indentation on the upper part of the body to carry and keep in position, a stick or other support to the plant.
68327	21 February	1887		Shape of a flower or lamp bowl with sides turned down or lapped over, showing from side view a crescent shape.
99911	10 May	1888		(Globe flower holder)
120451	27 February	1889		(Naturalistic flower holder)
199109	20 September	1892		(Pattern)
216157	3 August	1893		
216779/80	16 August			(Flower holder 216779)
217202	25 August			(Design for decoration)
217900	9 September			(Design for decoration)

239241

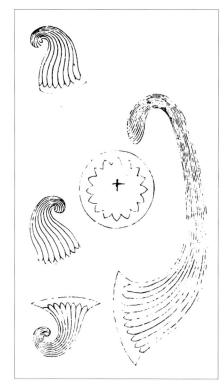

28 February 1870
Hodgetts, Richardson & Pargeter
Handle and ornaments for ewer and bowl.
† Base of ornamental parts

260649

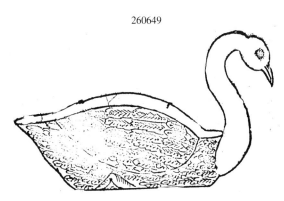

22 February 1872
Hodgetts, Richardson & Son. Swan shape.

260650

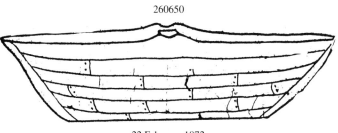

22 February 1872
Hodgetts, Richardson & Son

Henry G. Richardson & Sons

Registration No.	Date	Year	Design
261065/6	4 September	1895	(Unusual flower holders – 261066 'Lyre' shape)
287472	2 November	1896	
291659	8 January	1897	(Naturalistic fir cone holders)
317448	18 April	1898	(Naturalistic acorn flower holder)
318345	6 May		(Complicated bamboo cane flower holder)
331189	19 December		

395786

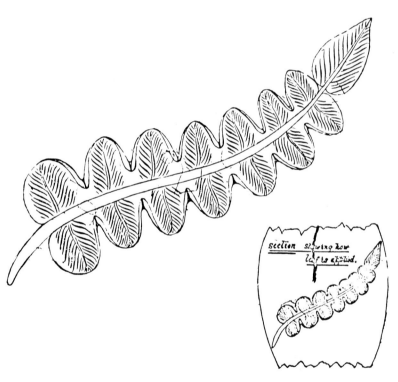

19 March 1883   Henry G. Richardson

15256
16 October 1884
Henry Gething Richardson

Thomas Webb & Sons, Dennis Glass Works, Stourbridge.
Design Registrations 1863-1893

In October 1867 Thomas Webb & Sons registered the handle, spout and feet design which is similar to that of Boulton & Mill's and Hodgetts, Richardson & Pargeter's designs of a few years later. Between 1868 and 1875 there were apparently no registrations. In 1875 there were a couple and in 1876 they registered both a top and a bowler hat design. After that there was nothing until 1879 when there was a "cock" jug. In 1882 the firm registered a rim, or lip of bowls and vessels and in 1883 an elephant handle, a pear shape and an apple shape. In the next couple of years they produced several scent bottles, which are important now, and in 1886 a series of patterns such as diapers of semi-circular lines forming a decorative pattern, diapers of irregular lines forming a watery or wavy pattern, and one for a cylindrical form tapering with six rows of arched corrugations. All of these were different to what had been registered previously and to the designs that came later on.

In 1887 there were two shapes for a particular form of edging and there was little else until 1891 and 1893. During these years there were some of the more important registrations of flower holders; some were multi-tiered and naturalisticly inspired and some were of a slightly fragile Venetian appearance. There were elaborate centre pieces and flower holders connected by turned glass rods, equally two flower holders suspending a third. There were about twelve registrations during these years depicting these fancy and somewhat fussy designs for the dinner table, although being Webb's they were in good taste for that era.

The variety and splendour of the glass made by Thomas Webb & Sons is well known and has been covered thoroughly in "British Glass" by Charles Hajdamach (ISBN 1 85149 141 4).

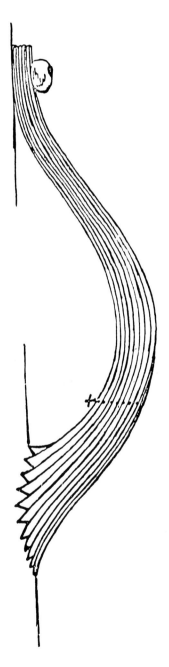

212674 & 212675

Shell.

Spout.

Section of handles x

19 October 1867

Thomas Webb & Sons

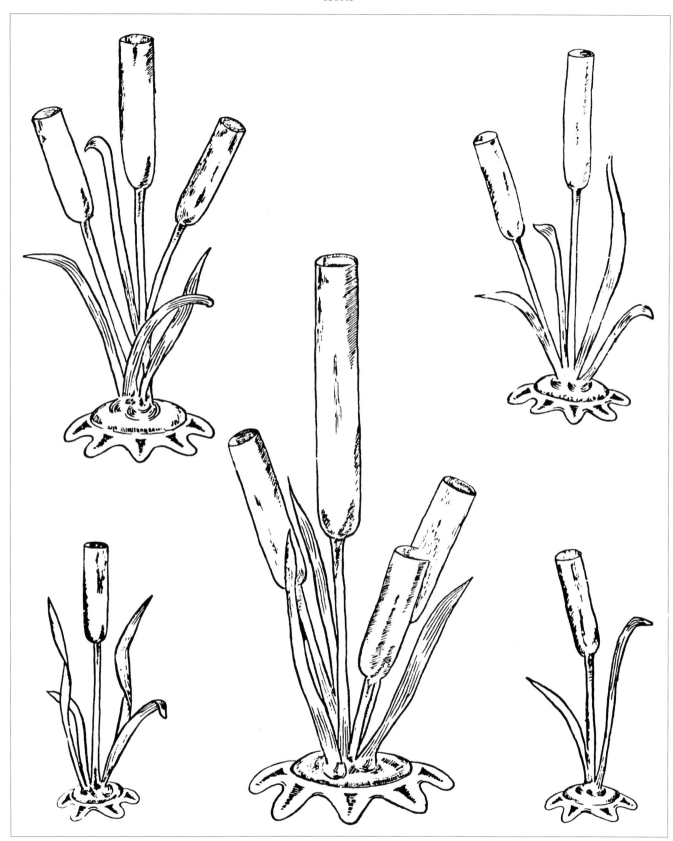

4 December 1899
Thomas Webb and Corbett Ltd.